D0883112

E
664
.F743
D48

206081

DEVINE

JOHN W. FOSTER

John W. Foster

*Politics and Diplomacy
in the Imperial Era,
1873-1917*

John W. Foster

Politics and Diplomacy
in the Imperial Era,
1873-1917

by
Michael J. Devine

OHIO UNIVERSITY PRESS

ATHENS, OHIO

London

Library of Congress Cataloging in Publication Data

Devine, Michael J   1945–
    John W. Foster : politics and diplomacy in the
imperial era, 1873–1917.
    Bibliography: p. 162. Foster, John Watson, 1836–1917. 2.   United
States—Foreign relations—1865–1921. 3.   Diplomats—
United States—Biography.
E664.F743D48   327.73′0092′4   [B]   80-17387
ISBN 0-8214-0437-7

FOR MAIJA

Contents

Acknowledgments

A project of this nature developing over a period of several years would be an impossible endeavor for any author, but especially for this one, without the advice, support, and assistance of numerous considerate individuals, who included interested colleagues, resourceful reference librarians, and conscientious critics, several of whom I would like to mention here. Of particular importance in guiding the early stages of this work were Marvin Zahniser, Alfred Eckes, and Li Tien-yi, who gave generously of their time and energy. I am indebted to John L. Gaddis of Ohio University for reading an early draft of the manuscript and furnishing necessary and constructive criticism. James Cunningham, also of Ohio University, read certain chapters and offered substantial advice, and Hal Williams of Southern Methodist University, Lawrence Gelfand of the University of Iowa, and Robert Ferrill of Indiana University all contributed valuable aid that greatly improved my manuscript. Marcia Brubeck provided indispensible editorial assistance. Despite their best efforts, I must accept full responsibility for errors and misinterpretations that remain in this work.

The American Philosophical Society awarded me a grant to support my research and writing, for which I am grateful, and I appreciate the society's interest.

My research was facilitated by the dedicated staffs of the libraries I visited, and I was continually impressed by the dedicated service rendered by the hard-working professionals at the Library of Congress, Rutherford B. Hayes Presidential Library, Indiana Historical Library, and Princeton University Library. I am also indebted to Mrs. Eleanor Lansing Dulles for allowing me access to transcripts of her tapes and copies of photographs in her possession.

Finally, my wife, Maija, is entitled to more eloquent recognition than I am able to render for enduring many hardships in order that I might complete this volume. Besides helping to earn the income, she cared for our family and deciphered hundreds of illegibly written pages while typing various early drafts. Without her this book could not have been written.

John W. Foster

Politics and Diplomacy
in the Imperial Era,
1873-1917

Introduction

My grandfather, whose name I bear, exerted a great influence over my life, and he had ideals and purposes which I have tried to make my own. He was a deeply patriotic American. He belonged to the period which saw this country rapidly developing from a small Atlantic coast group into a nation that spread across the continent. He fought to preserve the Union; and then on diplomatic missions and as a Secretary of State he helped to spread the influence of this nation throughout the world of Europe and Asia.

John Foster Dulles, 1955

During the final decades of the nineteenth century Americans began to look outward upon the world with a sense of destiny and mission. Having met most of their internal challenges, the restoration of the Union, the settlement of the West, and the development of an industrial economy, Americans turned their attention to foreign affairs. They began to consider the idea of exporting the American experience, thereby bestowing the blessings of American democracy, the free enterprise system, and Anglo-Saxon values upon peoples of the earth. Compounded by economic, diplomatic, and humanitarian factors, a fervor grew within the nation, and Americans thought they saw the opportunity to redesign the world in their own image. Meanwhile, powerful voices emerged, demanding a more aggressive United States foreign policy.

Among those calling for a new assertiveness in United States foreign relations was John W. Foster, perhaps the most capable and experienced American diplomat of his time. His wide diplomatic experience, literary fame, and legal contacts made him an extremely influential figure in the State Department during the period in which the United States embarked upon an era of expanded diplomatic relations and insular imperialism. He was

3

involved in the formation of United States foreign policy in every administration from that of Ulysses S. Grant to that of William McKinley and served in many diplomatic posts, including as minister to Mexico, Russia, and Spain, and was secretary of state for nine months in the Benjamin Harrison administration. Highly regarded as an international lawyer, Foster's many clients included the Washington legations of Mexico, Spain, Russia, Chile, and China. He was a central figure in the international arbitration movement and a founder of the American Society of International Law, the Carnegie Endowment for International Peace, and the American Red Cross. A widely known and eminently knowledgeable lecturer, he also authored several important books and dozens of articles on American diplomacy and international law.

In many respects, Foster occupies a position as a significant figure of both the nineteenth and twentieth centuries. A youthful abolitionist in frontier Indiana, Foster earned a degree from Indiana University, studied law at Harvard, and served with distinction as an officer during the Civil War. For a period of seven years he edited the Evansville *Daily Journal* in his home town and labored in state Republican party politics before embarking upon a diplomatic career with an appointment as minister to Mexico in 1873. In the remaining four decades of his life, Foster never left the diplomatic arena. Even during his final years in retirement, he remained close to the vortex of American policy making, where he advised his son-in-law, Robert Lansing, Woodrow Wilson's secretary of state, and monitored the nascent careers of his precocious grandchildren, John Foster and Allen and Eleanor Lansing Dulles.

In the past two decades, a myriad of significant historical studies has added to our understanding of American diplomacy during the era in which the United States emerged as an imperial power. Yet historians of this period disagree over whether the role that the United States assumed after 1898 was a "new departure," a "diplomatic revolution," or rather the coming into full fruition of the policies that the nation had been pursuing consistently since the Civil War. An examination of Foster's diplomatic record that spans the period in question and extends to the entry of the United States into World War I demonstrates clearly the continuity in the evolution of American foreign policy from Ulysses S. Grant to Woodrow Wilson. Foster's diplomatic record provides a means for understanding the inner workings of the State Department during this transitional period in American history, and his career illustrates the intimate relationships between domestic politics and foreign policy throughout the course of the United States' emergence as a world power.

Recent studies of American foreign policy mention Foster as a leading figure in the diplomacy of his era, yet none explores his role in depth or makes an attempt to analyze his complex and sometimes self-contradictory views on

American foreign policy. The twofold purpose of this study is, first, to review the details of Foster's long diplomatic career, tracing his political and diplomatic movements through long years on intricate negotiations and complicated diplomatic maneuvers, and second, to offer an assessment of his unique contributions to the development of American foreign policy during the era of imperialism.

The chapters in this biography of the man viewed by his colleagues as America's "first professional diplomat" focus on Foster's public career in politics, international law, and diplomacy. Attention has been directed to his diplomatic efforts to acquire insular possessions (in particular the Hawaiian Islands), his writings justifying American imperialist policies, and his wide participation in peace organizations that attempted to impose Anglo-Saxon standards of order and law on non-western peoples.

I

Midwest Origins

Republicans loyal to the incumbent President Ulysses S. Grant found his campaign for reelection in 1872 to be far more difficult than they had ever anticipated, and as the election day drew near they knew that only a concerted effort by the party faithful would assure another victory. A Liberal Republican party had risen up to challenge the old guard or "Stalwart" Republicans loyal to Grant, and this splinter group had named Horace Greeley as their candidate; meanwhile, the Democrats, lacking a strong candidate of their own, joined the Liberals and also nominated Greeley at their convention. In addition to facing the combined challenge of the renegade Republicans and the Democrats, Grant's forces were burdened with unpleasant political issues, including the administration's involvement in an ill-conceived filibuster to annex Haiti, persistent racial troubles in the occupied South, the scandalous conduct of the William M. Tweed "Ring" in New York City, and the popular demand for civil service reform—a cause that the Liberals had made central to their program. Everywhere the campaign was waged with the utmost bitterness, but perhaps no state witnessed greater political vehemence than Indiana, a key state in the aspirations of both sides, where Grant's foremost loyalist, Senator Oliver P. Morton, fought desperately for his own political life as well as for the reelection of the president. A ruthless and tenacious veteran of innumerable political wars, Morton believed with grim determination that his only chance for survival was to keep the Republican party in his state united by firing the hatreds of the recent Civil War while at the same time keeping his political machinery well lubricated with generous doses of campaign money, which flowed steadily

7

into the party office.[1] To provide the victory he so desperately wanted, Morton depended heavily upon a capable, energetic, and ambitious thirty-seven-year-old lawyer and newspaper publisher from Evansville who had recently been elected chairman of the Republican State Central Committee. His name was John Watson Foster.

Early in the campaign the senator ordered Foster to patch up local differences for the coming election. Morton advised his young protégé that money was being raised, and he offered encouragement: "We have the greatest faith in your ability to organize the party . . . and believe you have already succeeded in alarming the Democrats."[2] Still, the election of Democrat Thomas Hendricks as governor in October worried the Republicans, even though they won the other state offices and a large majority in the state legislature. To assure victory in the November presidential election, Morton hastily dispatched a lieutenant to New York with instructions to bring back thousands of dollars in additional funds, and Foster intensified his efforts with the party workers.[3] At a rally in Indianapolis he congratulated party members for overcoming "disaffection in our own ranks" and claimed that the governorship was lost only because of "the personal slanders and frauds of our opponents." He urged loyal Republicans to keep working until the presidential election in November, reminding them, "we have one more assault to make upon our opponents." The campaigning continued relentlessly until election day, when Foster's newspaper, the Evansville *Daily Journal*, confidently predicted: "If every Republican votes once, and no Democrat more than once, Grant will have a six hundred majority in Vandenburg County."[4] Ultimately the intensive campaigning and enormous expenditures paid off—Indiana joined those states that provided Grant with an overwhelming victory over Horace Greeley; as the Indiana state legislature remained in Republican hands, Morton had assured himself of another term in the United States Senate.

The months following the victories of Grant and Morton were a time for paying political debts and rewarding party loyalists. Naturally John W. Foster ranked among the first to be considered. His work in the campaign had won him the gratitude of Indiana Republicans and had attracted the attention of national party leaders, including the charismatic Speaker of the United States House of Representatives, James G. Blaine.[5] Foster was soon invited to Washington, where he met with President Grant in the White House. Senator Morton instructed him to look for a good position for himself by browsing through the register of federal offices, known then as the "Blue Book," advising him not to concern himself with such matters as qualifications or experience. Taking Morton's statements to mean that the senator had the influence to secure virtually any appointment, Foster discussed the situation with his wife and announced, "A brief residence in Europe would be both pleasant and useful." His request for assignment to

Switzerland was denied, however, as even Morton could not procure this choice position, which had been set aside for one of the president's cronies. Instead, Morton offered Foster the prospect of an appointment as minister to Mexico. Nearly four decades later Foster recorded his reaction to Morton's suggestion in his *Memoirs*:

I was bewildered by the proposition. It was with much misgiving as to my fitness for the office [that] I had chosen the Swiss Mission, one of the lowest and most unimportant of the diplomatic posts; and now I was tendered the highest and most difficult mission on the American hemisphere. I frankly told the Senator that I very much doubted the wisdom of accepting such a post with my entire inexperience in diplomacy. I at the time spoke no foreign language, had never been out of my own country, and had only a textbook knowledge of international law. But the Senator only smiled at my hesitation, reasserted his confidence in my ability, and said I was much better fitted than most of those who were appointed to our diplomatic service.[6]

Morton's confidence in Foster would prove well founded. His protégé soon demonstrated remarkable diplomatic skill in volatile situations, and while his selection had been made in a rather random fashion, he was probably the best available choice for the appointment. Although characterized by a certain narrowness, inexperienced in diplomacy, and unfamiliar with world affairs at the time, Foster was not unsophisticated. Extremely well educated by any standards of his time, he was as well versed in Greek, Latin, and the classics as many polished European diplomats were. Furthermore, he was trained in law and familiar with newspaper publishing and other business enterprises, and his participation in domestic politics had provided him with an opportunity to develop his talent for pragmatic politics. Following his appointment to Mexico, Foster was never to return to live in his native Indiana; he was destined to spend the next forty years in the world of international diplomacy.

The new minister to Mexico was born and reared among the rugged hills of southwestern Indiana. His father, Matthew Watson Foster, had immigrated to the United States with his family from England as a lad of twelve, and after living with his family in New York for a few years, Matthew set out for the West on his own. He worked his way down the Ohio River and in 1819 settled on eighty acres in Pike County, Indiana. The frontier was an ideal environment for the energetic and resourceful young pioneer, and he quickly prospered. Furthermore, his marriage to Eleanor Johnson brought him a high degree of social prominence in the community; his bride was the daughter of John J. Johnson, an aide to General William Henry Harrison, a member of Indiana's first territorial legislature. A few years after his marriage, Matthew moved his family (which now included two children) a short distance to the town of Petersburg. Now a naturalized citizen, an officer in the local lodge of

Free and Accepted Masons, and a man of influence in the Whig party in Pike County, he operated a general store and won election as a probate judge. It was here, too, that the couple's third child, John Watson, was born on March 2, 1836. Soon Matthew's business interests outgrew Petersburg, and in 1839 the family moved again, this time to the bustling commercial town of Evansville on the Ohio River, where "Judge" Foster enjoyed success in the wholesale grocery business and acquired interests in banking and railroad ventures. Described by a contemporary as one of the community's "most enterprising, upright, enlightened and philanthropic citizens," Matthew headed a household of ten children—eight by Eleanor, a conscientious and pious woman who died helping the victims of a riverboat disaster in 1849, and two by a second wife, a sophisticated and socially prominent widow named Sarah Kazar, whose husband had been lost while searching for his fortune in the California gold rush.[7]

Calvinistic discipline and hard work characterized the Foster home. Matthew carefully monitored the education of all his children and enrolled them in private subscription schools (public education was not yet known to this developing region). John Watson, a particularly bright and gifted student with a reserved and scholarly disposition, was sent to the Evansville Academy, conducted by a New Englander named Myron Stafford who had graduated from the Lane Theological Seminary in Cincinnati. A man of high moral principles and sincere dedication to his pupils, Stafford encouraged John Watson to attend college and provided the necessary instruction in all subjects except Greek and Latin, for these a tutor was provided in the person of a young law clerk in the office of attorney Conrad Baker.[8] At the age of fifteen, John Watson was enrolled at the University of Indiana at Bloomington, a choice about which Matthew felt comfortable because the Presbyterian church dominated the University's board. Young Foster studied a curriculum based on the classics, joined a "Greek" fraternity, received repeated scoldings from his father for not writing home with regularity, and graduated in 1855 as the valedictorian of his small class. Following a year of study at Harvard University Law School and a brief apprenticeship in Cincinnati with Algernon Sullivan (later a founder of the powerful Wall Street firm of Sullivan and Cromwell), he started his own private practice in Evansville at the age of twenty-one.[9]

During the few short years between his return to Evansville and the outbreak of the Civil War, the aspiring young attorney made a number of important associations that he would maintain throughout his life. Certainly the most significant of these was his marriage in September 1859 to Mary Parke McFerson, a bright, prim and proper young lady whose mother headed the Female Seminary at Bloomington. An exceptionally well-educated woman, Foster's bride, whom he always affectionately called "Parke," was, like her husband, a student of the classics. She was also a gifted linguist, and throughout their many world travels and long residences in foreign lands she always found the native tongue easier to master than her diplomat husband did.[10] While busy in his legal practice, Foster also became active in community affairs. A member of the Evansville Library Association, he was elected corresponding secretary and served as an officer of the organization.[11] Also on the association's board at that time were attorney Conrad Baker, a rising Republican political figure who would within a few years become governor of Indiana, and Charles Denby, a courtly Virginian and Democrat destined to gain prominence as United States minister to China.

While occupied with his legal work, new family, and civic affairs, Foster still found time for involvement in his most burning interest—politics. As a student in college he had developed an intense interest in Republican party politics, and his outspoken views on the slavery issue had caused the disapproving label of "abolitionist" to be given him by his classmates at Bloomington. Nevertheless, he worked for John Charles Fremont in the first Republican presidential campaign in 1856 and became ever more deeply involved in the presidential election of Abraham Lincoln four years later.[12]

When Lincoln's inauguration led to the secession of the South, Foster, like many abolitionists, viewed the coming war as a kind of crusade to purge the nation of the evils of slavery. "My whole soul was enlisted in the anti-slavery cause", Foster recalled in his *Memoirs*, "and when the Civil War . . . burst upon the country, my first impulse was to join the army of the Union. . . ." Not at all anxious to adopt the hardships of military life, he nevertheless felt that his moral convictions left him no choice but to fight for what he viewed as a righteous cause. When the war broke out, Foster and his bride were settled in a comfortable home in Evansville with their infant daughter and were greatly relieved that the initial rush of volunteers to the Union cause was so great in Indiana that the supply of manpower easily exceeded all apparent need. After the defeats suffered by the Northern armies in the first months of the war, however, Foster felt compelled to answer President Lincoln's renewed request for volunteers. Having been an outspoken abolitionist and a loyal Republican, he believed "the call was loudest upon those who had professed devotion to the anti-slavery cause." Following the news of the disaster at Bull Run, he journeyed to Indianapolis and enlisted.[13]

Despite his own self-doubts and pacific nature, Foster soon proved to be a capable soldier. During his college days Foster had regarded himself as a "peace man" and had entered the army with serious reservations about his fitness—physical and mental—for the life of a soldier. Although he was completely lacking in military training and inclination towards the martial arts, because of his political connections he received a commission from Oliver P. Morton, who had been inaugurated as governor of Indiana in January 1861. As a twenty-seven-year-old major in the Twenty-Fifth Indiana Volunteer Infantry, Foster rapidly learned the ways of war at the old fairgrounds in Evansville while he trained with raw recruits who were mostly farm lads from the nearby countryside. After a mere two weeks in which to learn the basics, the Twenty-Fifth was ordered to St. Louis, where it was involved in periodic efforts to pursue rebel forces in the surrounding areas. Following almost six months of relative inactivity, the Indiana volunteers boarded steamers and proceeded down river to Cairo, Illinois, where they joined the forces under the command of Ulysses S. Grant.[14]

Foster's leadership under fire would soon be tested in two of the war's bloodiest battles. The men of the Twenty-Fifth Indiana Volunteer Infantry arrived at Fort Donelson on February 13, the day preceding the opening of the battle, and took up positions from which they would attack the enemy's center when the struggle commenced. The fort fell after two days of savage fighting, and Foster's first experience leading men under fire won praise from his commanding officer for "fearless and energetic" leadership displayed in carrying out his assignments.[15] Two months after the capture of Fort Donelson, the men of the Twenty-Fifth were encamped with Grant's army at Pittsburg in western Tennessee near the country church of Shiloh. On Sunday, April 6, while the troops were finishing breakfast, their camp was suddenly attacked by a large Confederate force under the command of General Albert Sidney Johnson. Immediately caught up in the heaviest fighting he would ever experience, Foster was called upon to assume command of his regiment when the lieutenant colonel was severely wounded and forced to retire from the battlefield. Finding his troops nearly surrounded by a superior Confederate force, he had his men fall back in an orderly fashion for nearly a hundred yards, where they set up a new line and held their ground. For two days the young officer rallied his troops and kept them in order despite the lack of water, rations, or time to sleep. The young major's coolheaded and decisive leadership at the Battle of Shiloh brought him praise from his commander and a promotion to the rank of lieutenant colonel.[16]

Following the Battle of Shiloh, Foster was transferred out of the Twenty-Fifth and spent the remainder of his wartime service as a commander of mounted infantry in pursuit of rebel guerrilla forces in eastern Tennessee and Kentucky. He returned to Evansville in June 1862, accompanying the body of his brother-in-law, Lieutenant Alexander McFerson, who had died of typhoid fever while fighting in Tennessee. Instead of rejoining the Twenty-Fifth following his leave, Foster was assigned to assist General Ambrose Burnside, commander of the Army of Ohio, in the campaign to drive rebel forces out of eastern Tennessee and assure the security and safety of that significant portion of the population sympathetic to the Union cause.[17]

In the border regions of Kentucky and eastern Tennessee, Foster was placed in command of the Union forces and charged with maintaining civil order. In January 1863 rebel guerrillas caused serious disruptions by stopping mail deliveries, interrupting river traffic, and forcing some men of Union sympathies to flee their homes. Foster described the tactics of the Confederates in the area as "cowardly and cruel and entirely unwarranted [*sic*] by the rules of civilized nations". Realizing that the guerrillas could operate only with the support of local sympathizers, Foster forced a harsh levy on individuals suspected of aiding the Rebels and then arranged to have the revenue distributed to Union families "in proportion to their necessities and losses."[18]

Immediate protests against Foster's actions from prominent Democratic politicians in Kentucky and border states reached President Lincoln, who decided that the young officer's conduct "though just and politic in some cases, is so liable to gross abuse as to do great injustice to some other and give the government immense trouble."[19] Foster denied that the confiscations of Rebel property involved any personal wrongdoing and sent his commander a detailed report on the subject.[20] Ultimately, his activities were judged appropriate by his superiors. Nevertheless, he requested and received a transfer.[21]

In August 1863 Foster's regiment was ordered into eastern Tennessee to take part in a planned invasion of that area of pro-Union sentiment. Again he demonstrated a deep concern about the condition of Union sympathizers in the area and was deeply moved by the warm welcome that he and his men received from the local populace. "It does soldiers good to fight for such people," he wrote to his wife, "It's a labor of love."[22] In command of the Sixty-Fifth Indiana Mounted Infantry, Foster took Knoxville in September 1863 and occupied that city. On September 21, near the village of Blountsville, his troops drove off a Confederate force of more than three thousand following a "considerable skirmish" that inflicted heavy losses on the enemy. Two weeks later, however, Foster's troops were the victims of a surprise attack near Kingsport, Tennessee. As a result, his forces were unable to cut off the retreat of a large Confederate army near Greeneville, and the Rebels escaped.[23]

As with all the young men of his generation who survived the Civil War, Foster was profoundly sobered and matured by his wartime experience. He emerged from the war a proven leader with a new self-confidence gained from leading men in desperate conflict. Despite hard campaigns, poor living conditions, and despicable medical facilities, Foster's health apparently improved during the war; the rigorous outdoor life seemed to agree with him, and he returned from the service with a new physical vigor.[24] Furthermore, the wartime experiences deepened his religious conviction. "I will not forget my Christian standing," he wrote to his wife, "I want to come home as good a Christian at least as when I left, though the temptations to evil and bad habits are great." Unlike many of his fellow officers, he scrupulously kept the Sabbath, attending services wherever possible and longing for the day when he could spend his Sundays attending services with his family. Before leaving to join the army he had established the Mission Sunday School in Evansville, and the survival of this effort was constantly on his mind. In his letters to Parke, he gave detailed instructions for the school's operation during his absence.[25]

Foster participated in the war because he believed he had a moral obligation to fight for the righteousness of the Union cause. His wartime adventures took place almost entirely in the border regions, where he viewed firsthand the sufferings of Union sympathizers, and the situation he witnessed hardened his convictions. Because he was so committed to the cause for which he fought, Foster was tempted to pursue a military career. In August 1864 he wrote to his wife, "I take so much interest in the war and am so thoroughly satisfied with the correctness of the principles for which it is being prosecuted, that I must confess I do not like to leave the army. . . ."[26] But the strenuous objections of his wife and increased family responsibilities following his father's death compelled him to leave the military in September 1864, when his period of enlistment ended.[27]

At the conclusion of the war Foster spent a few uncertain months in Cincinnati, associated with his relatives in a firm called "Foster Brothers," a wholesale grocery business, but he was soon back in Evansville and involved in state politics more deeply than ever. Even during his military service he had remained in touch with political issues. He was readily available in 1864 to answer Governor Morton's call for the raising of regiments of "100 Days Men" to provide logistical support for General William Tecumseh Sherman's army as it moved through Georgia and smashed the Confederacy. Commissioned colonel of the One Hundred and Thirty-Sixth Regiment, Foster raised a regiment comprised of recruits from his home county of Vandenburg and those adjoining it. Following an uneventful march through Kentucky and eastern Tennessee, a part of the country now very familiar to him, Foster again returned to private life—with one more political credit in his store.[28] When the war ended, Governor Morton decided to run for the United States Senate, and Foster was active in organizing southwestern counties.[29] Meanwhile, he practiced law and invested in a promising business venture, the Evansville *Daily Journal* Company, which published an extremely partisan daily paper and also manufactured blank books, did steam printing jobs, dealt in stationery, and produced a couple of small weekly newspapers. As a partner in the company Foster had a steady source of income as well as a political forum.

In the years immediately following the Civil War, Republicans enjoyed considerable successes, and Foster's fortunes rose along with those of his party. In 1868 he worked long hours with the state central committee in planning political strategy, electing local slates, and corresponding with Republican leaders in neighboring states. His longstanding friendship with Conrad Baker, now Governor of Indiana, brought him new contacts in Indianapolis, including Benjamin Harrison, the aspiring grandson of the legendary Tippecanoe.[30] There were also political plums to be distributed, and Foster did not miss the opportunity to collect his; in 1869, following considerable lobbying of both Morton and Baker, he was named postmaster for the city of Evansville and was provided with a $200,000 appropriation to construct a new post office in his home town.[31] But the biggest prize was to come after the Republican triumph in the elections of 1872, and Foster knew it would change his life. He sold his interests in the Evansville *Daily Journal* the day after Grant won reelection.[32]

Foster's diplomatic career resulted entirely from his service as a Republican party loyalist. At the time of his appointment to Mexico he was thirty-eight years old, and like most Americans of his time, he had indicated little concern for foreign affairs and seemed uninterested in international diplomacy. He had no diplomatic experience, had never been abroad, and spoke no foreign language. He was a diligent, scholarly individual, however, and he quickly learned the art of diplomacy and became an astute and capable diplomat. Throughout his diplomatic career, Foster would be well served by his practical and diverse Midwestern background in politics, journalism, law, and the military.[33] His involvement in the rugged world of Indiana state politics had provided him with an excellent education in the art of political tactics. From the pragmatic Senator Morton, Foster had acquired a sense for political expediency, and he had emerged from the war with recognizable qualities of leadership and the confidence of knowing that he could perform efficiently under the most severe pressure.

Although Foster had been educated in the classics, he had traveled little. Despite this handicap and a manner that caused him sometimes to be considered abrupt, humorless, and sober, he nevertheless established cordial and often exceedingly friendly relations with people of many cultures. He was successful in these relationships because he was consistently effective, reliable, and worthy of confidence. His undeniable ability and personal integrity made up for his lack of outward amiability. Throughout his career he was also relentlessly loyal and extremely partisan, traits that caused him to irritate opponents while endearing him to friends.

Mexico

Early in 1873 the United States looked with favor upon the liberal administration of Mexican President Sebastián Lerdo de Tejada, and an increasingly cordial relationship with his government was anticipated as expanded commercial relations between the two countries appeared likely. Lerdo had become president in 1872 following the sudden death of Benito Juárez and appeared to have wide popular support. A man of great intellectual accomplishments, Lerdo offered amnesty to the followers of Porfirio Díaz who had opposed Juárez, and Díaz himself accepted a full pension and returned to sugar planting.[1] Despite the persistent problem of looting by bandits and Indians along the United States border, no exceptional or urgent matters seemed to await Foster in Mexico City, where his primary assignment was to be the encouragement of friendly relations between the United States and the republican government in Mexico.[2]

Before leaving to assume his post, the new minister had an opportunity to express his views on the prospects for increased trade and improved relations with Mexico. His remarks demonstrated that he had already given some thought to his assignment and indicated that he had directed some attention to matters of commercial intercourse.[3] While delayed in New Orleans awaiting his instructions and credentials, Foster responded to a request from the New Orleans Chamber of Commerce and addressed its gathering on May 14.[4] Aware that this Southern city was anxious for increased trade with Latin America, Foster cautioned his listeners that commerce and prosperity depended on domestic order and peaceful submission to constituted authorities; he also stated that the establishment of a direct steamship line between New Orleans and Vera Cruz would be useful. The remarks seemed to make a favorable impression on the audience of businessmen, whose fortunes had not been very happy since the Civil War years.[5] Despite his interest in improving trade with Mexico, because of political turmoil Foster would find little opportunity to address himself to this subject until the final years of his time in Mexico.

Foster's first months in Mexico were relatively uneventful, and upon arriving in the Mexican capital he quickly set himself to the tasks of acquiring a working knowledge of Spanish and becoming familiar with the diverse community of United States citizens living in Mexico.[6] During this time he made routine reports to Washington on Apache Indian activities along Mexico's border with the United States,[7] and in December 1873 for the first time he relayed information concerning violent political protests and armed uprisings in Yucatan.[8] The difficulties facing the Mexican government at this time did not appear serious, however, and there seemed to be good reason to believe that Lerdo's government would provide domestic stability. Hoping to help the friendly Mexican regime, Secretary of State Fish instructed Foster to urge support for Lerdo and to avoid saying anything that might weaken his administration.[9]

While the United States continued to hold hope for the Lerdo regime, powerful anti-government forces within Mexico were gathering strength. In January 1874 the Mexican Congress demonstrated strong opposition to Lerdo's administration. Alarmed at the president's increasingly dictatorial methods, many newspapers that had previously been pro-government now turned against the administration.[10] In 1874 Lerdo survived an attempted coup and demanded from the Mexican Congress exceptional executive powers to meet what he recognized as a crisis.[11] By this time, however, the economy of the country was completely paralyzed, as guerrilla bands rampaged through the countryside and tension between the president and the legislature increased.[12]

The leader of the revolutionary forces, General Porfirio Díaz, operated along the Rio Grande River, and established headquarters in Brownsville, Texas, leading raids into Mexico with great success.[13] The strength of Díaz's forces increased throughout 1876, and on November 21 Lerdo was forced to evacuate the capital.

As the triumphant Díaz entered Mexico City, worried diplomats from various countries gathered with Foster in the United States legation to discuss policy.[14] Díaz created many problems for the United States. As a revolutionary leader attacking a government friendly to the United States, he had interrupted lines of communication, forced United States citizens living in Mexico to loan money to his cause, and repeatedly crossed into United States territory.[15] Furthermore, Díaz had denounced all foreign investors and accused the Lerdo government of sacrificing the country to foreigners. In his

Plan of Palo Blanco of March 31, 1876, a modification of his earlier Plan of Tuxtepec, Díaz claimed that Lerdo was attempting to "rob Mexicans of their future, and sell the country to foreigners."[16] After the generally moderate and constitutional governments of Benito Juárez and Lerdo, the arrival of the apparently revolutionary Díaz caused consternation and alarm in Washington.[17]

As Díaz took control of the capital, Foster summarized the situation for Secretary Hamilton Fish and asked for instruction. While admitting that he could not immediately assess the ability of Díaz to govern all of Mexico effectively, the minister did feel that the revolutionists at least had the military capabilities necessary to hold the capital. Foster also advised Secretary Fish that Díaz would make an effort to produce a payment on a claims settlement to the United States in January as a means of prodding Washington into giving him diplomatic recognition. Realizing that the Grant administration would want to proceed with caution, Foster concluded, "I have to respectfully request your views upon the situation at as early a day as possible, even though you and the President may not be prepared to take definite action."[18]

The question of extending diplomatic recognition to Díaz troubled Secretary of State Fish, and he delayed making a decision. By January 1877 Foster had still not received orders from Washington; thus, in the hope that his suggestion might help the formulation of a policy in Washington, the minister offered an "unsolicited" opinion given in "confidential and unofficial form." Foster recommended that recognition of Díaz be withheld until after the Mexican elections, which were only a month away and would be largely controlled by Díaz. Since the elections would show Díaz to have a mandate, the United States could then logically extend recognition. Foster did not believe it likely that Díaz would survive his term of four years, but the minister did not see how the United States could delay any longer extending recognition to a de facto government in a country with which the United States had extensive contact.[19]

At almost the same instant that Foster was writing his dispatch to Fish, the secretary was sending Foster his long-awaited instructions. Fish's orders offered Foster little guidance, advising him only to use his "best discretion" on the whole matter. Fish could not see how the United States could possibly receive a payment from a government it did not acknowledge, and he left the decision regarding recognition entirely in Foster's hands.[20] Fish demonstrated great confidence in Foster's judgment, and had the minister been allowed to make policy on his own, diplomatic recognition would probably have been extended to the Díaz government following the Mexican elections.[21] But the Grant administration was replaced in March 1877 by that of Rutherford B. Hayes, and the new secretary of state's instructions soon reflected a hard-line policy toward Mexico. While Foster was becoming increasingly enthusiastic about General Díaz, the Hayes administration and the new secretary of state, William M. Evarts, responding to domestic pressures, adopted an increasingly unfriendly and at times belligerent posture toward Mexico.

Foster soon came to believe that Díaz demonstrated genuine qualities of leadership, and he felt that the United States' failure to grant recognition created an additional hardship and embarrassment for the new government in Mexico. In April he urged Secretary of State Evarts to consider recognition, arguing that Díaz embodied "the only hope of the country from within itself, much as I deprecate his revolutionary conduct." Foster maintained that without Díaz the country would "fall into anarchy" and claimed that the return of Lerdo would only bring continued guerrilla warfare. Foster further pointed out that many of the problems between the United States and Mexico could be better resolved if formal diplomatic recognition existed.[22] Foster continued for several months to urge a policy of moderation and recognition as the best course of action for the United States.[23] But while the Hayes administration heard the minister's argument, it was listening to other voices.

The problem of checking the depredations of bandits along the Rio Grande frontier had a long and sordid history by 1877, and prominent Texans and the military exerted great pressure on Hayes to end the border problems permanently by means of written guarantees or treaties prior to recognition.[24] Hayes and Secretary of State William Evarts took the position that the problems existing along the Rio Grande border needed settlement before recognition could be considered, and the administration demanded that the Mexicans cooperate in ending border incidents, even to the extent of permitting United States troops to enter Mexican territory in pursuit of outlaws.[25] The Mexican government was disturbed by the United States' refusal to grant diplomatic recognition, and the situation became further complicated by two events over which Foster had no control. The first involved the strange mission of General John B. Frisbie, a would-be American railroad entrepreneur who suddenly appeared in the Mexican capital with his father-in-law, General M. G. Vallejo, a well-known figure in the fight for California's independence. Evarts had advised Foster that the two men were coming, and they seemed on the surface to be interested in winning a legitimate railroad contract from the Díaz government. But the railroad project fell through, and the real purpose of their mission was exposed. The two men were involved in an attempt to pressure Díaz into selling a large part of northwestern Mexico to the United States. The extent to which Secretary of State Evarts had involved himself in the scheme was unclear, but the incident aroused Mexican public opinion against the United States.[26] The second and considerably more serious development that further strained the already tense relationships between the United States and Mexico concerned the attacks by General E. O. C. Ord on bandit strongholds inside Mexico.

Pressure within the United States for such military operations had not deterred the Grant administration from a moderate course. But Hayes was not politically strong enough to withstand the demands for action.

The tough stand toward Mexico was motivated in large measure by factors not connected with problems along the Mexican frontier. Hayes had been urged by some of his Republican supporters to seek a war with Mexico "to turn public thought from our unhappy internal affairs" and because war would "furnish immediate employment to thousands now starving for bread."[27] Although Hayes may not have desired war himself, powerful forces within his administration were clearly anxious for hostilities.[28] Meanwhile, Foster received information "on good authority" that certain influential figures believed "it would divert attention from pending issues and tend greatly to consolidate the new Administration, if a war could be brought on with Mexico and another slice of its territory added to the union."[29] In this volatile atmosphere General Ord received authorization early in June 1877 to chase desperados across the United States border and into Mexico.[30]

The Mexicans were understandably suspicious of any United States military operations along their northern frontier and viewed Ord's operations as either an attempt to return Lerdo to power or a filibuster aimed at provoking war.[31] Foster now had the responsibility of assuring the Mexican government that Ord was acting in a limited operation aimed only at ending border incidents, and he explained the United States' position to the Mexican government in dispassionate and reasoned language. Several weeks after Ord's military operations started, Foster sent the Mexican Foreign Office a carefully worded memorandum explaining the reasons behind the extreme measure. Foster stated that the instructions given to Ord were not entirely original; he reminded the Mexicans that the United States had frequently suggested such a plan and had informed Mexico of the possibility of such action. He claimed that the depredations of the past four years were not common to both sides of the frontier, since bandits from Texas did not raid Mexican territory. He asserted that adequate measures to prevent raiding and punish criminals had not been employed with vigor by the Mexican authorities, and he reminded the Mexican government that it had even acknowledged its inability to cope with border problems. He explained that the instructions to General Ord were "not unconditional": the U.S. commander was ordered initially to seek the cooperation of local Mexican authorities and to pursue bandits into Mexico only as a last resort. Finally, Foster protested the public claims by the Mexican minister of war that the United States was seeking to discredit the Díaz government or support the ambitions of Lerdo's anti-government forces.[32]

Foster believed that his government was following an unwise course of action with regard to Mexico and suspected that the administration did not understand the situation in Mexico and the true nature of the Díaz regime.

Therefore, he requested permission to visit Washington to present his views directly, but Evarts rejected Foster's petition, stating that he expected that Foster's actions would "continue to be discreet, judicious and energetic."[33] Nevertheless, the minister was soon called back to Washington to testify before Congress; the Mexican question had become such an important political issue that both the House and Senate were holding investigations of the Hayes administration's handling of Mexican policy.[34]

In presenting his testimony Foster skillfully presented his arguments for recognition without appearing to be at odds with the president or secretary of state. Foster testified before a House subcommittee on February 9, 1878 and stated that in his opinion Díaz was making a genuine effort to control the border situation. He claimed that Díaz surpassed his predecessors in efforts to police the frontier regions. But Foster refused to answer when he was asked what his policy would be regarding recognition, pointing out that policy making should be left to the president and the secretary of state.[35] Testifying again one week later, Foster was careful not to contradict official policy, but he did go as far as to state that nonrecognition had a negative effect on commercial intercourse and had "a tendency to irritate the Mexican people [who viewed it] as an unfriendly act." Foster also urged improved transportation facilities, particularly the construction of railroads, which would assure American trade "a great advantage over European nations."[36] Apparently Foster's presence in Washington helped alter United States policy toward Díaz. Before returning to Mexico Foster received a new set of instructions that authorized him to recognize the Díaz government.[37] These orders were drafted by Foster himself in cooperation with Assistant Secretary of State Fredrick W. Seward, who had been informed by Evarts that the minister could have the exact instruction he wanted.[38]

The recognition of Díaz ended an anxious and unpleasant situation, but border raids continued to be a serious problem for several years; and in spite of official recognition, obstacles to improved commercial relations still existed. For the remainder of his tenure in Mexico, Foster spent long hours reporting on border incidents and making protests to the Mexican government that "criminals habitually take refuge with their plunder in Mexican territory."[39] Foster demanded that the Mexican government agree to extradition for those committing crimes in United States territory, but the Mexicans insisted that the United States agree to reciprocity in such cases.[40] The order allowing General Ord to pursue bandits into Mexico was revoked in March 1880, much to the delight of the Mexican government.[41] Finally, in 1882 (after Foster had departed from Mexico), a convention was signed providing that "regular federal troops of the two Republics may reciprocally cross the boundary line of the two countries" in pursuit of bandits and Indians.[42] This agreement became a major step in improving border conditions.

During his years in Mexico Foster devoted considerable energies to improving commercial relations. The recognition of Díaz's government improved United States relations with Mexico; still, Foster viewed the revolutionary nature of Mexican politics and the poor lines of communication between the two countries as principal obstacles to increased trade.[43] Rejecting all schemes for establishing a type of protectorate over Mexico as a means of exploiting commercial opportunities, Foster maintained, as Porfirio Díaz relentlessly consolidated his power, that "the only pressure or influence we ought at present to exert in the internal affairs of this country is that which will secure the peace and good order of our frontier and the protection of American citizens and their interests in this Republic."[44] He believed that United States interests were best served by a stable and independent Mexico at peace with her northern neighbor and open to foreign investors. Foster also considered the construction of railroads connecting Mexico with major United States cities in the Southwest of paramount importance if the United States were to enjoy advantages over European investors.[45]

Foster viewed commercial reciprocity as a device that could improve the position of the United States in trading with Mexico. Shortly after arriving in Mexico City, he had initiated informal discussions on the topic of reciprocal trade with the Lerdo government, even without instructions to do so, and he forwarded to Washington information favorable to a reciprocal trade agreement.[46] In January 1876 he had welcomed representatives from the New Orleans Chamber of Commerce who were interested in "the cultivation of more intimate commercial intercourse between New Orleans and Mexico." In his report to Secretary of State Evarts, Foster noted that the delegates had stressed the need for an agreement on reciprocity.[47] Several months later Foster transmitted to Washington an article by a prominent Mexican politician that expressed the desirability of a reciprocal trade agreement with the United States.[48] Any hopes for reciprocity with Mexico in the 1870s were destroyed by the confusion that followed the fall of Lerdo, but the idea of commercial reciprocity gained considerable popularity among United States foreign policy makers in the following decades, and Foster would play a prominent role in seeking important trade agreements with Latin American states. While his efforts to promote commercial reciprocity at this time proved premature, his work in this area was nevertheless significant.[49]

Always an advocate of improved railroad connections between the United States and Mexico, Foster found that Mexicans did not share his enthusiasm for trunk lines linking central Mexico with the United States. Soon after arriving in Mexico, Foster reported that a contract to construct a railroad joining Mexico with Texas had been awarded to Edward L. Plumb of the International Railroad Company of Texas; however, the plan met opposition in the Mexican Congress, where there was fear that the powerful neighbors to the north might use the lines as a future invasion route. Foster sympathized with Plumb's efforts, but after long delays Plumb withdrew his project when Díaz gained control of the government.[50] Congressional opposition in Mexico also halted a plan to connect Mexico City with California during the first years of the Díaz regime; and although a New York company did win a contract to construct a railroad on the Isthmus of Tehuantepec, for almost a decade the Mexican government continued to refuse to allow for lines connecting the center of its country with the United States.[51]

In the years following the recognition of the Díaz government, commercial relations improved, despite lingering problems. In February 1879 a trade delegation from the United States visited Mexico and found that the situation appeared favorable.[52] Foster reported that this group was well received by their Mexican hosts and that President Díaz had greeted the businessmen personally. Foster was enthusiastic about the possibilities of expanded trade and "regretted that the representation of the commercial interests of the United States was so meager." But Secretary of State Evarts lacked Foster's optimism and was not in favor of increased trade with Mexico while border conditions remained unsettled and danger to the lives of citizens and property of the United States in Mexico persisted.[53] Foster was not blind to the difficult conditions that existed, nor did he seek to gloss over the problems that awaited United States investors.[54] In fact, Foster's candid and realistic appraisals of conditions in Mexico on occasion upset both Mexican officials and foreign investors.[55] Nevertheless, he remained committed to the goal of increasing United States trade with Mexico, despite numerous discouragements.

Foster's admiration of the character and ability of President Porfirio Díaz led to the development of a close personal friendship with the Mexican dictator, and a profitable business relationship resulted some years later when Foster became the legal counsel for the Mexican legation in Washington.[56] While Foster was minister to Mexico, Díaz frequently visited the United States legation for social affairs. At one of the Fosters' usual Tuesday night receptions, the Mexican president was introduced by Mrs. Foster to the beautiful daughter of a wealthy Mexican landowner. The young woman eventually became the wife of the president, and the friendship of the Fosters with Díaz became even more intimate as a result. Because of Foster's close relationship with Díaz, Secretary of State Frederick Frelinghuysen asked Foster in the spring of 1883 to act as President Chester A. Arthur's special representative in escorting the Mexican leader, his wife, and her parents on a tour of the eastern United States.[57]

As Díaz demonstrated the ability to establish order and promote material progress in Mexico, Foster remarked that credit was "to be attributed, in great measure, to the personal qualities of President Díaz. Probably no other individual in the republic could so fully have controlled the turbulent and discontent elements of his own revolutionary party, or have inspired so much fear in the ranks of his opponents."[58] After 1880 Díaz grew increasingly receptive to foreign investment in Mexico, and during his long period of dictatorial rule, known as the *porfiriato*, industry and commercial interests expanded while foreign investments increased. Díaz provided order and stability by using harsh, repressive measures. His principal advisors, trained in *laissez-faire* economics and the philosophy of positivism, created a government that concentrated on materialism while neglecting human needs. Meanwhile, individual rights and civil liberties were put aside in the name of economic progress and prosperity. After 1880 Díaz was viewed favorably in the United States, and throughout his regime he enjoyed a close relationship with administrations in Washington.[59] During the time Díaz held power in Mexico, Foster served as a spokesman for his regime in the United States. Writing in 1909, two years before the aged dictator was finally driven into exile and the *porfiriato* ended. Foster still viewed Díaz as a man who had done remarkably well for his country:

> *President Díaz was able, through his successful administration of affairs, to accomplish what at the time seemed hopeless. He gave the country a long era of peace and order. He forced the Congress to grant liberal concessions for railroads connecting with the United States. He established protection and security to life and property. He restored public confidence. He brought about great development of the resources of the country. Under his regime, commerce, internal and foreign, flourished beyond the dream of the most hopeful.*[60]

Obviously Foster considered the maintenance of order and stability of greater importance than attention to social needs.

In a number of ways Foster proved to be a welcome change from the usual type of diplomat representing the United States. He traveled widely in Mexico, met and mixed with the people, and unlike previous ministers to Mexico, he learned to read and speak Spanish with skill. United States citizens in Mexico generally found Foster to be a conscientious and capable diplomat whose official residence served as "the center of social hospitality."[61] The British citizens in Mexico also thought highly of Foster and were grateful to him for the work he did on their behalf in the absence of representation by their own government.[62]

Before accepting the position in Mexico, Foster had been just another Midwestern politician who would have been content to accept a minor diplomatic mission in an obscure but pleasant European capital as a reward for political services, but following his seven years in Mexico, Foster was a proven diplomat with ambitions beyond returning to a routine legal practice in Evansville. In 1880 Foster received word of his nomination by President Hayes to be minister to Russia, and he viewed the appointment as recognition of his accomplishments in Mexico on the part of the administration in Washington. Indeed, the secretary of state was pleased with Foster's performance, and in spite of differences that they had endured, Evarts wrote, "It pleases me that the Russian mission has fallen into such competent hands as yours. There are international opportunities there, waiting for the man with the ability and the desire to improve them."[63]

The appointment to Russia marked a turning point in Foster's career. Still in his early forties, Foster had already served seven turbulent years in a difficult diplomatic post and had distinguished himself. Furthermore, he was a Republican with an honorable war record—a prerequisite for political advancement in the post–Civil War era. In 1876 he had returned briefly to Indiana to aid in the presidential campaign of Rutherford Hayes, the governor of Ohio. Foster became involved in questionable campaign tactics, including the raising of $35,000 to purchase and finance secretly a Greenback party newspaper in Indianapolis that would urge soft-money Democrats to desert Samuel Tilden in favor of the third party candidate, Peter Cooper. Operating what one campaign worker described as "a sort of side committee," Foster maintained a special fund to pay off Greenbacks who were willing to support the Republican candidate.[64] The brief but eventful return to Indiana provided the opportunity to renew old contacts, and his political efforts earned consideration for a cabinet position in the Hayes administration.[65] By 1880 Foster was clearly a man with a promising future in national politics.

The experience in the Mexican capital provided a valuable diplomatic education as well as an opportunity for Foster to exhibit his talents. Quick to recognize the political and military strength of Porfirio Díaz, Foster demonstrated skill in negotiating the recognition issue and sound judgment in handling the problems concerning border raiding. He established firm and genuine friendships with Díaz and key members of his administration and became popular with the Mexican officials and American residents who, like the British citizens in Mexico, found him not only competent but approachable. Foster's diplomatic ability was not overlooked in Washington, where Secretaries of State Fish and Evarts followed his sound advice and allowed the minister considerable initiative in making policy.

A self-righteous Presbyterian and nationalistic Midwesterner, Foster would never shed certain aspects of provincialism. Although he was interested in Mexican culture, Foster never doubted the superiority of his own values. He considered the Catholic church in Mexico to be unenlightened, although not hopelessly backward, and he felt confident that the activities of Protestant missionaries in Mexico would create "a spirit of rivalry in the old religion and awaken its energies to new life and activity." While the Mexicans celebrated Sunday with dancing, parties, and bull fights, Foster remained at home and spent the Sabbath in quiet seclusion with his family, exactly as he would have in Evansville, Indiana, and much to the consternation of the diplomatic community in Mexico City, only "tea and light refreshments" were ever served at gatherings in the United States legation while Foster was minister.[66]

In Mexico Foster displayed characteristics and interests that would mark his entire career in diplomacy. His long interest in reciprocity as a device for bringing Latin America into closer economic ties with the United States began during his tenure in Mexico, and eventually his unique expertise was employed in efforts to secure a reciprocity treaty with Spain for the islands of Cuba and Puerto Rico. Foster's knowledge of reciprocity matters also led to a key appointment in the Benjamin Harrison administration as a special assistant and counselor to Secretary of State James G. Blaine. While he was in Mexico, Foster disagreed with those who urged United States territorial expansion in Latin America. His stand in opposition to those who would have welcomed a war with Mexico as an opportunity to secure areas of land adjacent to the southern border of the United States was to be repeated decades later when, as a senior American statesman, Foster would voice opposition to the acquisition of Puerto Rico and Cuba as well as the Philippines. To Foster, the United States interests in Latin America were commercial and economic, and he viewed the inclusion of enormous masses of non-Anglo-Saxon Spanish-speaking peoples into the Union as a potential political disaster.

Because he judged progress and order in Mexico to be directly related to the economic influence of the United States, Foster believed that domestic political order and stability should be the paramount concerns for any Mexican government. Porfirio Díaz, using efficient, forceful, and often brutal means, managed to bring to Mexico the order and stability that Foster viewed as a prerequisite for the United States investment necessary for progress in Mexico and profits for the investors. As Foster prepared to leave Mexico, the Díaz government was becoming increasingly friendly to foreign investors. During the thirty years of the *porfiriato*, Mexican governmental operations were centralized, internal lines of communication and transportation saw improvement, and the country was opened to extensive foreign economic penetration. Dismissing the dictatorial aspects of the *porfiriato* as unavoidable, Foster firmly established a close, harmonious, and mutually profitable relationship between the United States and Porfirio Díaz. In addition, Foster would have the opportunity for personal gain.

In the appointment to St. Petersburg, Foster was presented with an opportunity for a career in international diplomacy. His first experience in foreign affairs had been a marked success, and he had every reason to expect that a brilliant future awaited him. But the 1880s were to be an uncertain decade in American foreign relations, and John W. Foster would find himself charting an ambiguous and irregular course.

Politics

The 1880s proved to be an uncertain period in United States foreign relations as the expanding nation took tentative and uneasy steps towards an enlarged influence abroad. Those Americans desiring an active foreign policy hoped in 1881 that President James A. Garfield and his dynamic secretary of state, James G. Blaine, would herald a new policy of increased foreign trade, extended coastal defenses in the Pacific and Caribbean, and greater prestige abroad. Garfield and his successor, Chester A. Arthur, failed to realize their designs for a more internationalist policy, but they did focus attention on foreign policy problems and alternatives from which Americans would eventually be forced to choose.[1] But as yet Americans recognized no great need for a professional diplomatic service, and many isolationist-minded Americans viewed the State Department as a waste of money. When John W. Foster assumed his duties in St. Petersburg, he was one of only twenty-five ministers in residence representing his country in a foreign capital.[2]

Throughout the 1880s Foster's diplomatic career was characterized by frustration, vacillation, and uncertainty; these years were an important time, however, because they provided an opportunity to acquire knowledge and experience that would later prove invaluable. This was the case particularly with respect to the issue of commercial reciprocity. While Foster was to find his initial endeavors fruitless, his frustrated efforts to secure reciprocal trade agreements would qualify him for an important appointment in the Harrison administration that led ultimately to the office of secretary of state. Twice during the 1880s Foster resigned from diplomatic service to pursue an exceptionally profitable career in international law, and at the time of each

27

resignation Foster claimed he was leaving government service forever. Still, it seems that he never really intended to drift far from the State Department; his residence in Washington and his legal work kept him in close personal contact with the shapers of United States foreign policies. He also remained involved in Republican party politics, although his political fortunes suffered temporary setbacks. Perhaps he would have secured a cabinet post for himself, had he not twice supported Walter Quinten Gresham's unsuccessful attempts to secure the Republican party's presidential nomination.

Foster's tenure in Russia did not last much beyond a year, and his record at St. Petersburg left no discernible impact on United States relations with Russia. To Foster's great disappointment the prestigious assignment to St. Petersburg proved dull and uninteresting, compared to the challenge of diplomacy in Mexico. The most urgent and time-consuming matter with which he dealt concerned the unjust and discriminatory treatment of Jewish citizens of the United States who resided in or traveled through Russia, and on this subject Foster displayed all the zeal he had once known as a youthful abolitionist. Foster not only protested the unfair treatment of Jewish Americans but also lectured the Russian regime on the evils of religious discrimination. Not surprisingly, despite Foster's protests the history of Russian antisemitism continued, and it is doubtful that the sermons of the United States minister received much attention. Beyond the protesting of mistreatment to United States citizens, Foster's duties proved quite routine, but because this was his first assignment in Europe, the time in Russia was not without some importance in Foster's diplomatic education.

Upon his arrival in St. Petersburg in June 1880, Foster found a dispatch from Secretary Evarts awaiting his attention. The message stated that the Union of American-Hebrew Congregations had expressed anxiety about the conditions of Jews in Russia, and the secretary advised Foster to look into the matter, cautioning the minister that it "would of course be inadmissible for the government of the United States to approach the government of Russia in criticism of its laws and regulations, except so far as such laws and regulations may injuriously affect citizens of this country, in violation of natural rights, treaty obligations or provisions of international law. . . ."[3] Foster soon discovered that the legation's chargé ad interim already had in his hands the case of Henry Pinkos, an American Jew expelled from St. Petersburg, where he had been involved in a modest business. Because of assassination plots aimed at Emperor Alexander II, in which some Jews were rumored to be involved, a decree had been issued, demanding that all Jews leave St. Petersburg. Apparently United States citizens such as Pinkos were not to be exceptions. Foster's orders were to protest the expulsion of a citizen of the United States because of his religion.[4]

The case of Henry Pinkos and his family, along with that of Marx Wilczynski, who was expelled from St. Petersburg under circumstances similar to Pinkos', formed the basis for a number of exchanges between Foster and Russia's minister of foreign affairs, the courtly Nicholas de Giers.[5] During one conversation Foster went beyond the mere protestation of the treatment of United States citizens. In a dispatch to the secretary of state, Foster reported:

In the course of the conversation I stated that while the object of the interview was to obtain proper recognition of the rights of American Jews, my government took deep interest in the amelioration of the condition of the Jewish race in other nations, and I was satisfied that it would be highly gratified at the statement of the minister that a commission was now considering the question of modification in a liberal sense of the Russian laws regarding the Jews.[6]

This remark did not seem to move Giers; he calmly retorted that few nations escaped the problem of race prejudice, including the United States. Concerned that his minister was becoming overly self-righteous, Evarts felt compelled to remind Foster that the United States protested Russian policy "not because they [United States citizens] are Jews but because they are Americans."[7] Evarts was pleased, nevertheless, with Foster's spirited defense of American policy and his vigorous presentation of the United States position in the Pinkos and Wilczynski cases.[8]

Through the final months of 1880 Foster witnessed and reported to Washington on growing civil discontent in Russia. However, the minister misread the nature of the radical opposition to Alexander II, believing that there had "not developed any widespread or very alarming conspiracy against the government."[9] Because the tzar's ruthless police appeared to have quieted the capital, Foster was completely shocked by the brutal assassination of Alexander II by a terrorist's bomb.[10] The United States government had viewed the liberal and reform-minded Alexander II as a friend because of his neutrality during the Civil War, and Foster immediately made an official expression of sympathy on behalf of the United States.[11]

The excitement and drama surrounding the death of Alexander II probably provided the single most profound experience of Foster's tenure in Russia. Foster had been in Russia only six months when he began to show concern about being removed from his position as the new and unfamiliar Republican administration of former congressman James A. Garfield began. Following the elections in November, Senator Benjamin Harrison of Indiana wrote to assure Foster that he need not worry that President Garfield would have him replaced.[12] Nevertheless, Foster announced that he was "quite ready to give way to some Indiana or other patriot who is anxious to serve his country and spend his money for the government."[13] Apparently Foster had found court life in St. Petersburg beyond his means. In August 1881 he took a leave of absence and returned to the United States, tendering his resignation a few months later without ever returning to Russia. Although both the new secretary of state, James G. Blaine, and the president would have preferred that the minister remain at his post or take a diplomatic assignment elsewhere, they accepted his wishes to enter a private law practice in Washington.[14]

Foster was not pleased with what he saw of Russian society. Concerned about the treatment of Jews, Foster considered the Russian government brutal, unenlightened, and autocratic. To the God-fearing, moralistic Foster, it seemed that "the country must pay dearly in the end for the unjust treatment of six million of its people."[15] The violent attacks against the government by youthful nihilists also upset Foster, and he came to believe that orderly reform in Russia would be impossible. Through his diplomatic career Foster would maintain an unfavorable view of Russian foreign policies, particularly with regard to Russia's ambitions in the Far East. Clearly, Foster's experience in St. Petersburg did nothing to provide him with reason to be sympathetic to the Russian rulers.

For more than a year following his resignation from the State Department, the former diplomat applied his energies to the pursuit of fortune. Foster was concerned about "accumulating a competency" for his family and providing his two teenage daughters with an education in their homeland. The legal work went extremely well, and his practice proved profitable beyond his expectations, offering great prospect for an even more profitable future. It was therefore with some misgivings that Foster received a note from Garfield's successor, President Chester A. Arthur, asking that he call at the White House on February 21, 1883. Foster met with the president and discussed the possibility of an appointment to Spain as a special envoy.[16] After considering the matter with his wife and political associates, principally Senator Harrison of Indiana, Foster accepted what he considered "an appeal too flattering to my pride and patriotism to be resisted."[17]

President Arthur was anxious for a reciprocity treaty with Spain for that nation's colonies of Cuba and Puerto Rico. Already, former President Grant, serving as a special agent, had followed up on Foster's earlier efforts and had negotiated a reciprocal trade agreement with Mexico. Arthur hoped that additional reciprocity treaties would further increase Latin American trade with the United States. Other matters of importance awaiting settlement involved claims of United States citizens against Cuba stemming from personal losses suffered in a recent rebellion.[18] The government viewed the problems regarding Spain's Caribbean colonies as extremely serious, and Foster was apparently chosen for the assignment without regard for political considerations; rather, Secretary of State Frederick T. Frelinghuysen chose Foster because he knew the Spanish language and had experience in sensitive diplomatic situations.[19]

Arriving at the court of King Alfonso XII on June 16, the American envoy read a brief statement in which he expressed the hope that "through increasing and improved commercial relations the United States and Spain may reciprocally share each other's prosperity."[20] Despite a gracious welcome and public statements favoring reciprocity, the Spanish government demonstrated no real enthusiasm about an agreement. Cuban members of the Spanish Cortes, or National Congress, favored reciprocity, especially after the Grant-Romero Treaty created reciprocity between the United States and Mexico. This agreement hurt Cuban plantation owners: it provided Mexican sugar with free entry into the United States, and Cuban growers realized the importance of the North American market. Despite exorbitant duties, trade between the United States and Cuba totaled $82,585,476 in 1882, while trade with Spain amounted to only $12,674,157. Naturally, the government in Madrid feared that a reciprocity agreement might further weaken Cuba's ties with the mother country, possibly leading to rebellion, independence, and even eventual annexation by the United States.[21]

The hesitancy of the Spanish government to agree to a reciprocity treaty was made apparent by the stalling tactics employed by the Spanish negotiators. Foster unkindly attributed much of the delay to "the Spanish temperament [which] does not admit of celerity in the dispatch of public business." He also acknowledged the more significant obstacles; the tour of Alfonso XII to Berlin and Paris, which caused an international uproar, the strong *Carlist* movement which sought to place the pretender Don Carlos on the throne, and numerous ministerial changes.[22] When given the opportunity for discussion, Foster negotiated with force and vigor, threatening with United States trade reprisals in order to pressure the Spanish into an agreement. Finally on January 2, 1884, Prime Minister Antonio Cánovas del Castillo consented to remove differential levies and consular fees from products imported from the United States; in return, he was assured that the United States would remove a recently imposed retaliatory duty of ten percent.[23] Following the signing of a temporary agreement in March, which anticipated a future reciprocal trade agreement, Foster optimistically advised the State Department to proceed with plans for a reciprocity treaty. Viewing reciprocal trade as "the true *American commercial* system, as it combines the best element of 'protection' and 'free trade,'" Foster was now convinced that the United States could drive for a treaty with Spain that would secure for the United States "almost the complete monopoly or control of the rich commerce of these islands."[24] At this point Foster seemed to feel that the matter was virtually resolved.

With the coming of the presidential election campaign of 1884, Foster's attentions turned suddenly from diplomacy to Republican party politics. Negotiations in Madrid had reached a point where there would be delay before Foster could proceed to a permanent reciprocity agreement, and although Foster was authorized to continue on in the Spanish capital, he requested and received orders to return to Washington for consultations with Secretary of State Frelinghuysen.[25] Foster did not really want or need discussions on reciprocity; his real motive for arranging his own recall at this time stemmed from his desire to assist the political campaign of his close personal friend, Walter Q. Gresham, the postmaster general, who was now serving along with Frelinghuysen in President Arthur's cabinet. The two had been political allies and warm friends since before the Civil War, and Gresham lived in the Fosters' home in Washington while the minister and his family were in Spain.[26] A liberal Indiana Republican with great popularity in the Midwest, Gresham was anxious to have Foster's support in taking the Republican party's nomination away from the incumbent president. As Gresham began maneuvering for the nomination, Foster returned home to attempt to "turn the tide" and keep Indiana's Senator Benjamin Harrison from "antagonizing" Gresham's support in their home state, where Foster felt he still had some influence, despite his years abroad.[27]

Foster viewed Gresham as an ideal candidate. A favorite of General Grant, Gresham had an exceptional war record and was highly regarded among the liberal wing of the Republican party. He was bright, sensitive, "incorruptible," and blessed with a "winning smile." Furthermore, Foster hoped Gresham could emerge as a possible compromise candidate, "not mixed up in the old quarrels and yet one who had a good record and [had] shown administrative ability."[28] But this was not to be the year for such a nominee. Indiana's Senator Harrison demonstrated unexpected strength in his own delegation, and at the Republican party convention a "Harrison movement" emerged. While leading the Gresham forces, Foster tried to resist Harrison's pressure on Indiana delegates by supporting President Arthur as a tactical ploy, hoping to swing the delegation to Gresham if Arthur failed to receive the nomination. Despite such tactics, Harrison people in the Indiana delegation succeeded in winning the right to place their man's name in nomination.[29] On June 6, Foster telegrammed Gresham from the convention to inform him that Harrison's men had made a deal with James G. Blaine that would assure the Republican nomination for the powerful senator from Maine. Later the same day Foster sent word to Gresham that he was being considered for the vice-presidential nomination and asked his friend for directions regarding this possibility. Gresham quickly rejected the idea and suggested Harrison as a suitable running mate.[30]

Both Foster and Gresham were disappointed with the outcome of the convention, not only because their ambitions had been checked but because they intensely disliked the man chosen to be the party standard-bearer. Foster remained a solid party man, although unenthusiastic about the campaign, which he viewed as "one of filth beyond precedent." Blaine's campaign against the Democratic candidate, Grover Cleveland, produced such scandal that Foster believed Gresham fortunate not to be on the ticket. Following the

Republican defeat by Cleveland, Foster confided to Gresham that during his return to the United States for the convention and campaign, he had "learned things which confirm my anxieties that he [Blaine] would have been an unsafe ruler." For his part, Gresham completely avoided campaigning for the Republican nominee. He openly expressed admiration for Cleveland and began to publicly express grave disillusionment with the party of Lincoln.[31] Despite their disappointment, Foster and Gresham would team up again in 1888.

A few weeks after the Republican convention, Foster was back in Madrid and prepared to pursue negotiations with increased force and determination. He returned to Spain with a draft for a reciprocity agreement that had the secretary of state's approval. Foster had been given full power to make necessary alterations. The Spanish appointed Salvador de Albacete to hold discussions with Foster and facilitate the negotiating process. The two diplomats conducted prolonged and complicated sessions over a period of several months, with Foster exerting pressure on the Spanish negotiator that approached outright threats.[32] At one point Foster employed "a little plain speaking" to present the Spanish plenipotentiary with three reasons why Spain should agree to reciprocity: first, the lack of a treaty would cause great dissatisfaction in Cuba against Spain and would lead to the "early loss of the island to the Spanish crown"; second, the United States would make trade agreements with other tropical countries that would ruin the economies of Cuba and Puerto Rico; and third, failure to make a treaty "would cause such disappointment and resentment in the United States as would almost inevitably affect unfavorably our present friendly relations" and would surely exacerbate the difficulties concerning unsettled claims against Spain.[33] Faced with such alarming prospects, the Spanish agreed to a treaty in November, and Foster hurriedly returned to Washington with the document. He believed that Cuba's destiny was to be independent of Spain and economically, but not necessarily politically, tied to the United States. While negotiating with the Spanish, he wrote to Gresham:

Cuba lives off the United States, . . . and if Spain away off here in Europe is not willing to make a fair treaty with us relative to trade, it will be in our interest to see the island independent in the hands of natives who are and will be our friends. And that can be brought about by a little sympathy or indifference to neutrality matters on our part. We have plenty of grounds for a quarrel with Spain, but I do not think we want Cuba, although a war might not be the greatest evil that could befall us just now.[34]

Ironically, after the Spanish government agreed to reciprocity, the treaty was killed by politicians in Washington—an eventuality that Foster had not considered possible. Among the opponents of Foster's reciprocity treaty were both Republicans and Democrats, protectionists and free traders. The free trade advocates viewed the reciprocity system as sugar pills that might satisfy the patient but could not cure the illness.[35] Many special interest groups within the United States also voiced strong opposition to the agreement.[36] Although the economic objections were considerable obstacles, political considerations, not economic arguments, finally defeated the reciprocity treaty. The Republican party had been beaten in November, and the ambitious diplomacy of the Arthur administration was about to be replaced by the more negative and essentially defensive foreign policy of Grover Cleveland, an enemy of reciprocity. The attitudes of Democrats favorable to reciprocity before Cleveland's election quickly cooled toward Foster's treaty as Cleveland prepared to assume office. Furthermore, the Republicans were not united behind reciprocity, and the still influential James G. Blaine headed Republican opposition to the treaty, possibly out of personal animosity for Arthur.[37] Foster's treaty also had the misfortune of going before the Senate at the same time as a number of important foreign policy measures, including a Nicaragua canal treaty and a reciprocity agreement with Santo Domingo. With all these matters awaiting action, it seemed to many that Arthur's "lame-duck" administration was attempting to push through last-minute legislation without proper deliberation.[38] Thus, Foster's treaty became a political football, kicked by both Blaine and Cleveland from different directions until it was entirely deflated.

The failure of the reciprocity agreement with Spain did not end Foster's involvement with the issue. Shortly after the Cleveland administration took office, the new secretary of state, Thomas F. Bayard, asked Foster to return to Spain to seek modifications to the reciprocity agreement that would satisfy those American business interests that had opposed reciprocity. Understandably, Foster was skeptical of achieving any success at this point, but he agreed to return to Madrid.[39] Again he encountered difficulties in trying to get the attention of Spanish officials, this time because of a cholera epidemic and internal political instability. Furthermore, the changes desired by Bayard could not be secured because the exchange products that the secretary of state wanted to omit were precisely those most desired by Spain. The failure of the previous treaty before the United States Senate also made the Spanish reluctant to enter into any new agreements. After a summer of travel across the Iberian Peninsula but no progress regarding reciprocal trade, Foster resigned and returned to his private law practice.[40]

Foster now focused his attention on his legal practice with increased vigor. Employing his vast network of diplomatic contacts, Foster built an international clientele that included the Washington legations of Mexico, Russia, Spain, China, Peru, Nicaragua and, according to the *New York Times*, more than half the republics in South America.[41] Foster described his work as counsel for foreign legations in Washington as a much-needed service for countries wanting to "profit from my diplomatic experience and knowledge of the institution of our country." He claimed that his role as legal advisor headed off controversies with the State Department and constituted, in his view "a service to our own and foreign governments." He was proud of the success he attained and boasted of the financial rewards his work brought him.[42] While he served a number of countries as their legal advisor in Washington, he simultaneously accepted cases for United States citizens against some of the very countries whose legations employed him.[43] The matter of possible conflict of interest never seemed to raise problems for him, and while he accepted handsome legal fees, he insisted that he scrupulously avoided business involvements in countries where he served in an official capacity.[44] Increasingly after 1885 Foster found that public and private careers conveniently complemented each other.

Throughout his career as an international lawyer, Foster enjoyed a particularly close relationship with the Chinese legation in Washington. While minister to Russia Foster had made the acquaintance of Marquis Tsêng, then China's ambassador to St. Petersburg. Their friendship led to a long association between Foster and prominent Chinese officials that lasted three decades.

During the 1880s the central issue between the United States and China concerned the protection of Chinese citizens in the United States and the mitigation of legislation aimed at prohibiting Chinese from entering the United States.[45] In 1885 Foster was involved in a sensational case that brought him national notoriety. An attack by an angry mob against Chinese workers in Rock Springs, Wyoming on September 2, 1885 left twenty-eight Chinese killed and fifteen seriously injured. Following this incident, Foster helped the Chinese minister draft a letter of protest to Secretary of State Thomas F. Bayard.[46] Cleveland and Bayard publicly expressed "strong feelings of indignation and commiseration," but refused to acknowledge that the United States owed an obligation of indemnity to the Chinese. When Bayard did submit the matter of indemnity for congressional consideration, he claimed he acted "solely from a sentiment of generosity and pity." Eventually he recommended compensation to the Chinese, but only because he thought such an act might put China's minister to Washington, Chang Yin-hoon, in a mood to negotiate a treaty to restrict Chinese immigration.[47] Congress did recommend compensation as a humanitarian gesture but refused to consider the question of liability.[48] As the Chinese government's legal counsel, Foster viewed the award as only a partial victory. He strongly believed that the United States needed federal legislation to protect resident foreigners in the same manner that the United States demanded protection for its citizens overseas. Foster viewed the issue in terms of reciprocity. He understood that protection of Chinese in the United States was necessary to insure the safety of American investments and missionary projects in China.[49]

Chinese exclusion was the subject of great political interest, particularly in those areas where cheap Chinese labor caused social unrest. Chinese exclusion became a political issue in the presidential election year of 1888, and on March 12, Bayard and Chinese minister Chang signed a treaty excluding most Chinese laborers for a period of twenty years.[50] The unfavorable initial reaction to the treaty in China made ratification by that country doubtful. Assuming rejection, Democratic Representative William L. Scott, a close associate of President Cleveland, proposed a bill excluding all Chinese laborers.[51] The bill was passed quickly and the president signed it on October 1. This politically motivated gesture failed to win reelection for Cleveland, and it also severely damaged relations with China.[52]

Foster had been involved in the work leading to the treaty of March 12, and he was pleased with the agreement.[53] Convinced that the Chinese government would ultimately ratify the treaty, he opposed the Scott Bill as unnecessary and undiplomatic. On September 19, Foster called at the State Department and had a conversation with John Bassett Moore, the brilliant third assistant secretary of state, who was just beginning his distinguished career. Foster told Moore that the reports about the Chinese having already rejected the treaty were false. He claimed that opposition to the treaty actually came from Chinese merchants in Canton and British traders in Hong Kong engaged in transporting Chinese laborers to the United States.[54] After the Scott act became law, Foster helped the Chinese minister draft letters of protest to the secretary of state.[55] The Chinese, although bitter about the unfavorable settlement of the immigration question, appeared to have been pleased with the efforts of their legal counsel. The Chinese Empire displayed its confidence in Foster by retaining his services, entrusting him with important matters, and seeking his advice on international problems.[56] Foster would continue for the next two decades to present the Chinese government's point of view before the American public.

In 1888 Foster once again supported Gresham for the presidential nomination. Following his unsuccessful bid to capture the nomination four years earlier, Gresham had been appointed federal judge of the Chicago district. Here he gained popularity for his tough stand against exploitation by the railroads. However, the friends Gresham had made in the Midwest among reform-minded or Mugwump Republicans and independents caused party stalwarts to be suspicious of him.[57] Foster, always the pragmatist, warned Gresham of the need to secure broad support early in the campaign and advised the judge to avoid friction with Senator Harrison, financier Jay Gould, or the powerful Blaine. Foster exhorted Gresham to present the impression that, if nominated, he could hold the party together. Assuring Gresham that he would receive support from newspaper men, Foster secretly managed to arrange for the *New York Herald* to print an account of Harrison's opposition to Chinese exclusion in an effort to undercut the Indiana senator's bid for the nomination. Foster also wrote editorials for the

Evansville *Daily Journal* in his old home town to help Indiana's Charles W. Fairbanks revive the "Gresham boom." As the party's convention neared, Foster carried word to Gresham that he had the support of the influential Senator Thomas Platt of New York, a man Gresham might have selected as his running mate.[58]

Although committed to Gresham, Foster tried to maintain unity within the Indiana delegation, and at the same time he carefully guarded his old friendship with Harrison. Foster spoke with the Indiana senator, explained his support for Gresham, and presented hopes for party unity. To some in Gresham's camp it appeared that Foster was hedging on his support for their candidate, and when Foster did not attend the party convention, it appeared to some that Foster had deserted Gresham for a position of neutrality.[59] While he had taken care to keep his fences mended on all sides, however, Foster did not deliberately desert Gresham's camp at the last minute; instead, Foster excused himself from participating in the convention because of the tragic death of his youngest daughter.[60] Actually, Gresham never had a real chance to secure the nomination; the Republican convention overwhelmingly chose the stalwart Harrison over the more idealistic Gresham and a number of other possible choices. Foster found himself once again on the losing side.

The outstanding characteristic of the campaign of 1888 was the extraordinary financing by capitalists in support of Harrison, who won the Republican nomination with the backing of big money and the party bosses.[61] Carl Schurz remarked that the party "gave itself over body and soul to the money-power interested in the protective tariff, expecting from it substantial aid in the election."[62] After the convention Foster expressed similar sentiments to Gresham, remarking that the party was making a mistake by so enthusiastically associating itself with protectionism.[63] Gresham became completely disillusioned and refused to support the Republican ticket; eventually he would leave the party all together. Foster remained a party loyalist, but he considered his political and diplomatic career at an end. Confiding to Gresham, Foster wrote:

. . . *personally it makes little difference to me who is President. I have a business in Washington from which I am accumulating a competency for my family, and I ought not allow myself, for the next few years, to be diverted from it by any official position and of which I have a surfeit already.*[64]

When Harrison narrowly defeated Cleveland in November, Foster could not have imagined that the most important and demanding aspects of his diplomatic career remained before him. Ironically, both Foster and Gresham were destined to hold the office of secretary of state, the former as an interim cabinet member during the final months of Harrison's administration, the latter as head of the Department of State when Cleveland returned to the White House in 1893. Foster was to be associated with the expansionist foreign policy of Harrison's administration, while Gresham was fated to become part of an administration that would repudiate Harrison's diplomacy as imperialistic.

In retrospect Foster's support of Gresham over Harrison in 1884 and 1888 seems peculiar—especially since Foster and Gresham were to appear so dissimilar in their approaches to foreign policies. During the 1880s, however, Gresham displayed almost no interest in diplomatic issues, thus he and Foster probably found little to disagree about. It seems probable that Foster allied himself with Gresham because the judge, an attractive and personable man with a record as a liberal and reformer, appealed to Foster's sense of idealism and concept of American mission. Although always cordial with Harrison, Foster saw the Indiana senator as uninspiring and unimaginative.[65]

The election campaign of 1888 demonstrated increased interest in foreign policy. Issues such as the protective tariff, the Bering Sea fur seal controversy, and the Sackville-West scandal drew considerable attention. The election results brought into office a Republican administration favoring an aggressive foreign policy and prepared to reverse the generally inactive diplomatic course set by Cleveland.[66] To regard the election of Benjamin Harrison as a mandate for increased national self-assertion would be a misinterpretation. Politicians of that era found it difficult to discern what the American public really wanted in terms of foreign policies, and attention focused primarily on domestic problems.[67] While the public may have been confused, uneducated, or unconcerned about foreign affairs, however, Harrison and his political backers clearly wanted to bring about a change in United States foreign relations, and the inauguration of Benjamin Harrison brought to an end an awkward period in American diplomacy.

This uncertain era in American foreign relations had provided Foster with experience in varied diplomatic activities that would be of value as United States diplomacy took on new direction. In Russia Foster had forcefully argued for the rights of United States citizens and sought to bring about the realization of an emerging American influence in St. Petersburg. In urging the Spanish government to agree to a reciprocal trade agreement, Foster educated himself in the complexities of international commercial treaties and Caribbean affairs. He was cognizant of the possibility that reciprocity could lead Cuba to independence from Spain and a dependent relationship with the United States, and he welcomed such a prospect. He fought Chinese exclusion not only because he was legal counsel for the Chinese legation in Washington but because he foresaw the danger of anti-American retaliation in China that would close that vast empire to American commercial and missionary activities. As the decade of the nineties commenced, Foster was the American diplomat most experienced in the policies and tactics necessary for an expansionist foreign policy, and his knowledge and skills soon were to be of service.

IV

"Spirited Diplomacy"

Benjamin Harrison brought to Washington an administration committed to an assertive and aggressive foreign policy that would start the United States on a course of insular imperialism. During Harrison's four years in the White House, the United States attempted to acquire the Danish West Indies, tried to secure a lease for Samaná Bay in Santo Domingo, sought the concession of the Môle Saint Nicolas in Haiti, and seriously considered the possibility of establishing a naval base in Chimbote, Peru. Meanwhile, the administration initiated a program of extensive naval construction under the able leadership of Secretary of State Benjamin F. Tracy. All of Canada was viewed as a legitimate area for outright acquisition, including sole jurisdiction of the Bering Sea and rights to the fur seal trade. The complete annexation of the Hawaiian Islands almost became a reality in the final months of Harrison's term of office. A protectorate in Samoa was successfully arranged, plans were drawn for an enlarged merchant marine, and renewed interest was devoted to the prospects of increased trade in the Caribbean, South America, and the Orient. In a diplomatic crisis with Chile, the United States took a belligerent stand that demonstrated a self-confidence bordering on arrogance. Although the ambitions of the Harrison administration were not realized, the successful imperialistic policies of succeeding administrations were possible because of the decidedly expansionist policies developed during the Harrison administration.[1]

Although John W. Foster was not initially a member of the Harrison administration, he was to become increasingly important in the direction of foreign policy. Foster's friendship with Harrison extended back through their early careers in Indiana politics, and the two men had somehow remained close in spite of Foster's support for the president's archrival, Walter Q. Gresham.[2] Both the president and his secretary of state, James G. Blaine, appreciated Foster's talent and experience and soon brought him into the administration as a special agent for negotiating important reciprocity agreements. Harrison and Blaine were never close, and as the secretary's health declined, the president sought Foster's counsel with increasing regularity. Finally, when Blaine abruptly resigned in July 1892, Foster was quickly appointed to head the Department of State. But by the time of his appointment as secretary of state, Foster had already been as deeply involved as Blaine in drafting and implementing the administration's foreign policy. Indeed, throughout Harrison's administration Foster had immediate and virtually unlimited access to the president and the State Department.

Harrison decided to choose Blaine for his cabinet only after considerable delay and tremendous pressure from powerful Republicans.[3] Blaine was anxious to return to the State Department and he had supported Harrison vigorously in 1888. However, the president-elect did not consult him about important appointments in the diplomatic service and only reluctantly extended an offer of the cabinet post to Blaine. Apparently Harrison was concerned that the popular and dynamic Blaine would try to dominate the administration.[4] Harrison's fears of Blaine's ambitions proved unfounded, however, as the secretary of state soon demonstrated that he had lost his old fire. Nevertheless, Harrison never trusted Blaine as a confidant or advisor.[5] Suspicious of his secretary of state, the president refused to accept Walker Blaine, the secretary's son, as assistant secretary.[6] Harrison wanted to be his own man and personally handled foreign policies to a great extent, especially during Blaine's long absences from Washington.[7] Left out of policy planning, Blaine had no interest in routine administrative tasks and was a poor administrator.[8] Of their strained relationship Harrison remarked: "My association with Mr. Blaine covers some of the most pleasant experiences of my public life, and some of the most trying."[9]

Although Harrison and Blaine were not personally close, they demonstrated no disagreement on major foreign policy objectives. Both were committed to making the United States the dominant power in the Western Hemisphere with a sovereignty over Canada, the Caribbean, and Hawaii. Blaine outlined for the president his vision of the course of United States expansion by stating:

I think there are only three places that are of value enough to be taken, that are not continental. One is Hawaii and the others are Cuba and Puerto Rico. Cuba and Puerto Rico are not now imminent and will not be for a generation. Hawaii will come up for a decision at any unexpected hour and I hope we shall be prepared to decide in the affirmative.[10]

Blaine viewed commercial reciprocity as an important diplomatic device for drawing Canada, Hawaii, and vital areas of Latin America into a special economic sphere dominated by the United States.[11] To this end Blaine used his considerable leverage in Congress to fight for an expanded reciprocity amendment to the McKinley Tariff.[12]

The crucial and complex task of negotiating numerous reciprocity agreements under the McKinley Tariff was assigned to Foster by the president upon Blaine's recommendation.[13] Foster had already been active behind the scenes in advising the president, the secretary of state, Representative William McKinley, and members of the Senate Committee on Finance regarding technical matters concerning commercial reciprocity. Once the McKinley Tariff became law, Foster quickly arranged for a reciprocal trade agreement with Brazil and was given an appointment to negotiate a reciprocal trade agreement with Spain for Cuba and Puerto Rico.[14]

During 1891–1892 Foster was involved in negotiating eight reciprocity agreements—the most important of them with Spain for the colonies of Cuba and Puerto Rico. In late January 1891, Blaine and Foster agreed that before initiating negotiations in Madrid, Foster should make an unofficial journey to Cuba to confer with the commercial and industrial leaders on the island. While still a private citizen, Foster spent ten days in Cuba, ostensibly for reasons of health and vacation, but he carried with him a handwritten letter from Blaine to the United States consulate general in Havana stating, "he [Foster] goes to you officially with the fullest credit and confidence of the State Department. Please respond to any and all requests he may make. I give no specific direction. Mr. Foster is accredited *carte blanche.*"[15] In Cuba he labored to persuade planters, exporters, and the governor-general that since a reciprocal agreement between the United States and Brazil had already been negotiated, failure to achieve a reciprocity treaty for Cuban sugar would be ruinous for the island.[16] After returning to Washington Foster sailed for Madrid, where the Spanish government proved anxious to reach an agreement.[17]

During March, conferences were held between Foster and Spanish officials. Negotiations proceeded smoothly, yet there remained two difficulties; first, Spain had treaties with European powers and might be obliged to grant these nations any favors given to the United States, and second, the Spanish government was in the process of converting the Cuban debt at a lower interest and feared reciprocity would reduce government income. To avoid the problem of European interference, Foster urged acceptance of the United States interpretation of the most-favored-nation clause, which granted favors "only for equivalent compensations." Foster believed that United States interests were best served by a list composed of articles with which European nations could not compete. Foster was confident that he could secure free admission for all cereals, meats, lard, fish feeds, seeds and oil, cotton, coal, naval stores, lumber, sewing machines, and crude petroleum. He also felt that he could secure such a low Cuban duty on flour as to give the United States "a complete monopoly and double (Cuba's) importation."[18] Harrison remained concerned about other nations, particularly Canada and Argentina, gaining access to the Cuban market through the most-favored-nation clause, but once the treaty had been agreed to in Madrid, he was anxious to have his secretary of state sign the document.[19]

Because of illness, Blaine found himself unable to consider matters of state at this point, and he expressed to the president his complete confidence in Foster's discretion regarding the treaty and indicated a willingness to let him sign the document.[20] While Blaine rested and tried to regain his former vigor, Harrison consulted frequently with Foster on reciprocity and "some matters that are his charge."[21] Since his return from Spain Foster had been a private citizen involved with his law practice in Washington.[22] However, he remained an unofficial advisor to the president with special privileges in the Department of State, and the subjects to which Foster now addressed himself included nearly every major foreign policy problem.

Charged with the major responsibility for negotiating reciprocity agreements, Foster held many meetings in a room set aside for him in the State Department or at his home. The British were anxious for reciprocal trade agreements for their colonies in the West Indies, and the Colonial Office was disposed to allow each colony to pursue its own negotiations. Throughout the autumn of 1891 delegations arrived from Barbados, Trinidad, and British Guiana; all were presented to Foster by Sir Julian Pauncefote, the British minister in Washington, and the secretary of the British legation, the youthful Cecil A. Spring-Rice.[23]

At the same time that Foster was working on reciprocity agreements with the British colonies, the arrangement of a protocol with the German government regarding American pork presented a major problem for the State Department. Again Harrison looked to Foster.[24] Count Arco Valley and Chargé d'Affaires Alfons von Munn Schwarzenstein conferred with Foster during the summer of 1891 while Blaine remained secluded in his retreat at Bar Harbor, Maine.[25] In August an agreement was reached at Saratoga, New York in which the German government promised to end its import restrictions on American pork as soon as the United States put into force the Meat Inspection Act of March 1891. The German government also agreed to admit American agricultural products at some reduced tariff rates in return for free entry for German sugar.[26]

Problems in the relationship with neighboring Canada were also brought to Foster's attention. Besides the fur seal controversy, which had been raging for years, disagreements with Canada included boundary disputes, Chinese immigration from Canada, jurisdiction along the Great Lakes, cattle and port regulations, railway competition, canal tolls, and reciprocity.[27] Foster viewed the United States' relationship with Canada as extremely important since Canada represented the presence of a major European power in the Western Hemisphere. Therefore, Foster regarded border problems with Canada as far more serious than similar incidents with Mexico.[28] Beginning with his work in the Harrison administration, Foster was to be deeply involved in long and difficult negotiations regarding the Alaskan boundary question and the fur seal trade.

The secretary of state asked Foster to participate in informal discussions with a delegation from the Canadian cabinet in early 1892.[29] Blaine believed that the economically troubled Canada needed reciprocity with the United States far more than the United States did. Convinced that Canada eventually would seek annexation to the United States, Blaine had previously demonstrated little enthusiasm for reciprocity with Canada. Harrison and Foster were also skeptical about reciprocity with Canada, but they nevertheless agreed to the discussions.[30]

Blaine and Foster held talks with the Canadian representatives during February, but they failed to produce an agreement on reciprocity; the secretary of state declined a proposal for reciprocity on natural products, and the Canadians rejected Blaine's plan, which amounted to a complete commercial union between the two countries. It was soon apparent that the Canadians were not sincerely interested in reciprocity but were in Washington for the purpose of boosting the popularity of the Conservative party in elections back home.[31] However, the conference did produce agreement for cooperation on several subjects, including the creation of a joint commission to investigate complaints of poaching on the Great Lakes and the establishment of a joint survey of the boundary between Alaska and British Columbia. Toward the close of the conference, the secretary of state, acting on Foster's suggestion, vehemently protested Canadian discrimination in tolls along the Welland Canal; and Foster prepared an anti-Canadian report of the conferences, which Harrison delayed sending to Congress so as to avoid aggravating the Bering Sea fur seal question, which was pending.[32] It seems that during the conferences Foster took a harder line on United States–Canadian relations than the usually assertive secretary of state did.

In June 1892, the question of canal tolls was again the topic of a conference between Blaine, Foster, and Canadian commissioners. Again this time Foster urged Harrison to assume a strong position on the canal toll issue as he might enhance his position in the coming presidential election.[33] Harrison apparently took this advice; he demanded and received from Congress power to retaliate against Canadian tolls.[34]

In the spring of 1892 one more additional matter fell under Foster's supervision. Again Blaine's illness prevented him from preparing the case of the United States regarding the Bering Sea fur seal question. Blaine and Great Britain's Lord Salisbury had agreed to submit the issue to international arbitration, and when Blaine's incapacity became known, the president asked Foster to handle the preparations for the United States.[35] Foster and a team of legal experts were engaged in this assignment when Harrison appointed his old friend to the office of secretary of state.

*   *   *

While he was involved in nearly every aspect of foreign policy making in the Harrison administration, no incident more clearly demonstrated the magnitude of Foster's influence within the State Department than the "Chilean crisis" of 1891–1892. In fact, Foster was in large measure responsible for causing the crisis that developed between the United States and the Chilean government of Jorge Montt. When revolutionary forces led by Montt wrested control from President José Manuel Balmaceda, Foster, legal counsel for Balmaceda in Washington, used his influence with Harrison and Blaine to reverse the State Department's neutral position to one of partiality to Balmaceda. This policy shift caused resentment on the part of the revolutionists. When Congressional forces emerged as the victors despite the United States antipathy, popular emotions exploded into a riot in which United States naval personnel were killed, and a dangerous and senseless international crisis ensued.

In January 1891 a large segment of the Chilean navy joined the Congressional party in a revolt against the administration of President Balmaceda, claiming that the president had assumed dictatorial power. Balmaceda held the loyalty of the army in Santiago. However, he could not move against the revolutionaries in the north because they controlled the navy; neither could the Congressional forces move against Balmaceda, since he had a superiority of fire power on land.[36] To break the stalemate both sides sought armaments in the United States. Balmaceda tried to purchase a man-of-war through the United States minister to Chile, Thomas Egan, but this request was ignored by the State Department. The Congressionalists, headquartered in Iquique, sent an agent, Ricardo Tumbull, to buy arms in the United States. Tumbull arrived in New York, purchased a large amount of arms and had them transported to San Diego, California, where they were to be shipped to Chile. Trying to maintain a neutral posture, the State Department rejected the idea of the United States government selling a warship to Balmaceda but did not view allowing the purchase of arms in the United States as an unneutral act.[37]

Balmaceda's minister in Washington, Prudencio Lazcano, became aware of Tumbull's mission and informed Blaine on March 10 that the government of Chile hoped the United States would take measures to prevent these weapons and munitions from leaving the United States.[38] Blaine asked John Bassett Moore, the third assistant secretary of state, to draft a reply to the Chilean note. Moore believed that the purchase of arms by the Congressional forces was legal under the Treaty of Washington of 1871. On March 13, Blaine signed the document Moore had prepared. It stated:

The laws of the United States on the subject of neutrality, . . . while forbidding many acts to be done in this country which may affect the relations of hostile forces in foreign countries, do not forbid the manufacture and sale of munitions of war. I am therefore at a loss to find any authority for attempting to forbid the sale and shipment of arms and munitions of war in this country, since such sale and shipment are permitted by law.[39]

This note received no reply from the Chilean minister. Meanwhile, the arms and munitions purchased by Tumbull reached San Diego and were ready for shipment to Chile aboard the *Itata*, a Congressionalist transport ship.[40]

The *Itata* might have sailed for Iquique unhindered if an unusual meeting had not taken place in Blaine's home on the night of May 3. Among Blaine's guests that evening were Foster, Minister Lazcano, and Charles R. Flint, a New York businessman and friend of Blaine with power of attorney from President Balmaceda. The object of meeting was to consider whether the war materials purchased by Tumbull should be seized and held for violation of United States neutrality laws. Reversing the position he had taken on March 13, Blaine was now persuaded to halt the arms shipment. Foster immediately drafted instructions for the attorney general ordering him to take prompt measures to prevent United States neutrality laws from being violated and injury from being done to a friendly government.[41] The instructions were written on ordinary paper and in Foster's own handwriting, and upon receiving these orders the district attorney in Los Angeles instructed the United States marshal at San Diego to keep the *Itata* from leaving port. But the vessel was able to escape and rendezvous at San Clemente Island with the schooner *Robert and Minnie*, which transferred its cargo of arms to the *Itata*. Soon the *Itata* was in open waters and sailing for Chile.[42]

Immediately orders were issued to United States naval forces to pursue and seize the *Itata* as a fugitive from custody. The skillful crew of the Chilean transport managed to reach Iquique, however, where the *Itata* and its cargo were surrendered to representatives of the United States by the Congressional government.[43] Meanwhile, in San Diego legal questions concerning the seizures of *Itata* and *Robert and Minnie* were pondered by Solicitor General William Howard Taft. Ultimately the court held that the ships and their crews should be released as they were involved in a legitimate commercial venture.[44] The loss of the *Itata* had no impact on the outcome of the war in Chile. In August, the Congressionalists were victorious, and President Balmaceda committed suicide. The whole matter might have been insignificant had not this incident, combined with other United States activities, created bitterness against the United States in Chile.[45]

As the relationship between the United States and Chile came increasingly before public attention, Foster took steps to assure that his involvement with the Balmaceda regime remained unpublicized. In the State Department, Moore kept a careful record of the inner workings of the administration as the *Itata* incident developed, and he noted that Foster soon found his position "growing warm." Moore observed that Foster was "apprehensive lest his connections with the matter might become known, and in view of his connections with the Department of State, and his great privileges and opportunities in it, be the subject of comment." Foster therefore employed an attorney to act as his go-between with the Balmacedists, but Moore knew that Foster's connection with the Chilean government continued. It would have been impossible for Moore not to have noticed what was taking place, as Foster was bold enough to draft a memorandum, ostensibly from Minister Lazcano, while using as reference works the law books in Moore's own State Department office.[46]

After the fall of Balmaceda the United States seemed prepared to establish normal relations with the Montt government. On September 1, Minister Egan reported from Santiago that the Congressionalists were now in control, and he asked for permission to recognize the new government. Several days later Egan informed Acting Secretary of State Wharton that the Congressional forces appeared to have the support of the majority of the people and claimed that his relations with "all members" of the regime were "entirely cordial."[47] There remained a problem regarding the status of refugees who had found asylum in the United States legation, however, and many Chileans harbored resentment against the United States for the *Itata* incident and other acts that they deemed to be intervention in the recent civil war.[48]

While Chile appeared outwardly to be at rest following the revolution, tension was still very strong, and the continued presence of the United States Navy in Chilean waters did nothing to relieve the situation.[49] On the night of October 16 an altercation erupted in a Valparaiso saloon in which United States sailors from the *Baltimore* were attacked by a mob. Two sailors were killed and several others were injured.[50] This incident caused a severe rift in United States relations with Chile and ignited jingoist emotions in both countries.

Following the attack on the seamen of the *Baltimore*, an already tense diplomatic situation was further irritated by an undiplomatic and insulting public circular from the Chilean foreign minister and by Harrison's demands for an apology and compensation to the injured crewmen of the *Baltimore* and the survivors of the dead sailors.[51] By January 1892, war seemed a very real possibility.[52] As the Chilean crisis ran its course Foster was a principal presidential advisor, although in an entirely unofficial capacity.[53] Meanwhile, Blaine's role in the administration regarding relations with Chile was not of great significance. Blaine was ill much of the time, and routine State Department business was handled by assistant secretaries Francis Wharton,

Moore, and Alvey A. Adee; Secretary of the Navy Tracy also played an important role, and his aggressive attitude on the Chilean matter was forcefully presented.[54] Even when he was well enough to work, Blaine proved unreliable. On January 2 he lost an important message from Harrison under a mess of paper on his cluttered desk. As a result, he failed to attend a crucial meeting at the White House where the Chilean crisis was to be discussed.[55] Blaine also disagreed with Harrison's hard-line position, which held the *Baltimore* incident to be a premeditated assault on the uniform of the United States and therefore an act that demanded prompt and complete reparation.[56] In January Blaine read the diplomatic notes of the Chilean minister to Washington, Pedro Montt (brother of the Congressionalist leader), and the secretary of state found these carefully worded documents to constitute an apology. To the president, however, Montt's messages did not seem conclusive, nor did they express the degree of contrition Harrison desired.[57]

Finding Blaine's attitude incompatible with his own, the president dispatched Foster to the State Department, where he unofficially reviewed the correspondence from Chile, checking and verifying the translations made by the department's language experts.[58] The State Department's strongly worded note of January 21 to the Chilean government reflected the jingoist spirit that Blaine had advised against. In demanding an apology and reparations from Chile for the *Baltimore* incident and thereby risking war with Chile, Harrison disregarded the advice of the secretary of state. Blaine was embittered that his Pan American policies were jeopardized by Harrison's demands on Chile, and the president was upset that his secretary of state had not shown greater concern over an affront to the uniform of United States servicemen.[59] From January the relationship between Harrison and Blaine declined steadily. At the same time Foster staunchly supported the president's position on the Chilean affair. He believed with the president that the attack on the sailors at Valparaiso was an attempt by the Congressionalist forces to "manifest their unfriendly feeling toward the United States," and he firmly held that a show of force was needed. "Our government," Foster wrote, some years later, "could not have done less and retained the respect of other nations, but its action has left a feeling of resentment in Chile."[60]

Relations between Chile and the United States were normalized in the summer of 1892 by Chile's proposal to pay an indemnity of $75,000 to the *Baltimore*'s injured crew members and relatives of the dead sailors. Ironically, it was Foster, as secretary of state, who informed Minister Egan in Santiago that the Chilean offer would "be accepted cordially."[61] Thus, the lawyer whose intervention in the State Department on behalf of his Chilean client had led to seizure of the *Itata* and the subsequent controversies, the man who gave counsel to both the Balmaceda government and President Harrison, ultimately signed the official documents that ended an ugly situation created by his meddling.

The heavy-handed methods employed by the United States in the Chilean controversy indicated a new confidence, if not belligerence, on the part of American foreign policy planners, and this attitude carried over into negotiations with Britain and other powers. This new aggressiveness was noted by Cecil Spring-Rice, a young British diplomat in Washington during the weeks when war with Chile seemed possible. He viewed the affair as indicative of an emerging American attitude and wrote, "the moral for us is: what will the U.S. be like when their fleet is more powerful, if the administration acts in a similar manner?"[62]

The central role Foster played in the *Itata* affair demonstrated the almost unlimited influence he enjoyed within the administration, whether or not he was in government service. Initially an unofficial advisor to the administration on matters pertaining to reciprocity treaties, he soon accepted a number of special temporary assignments. Following several months negotiating reciprocal trade agreements with Spain, Latin American nations, and the British Foreign Office, Foster began to take an active part in diplomatic matters ranging from the fur seals controversy to a pork importation dispute with Germany. As Blaine's health steadily declined, Harrison began to call upon his old acquaintance from Indiana. By the time of the *Itata* affair and the subsequent Chilean crisis, Foster was in many respects behaving as if he were already the secretary of state. It was only logical, therefore, that the president appoint him to the post upon Blaine's sudden resignation.

V

Secretary of State

On June 4, 1892, just three days before the opening of the Republican National Convention, James G. Blaine abruptly resigned as Benjamin Harrison's secretary of state, and his letter of resignation was immediately accepted.[1] Blaine's action was not entirely unexpected, as he had been unable to carry out his duties as head of the Department of State for several months because of poor health complicated by personal anguish over family tragedies, including the death of his son, Walker, who served as solicitor for the State Department.[2] There was also speculation that Blaine's resignation was timed to assist those party leaders who wanted to dump the colorless Harrison and once again make the "plumed knight" their standard-bearer.[3] Regardless of Blaine's motivation in quitting the cabinet when he did, he proved to be unable to command a significant following at the party's convention, and he ceased to be active in national politics. He lived for only six months following his departure from the administration.[4]

Harrison won his party's renomination and faced the matter of appointing a new secretary of state in the midst of an election campaign. Upon Blaine's resignation Assistant Secretary Wharton had been named acting secretary, and there was public speculation that he might hold the job permanently, or at least until after the election.[5] Secretary of the Navy Tracy was mentioned prominently in the press as a man well suited for the post, and the railroad entrepreneur Chauncey Depew of New York also figured in the speculation.[6] In selecting John W. Foster, a long-time political associate from his home state, Harrison chose a man who had already familiarized himself with the current matters at the State Department through both official and unofficial assignments; it appeared to be a "safe," sensible, and businesslike selection.[7]

But because of Foster's previous alliances with Walter Q. Gresham, who now publicly supported the Democratic nominee, Grover Cleveland, Foster probably did not add any political strength to the administration.[8] Actually, Foster may have been something of a political liability.

Although seemingly a practical choice, the nomination of Foster brought severe public criticism. The *Nation* noted that Foster appeared well qualified for the position but questioned his involvement in legal matters concerning foreign claims settlements.[9] The *New York Times* was exceptionally critical of Foster and argued that either Tracy or Wharton would have been better choices. The *Times* stated that Harrison should not have appointed a man who had been retained as a private counsel to prosecute claims against the United States government as Foster had done for the legations of China and Mexico. The newspaper predicted, "his secretaryship will be distinctly not 'brilliant' and not sensational." Regarding the sudden departure of Blaine and the selection by Harrison of an old political associate from his home state, the *Times* reported:

One secretary of state has just "thrown up his job" with about as much form and ceremony as a bricklayer might exhibit in a similar proceeding. Another secretary of state succeeds to the portfolio the news of whose appointment will be received with a shrug and a smile in more than one Foreign Office. There are still a few Americans, not all living east of the State of Indiana, who are capable of shame and mortification when our State Department is made the laughing stock of foreigners.[10]

On July 4 the *Times* featured the new secretary of state's career in an exposé entitled "Foster's Many Masters." Criticizing the Senate for approving of Foster's nomination without debate, the *Times* claimed that Foster's popularity with Porfirio Díaz while Foster was minister to Mexico had led to his employment in legal disputes between Mexico and the United States. The *Times* viewed it as significant that the new Mexican legation in Washington was constructed next door to the Foster's home on I Street. Since Foster also represented the interests of Russia and Spain in Washington, the *Times* suggested that Foster took diplomatic assignments in these countries to advance his legal practice. The article stated, "There is every reason to believe that Foster has been as prosperous in diplomacy as most commercial men have been in trade of a different kind." The matter of Foster's opposition to Chinese exclusion, an unpopular political position, was also discussed. Finally, the *Times* article reported that State Department sources had leaked word of Foster's work as agent for the Balmaceda government and his unofficial role in the administration during the Chilean crisis. "It may be," the *Times* stated, "that the blunders of the Chilean controversy, the wrong in the 'Itata' case, like the blunder in the Barrundia case, may be traced to Foster's door."[11]

While not bringing discernible political advantages to Harrison's reelection bid, Foster did have a familiarity with current affairs at the State Department that provided a consistency in the president's foreign policies. During the presidential campaign and through the final months of his administration Harrison pointed to the success of reciprocal trade agreements in increasing exports, and he promised to stand firmly by American negotiators in dealing with Great Britain over matters including Atlantic fisheries, the Pacific fur seal industry, and the Welland Canal tolls. In the interest of improved commerce Harrison supported the establishment by the International Monetary Conference at Brussels of a bimetallic money standard utilizing the free coinage of silver at a fixed international ratio. The president proposed an extension of foreign commerce through the restoration of the merchant marine with American-built ships. He called for enlargement of the navy to protect national interests and compel respect for the flag of the United States. The president also focused attention on American concern for Hawaii, advocating the placement of a communications cable connecting the islands with the West Coast. On other international questions Harrison's position favored the construction of a Nicaraguan canal, home rule for Ireland, and continued protest to persecution of Jews in Russia. The party platform reaffirmed the principle of the Monroe Doctrine and supported "the achievement of the manifest destiny of the Republic in its broadest sense."[12] During the final months of Harrison's administration Foster would work tirelessly in support of Harrison's goals, but the Republican defeat by Cleveland meant frustration for most of the administration's foreign policy initiatives.

Like his predecessor, Foster took a strong stand against British aggressions in what he believed to be American areas of interest. He did not consider Samoa to be vital to the United States, and he was not happy about the policy of joint ownership with the British.[13] In November 1892, Foster instructed chargé d'affaires Henry White in London to inform the British of the United States' concerns about British activities near Pago Pago in Samoa. Foster's powerfully worded message stated that White was to "make known the president's conviction that any attempt on the part of Her Majesty's government to occupy any part of the port of Pago Pago as a coaling or naval station could not fail to be regarded by this government as an unfriendly act, because tending to impair our vested rights therein."[14] Foster also took notice of British activities along the Mosquito Coast and protested the expansion of the British in the area of Nicaragua near the site of a planned canal.[15] In another matter, Foster vigorously demanded that the British take measures to assure that an illegal traffic in Chinese workers by the Canadian Pacific Railroad be brought to a halt.[16]

In keeping with the ambition of the Harrison administration to expand the defensive frontiers of the United States, the secretary of state sought bases for coaling stations. Foster attempted to secure a ninety-nine-year lease on

Samaná Bay in Santo Domingo. The plan fell through when the Haitian strongman Ulises Heureaux demanded cash and the appropriation was delayed in Congress. Eventually Heureaux secured a loan from New York bankers and lost interest in a sale of land that might have created domestic opposition in his unstable country.[17] Meanwhile, Foster tentatively explored the possibility of establishing a naval base for the Pacific fleet at Chimbote, Peru.[18]

The International Monetary Conference in Brussels seemed to offer commercial interests in the United States an opportunity for increasing the money supply through the free coinage of silver at an internationally fixed ratio and thereby improving conditions for international trade.[19] The secretary of state advised Harrison on the selection of a bipartisan delegation to represent the United States.[20] Foster issued instructions to the delegates that proclaimed the administration's faith that the free and full rise of silver "would very highly promote the prosperity of all the people of all the countries of the world." He informed the American representatives, "your first and most important duty will be to secure, if possible, an agreement between the chief commercial countries of the world looking to international bimetallism—that is, the unlimited coinage of gold and silver. . . at a fixed ratio in coinage common to all the agreeing powers." Should they fail to secure such a sweeping agreement, the United States delegation was instructed to attempt to bring about some understanding for the larger use of silver as a currency to end depreciation of that metal.[21] In Brussels the American delegates deviated from Foster's instructions as a tactical maneuver. Instead of first seeking a broad agreement for unlimited use of silver, Senator William B. Allison urged the conference in an opening statement to consider first those plans for a limited use of silver. The strategy failed, and after ten long sessions the conference disbanded without ever considering the Allison proposal and without a single vote being taken on any matter.[22]

Because Blaine had frequently absented himself from Washington due to his poor health, routine work at the State Department had been left unattended, and Foster was pleased to be able to report as he left the department that all business had been brought up to date.[23] This was a significant accomplishment, considering that much of Foster's time as secretary of state was occupied with two unusual situations. The most time-consuming was the preparation of the fur seal case, over which Foster continued to preside after his appointment to head the State Department. With Robert Lansing, his son-in-law and junior law partner, Foster often worked far into the night, pondering the legal questions involved.[24] The second extraordinary development occurred when a revolution in Hawaii by a pro-American group of white planters and merchants presented the possibility of annexation to the United States. The failure to bring about annexation in the weeks before the inauguration of Cleveland presented Foster with probably his greatest disappointment in diplomacy.

To a large extent the defeat of Benjamin Harrison in November of 1892 can be viewed as a repudiation of the foreign policies his administration had pursued, particularly with regard to the tariff and reciprocity. The McKinley Tariff had adversely affected the farmer and laborer, and Cleveland and his party relentlessly attacked the incumbent on this issue. The Democratic platform denounced the protection of American industry at the expense of the farmer and argued that reciprocity, as practiced by the Harrison administration, amounted to a "sham" that sought only to establish closer relations with countries whose major exports were almost exclusively agricultural, while the United States was itself producing a farm surplus.[25] Certainly a number of factors combined to bring about Grover Cleveland's return to the White House, but Harrison saw the tariff as the key factor, and he was bitter that the American public did not support the protection of the nation's emerging industry. Following the election, Harrison assessed the results in a letter to Whitelaw Reid in which the president stated, "the workingman declined to walk under the protective umbrella because it sheltered his employer also."[26] Harrison's rhetoric oversimplified an election campaign that had focused also on the colorless leadership of the incumbent, the generally depressed national economy, and the question of silver currency. Yet Harrison's "spirited" diplomacy and the tariff had been central issues, and Cleveland's victory gave the Democrats reason to believe that the public had repudiated the Republican's foreign policies.

When it became known that President-elect Cleveland had chosen Walter Q. Gresham, Foster's oldest personal friend, to be secretary of state, Foster attempted to cooperate with his successor. A week before he resigned, Foster sent congratulations to his old friend and offered to meet with the secretary-designate in New York.[27] A meeting was arranged for February 24, but Gresham first held a discussion with Cleveland at Lakewood, New Jersey in which the situation in Hawaii was considered.[28] It seems doubtful that Gresham informed Foster of Cleveland's intention to oppose the annexation treaty Foster had placed before the Senate. Gresham did assure Foster of support at the international tribunal in Paris but indicated a belief that the United States' case on the fur seal question stood little chance of success, since the tribunal's jurors were all European.[29] Cleveland and Gresham viewed the election as a repudiation of the aggressive and expansionist foreign policies of the Harrison administration and during their first months in office would do much to frustrate the foreign policy initiatives of the Harrison years.[30] Foster's friendly and cordial offer to "hold myself ready to do anything I can" was never accepted by the new administration.[31]

The actual foreign policy achievements of the Harrison administration appear meager and insignificant because Cleveland repudiated many of his predecessor's actions. Furthermore, the American public in the early 1890s seemed still to be generally unaroused by foreign affairs and unconcerned about overseas expansion. Yet the Harrison years were important, because his administration was the first since the Civil War to coordinate diplomatic planning.[32] Harrison's attention to an overall foreign policy can be seen in his naval building program, which placed the United States naval forces seventh in world ranking in 1893 as opposed to twelfth in 1889. Conscious of American prestige and image overseas, the administration sought to have the rank of the highest United States diplomats abroad raised from envoy extraordinary and minister plenipotentiary to ambassador extraordinary and minister plenipotentiary.[33] In seeking to extend the frontiers of the nation beyond the North American Continent, the Harrison administration drew renewed attention to Cuba, Puerto Rico, Central America, and Hawaii, and in so doing outlined areas of American expansion for the coming decade.

The extent to which Foster shaped foreign policies as secretary of state is difficult to measure, just as it is hazardous to attempt an assessment of Blaine's performance in Harrison's cabinet. While Foster was secretary of state for only nine months, and much of that period as a member of a lame-duck administration, Blaine's tenure as head of the State Department was marked by a strained relationship with the president and conspicuous absences. Further, State Department officials such as Wharton and John Bassett Moore, Secretary of the Navy Tracy, and Whitelaw Reid clearly had considerable influence.[34] Yet, Foster appears to emerge as the central connecting figure providing continuity throughout the administration. To judge his role in the administration on the basis of his nine-month tenure as secretary of state would be inadequate; one must look at Foster's activities during the whole of Harrison's term of office, since Foster was formulating and implementing foreign policies many months before he was appointed to head the Department of State. Had he not twice supported the independent-minded Walter Gresham, Foster would perhaps have been Harrison's choice in 1889 for the post of secretary of state. In many ways Foster was more knowledgeable and experienced in diplomacy than his predecessor, and he was obviously far more compatible with Harrison than Blaine could ever have been.

One can only speculate as to what Foster's role would have been had Harrison won reelection in 1892. It seems likely that whether or not Foster continued as secretary of state, his influence would have remained enormous. He would have urged a tough stand in negotiations in Britain. He might have maneuvered to bring areas of the Caribbean into an association with the United States. And he would certainly have labored tirelessly to bring about the annexation of the Hawaiian Islands.

Major John W. Foster

Courtesy of Eleanor Lansing Dulles

Mary Parke Foster

Photo courtesy of Eleanor Lansing Dulles.

Foster, standing, with the staff of the United States Legation in Mexico, about 1877.
Courtesy of Eleanor Lansing Dulles.

Members of Benjamin Harrison's cabinet pose for a group photograph in late 1892. From left to right: Stephen B. Elkins, Secretary of War; John W. Noble, Secretary of Interior; John W. Foster, Secretary of State; John Wanamaker, Postmaster General; President Benjamin Harrison; Benjamin F. Tracey, Secretary of Navy; Charles Foster, Secretary of Treasury; Jeremiah M. Rusk, Secretary of Agriculture; William Henry Harrison Miller, Attorney General. Photo courtesy of Benjamin Harrison Memorial Home, Indianapolis.

This family portrait, taken about 1910, includes two future secretaries of state, Robert Lansing (third from left), John Foster Dulles (far right), a head of the Central Intelligence Agency, Allen W. Dulles (far left) and a high ranking State Department official and economics expert, Eleanor Lansing Dulles, seated on left with dog.

John W. and Mrs. Foster, Photo taken about 1913 Courtesy of Ms. Eleanor Lansing Dulles.

VI

The Struggle for the Annexation of Hawaii

President Benjamin Harrison and his secretary of state, James G. Blaine, harbored a strong desire for the annexation of the Hawaiian Islands. They held this ambition in common with expansionist-minded administrations dating back several decades.[1] In listing policy priorities in August 1891, Blaine wrote to the president, "there are only three places that are of value enough to be taken that are not continental. One is Hawaii and the others are Cuba and Puerto Rico. Cuba and Puerto Rico are not now imminent and will not be for a generation. Hawaii may come up for decision at any unexpected hour and I hope we shall be prepared to decide in the affirmative."[2] When the "unexpected hour" arrived in January 1893, however, neither Harrison nor Blaine was prepared to take aggressive action. The once dynamic secretary of state had left the cabinet and lay near death at his secluded retreat at Bar Harbor, Maine; the president, defeated by Grover Cleveland in a bid for reelection, no longer demonstrated his former intense interest in foreign policy matters. The task of attempting to bring about annexation fell to Blaine's successor in the State Department, John W. Foster.

Foster labored unsuccessfully during the final weeks of the Harrison administration to bring Hawaii into union with the United States. Although he failed in this effort, his desire to make Hawaii a United States territory remained unaffected. He became a leading spokesman for annexation, involved himself in business ventures in Hawaii, and played a vital role in bringing about a joint congressional resolution for the annexation of Hawaii

61

in 1898. Perhaps no diplomat played a greater part than Foster in the imperial diplomacy that brought Hawaii into the American empire.

Throughout the Harrison administration the business and commercial leaders in Hawaii had grown increasingly favorable to the prospect of annexation by the United States. The McKinley Tariff, which severely hurt the island sugar economy and the authoritarian and nationalistic tendencies of the native Queen Liliuokalani, had convinced substantial numbers of the white residents that their interests would best be served through union with the United States.[3] Early in 1892 a prominent Hawaiian attorney, Lorrin A. Thurston, was dispatched to Washington by the secret Annexation Club to inquire about the administration's attitude regarding the Hawaiian situation. Upon his arrival in the capital, Thurston met with Secretary of State Blaine and explained that the Annexation Club would not attempt to depose the Hawaiian monarch unless she tried to promulgate a new constitution giving herself increased powers. Blaine, too ill to burden himself with the Hawaiian matter, sent Thurston to see Secretary of the Navy Benjamin Tracy, who interviewed the Hawaiian representative on behalf of the president. Tracy informed Thurston that the administration would be sympathetic if developments in Hawaii compelled the annexationists to act against the queen.[4]

In the summer of 1892, as tension between the queen and Hawaii's prominent white residents increased, Foster succeeded Blaine as head of the State Department and became heir to a policy that had encouraged pro-annexationist elements in Hawaii. Foster also inherited the irrepressible John Stevens, an elderly friend of Blaine and minister to Honolulu who enthusiastically encouraged the efforts of the Annexation Club.[5] While the Hawaiian queen struggled with the legislature over the creation of a ministry, Stevens kept Foster informed of developments on the islands. In September Stevens reported "considerable excitement here in regard to a new cabinet," and claimed that the queen was dominated by a Tahitian favorite, Charles B. Wilson, and other "persons in whom the best portion of the citizens had no confidence." To Stevens it seemed that the queen was being advised to "resist the responsible men of the islands and the majority of the legislature."[6]

By late October it appeared to Stevens that the queen had come completely under the domination of the Tahitian and his followers, including "most of the anti-American element" on the island. Stevens also reported that the queen's friends were supported by the British legation in Honolulu,[7] and he maintained that only the presence of a United States naval force near Honolulu kept the "Tahitian marshal and his gang" from inducing the queen "to attempt a *coup d'état* by proclaiming a new constitution, taking from the legislature the power to reject ministerial appointments."[8]

Knowing that the minister was in close contact with members of the Annexation Club and other politicians favorable to annexation, Foster instructed Stevens to take care not to mention his involvement in Hawaiian politics in his official diplomatic correspondence. The secretary advised the use of two separate reports, "one of which shall aim to give the narrative of public affairs in their open historical aspect, and the other to be of a strictly confidential character, reporting and commentating upon matters of personal intrigue and the like so far as you may deem necessary for my full understanding of the situation."[9]

In November the ministerial crisis in Honolulu subsided temporarily when the queen asked George N. Wilcox, a legislator of pro-American sympathies, to form a new ministry.[10] The restoration of political calm did not, however, deter Stevens from continuing his efforts on behalf of annexation. On November 20, he authored a confidential eighteen-page report on political, social, and economic conditions in Hawaii. He concluded his lengthy dispatch to Washington by stating that an "intelligent and impartial examination of the facts can hardly fail to lead to the conclusion that the relations and policy of the United States towards Hawaii will soon demand some change, if not the adoption of decisive measures, with the aim to secure American interests and future supremacy by encouraging Hawaiian development and aiding to promote responsible government in these islands." He also pointed to the distressing increase in Hawaii's Asian population. "Hawaii has reached the parting of the ways," wrote Stevens. "She must now take the road which leads to Asia, or the other which outlets her in America, gives her an American civilization and binds her to the care of American Destiny."[11]

Secretary Foster considered Hawaii vital to American interests in the Pacific,[12] and he believed Americans had a civilizing mission to perform in the islands. He viewed the decline in Hawaii's native population from more than 130,000 in 1822 to less than 35,000 in 1892 as evidence of racial backwardness and incapacity of the royal family in Hawaii to govern by western standards.[13] While sympathetic to the cause of manifest destiny in Hawaii, Foster realized the political problems that annexation presented—especially if it were attempted by a lame-duck administration.

Despite some misgivings, the secretary directed a weak effort to purchase the islands during the final months of 1892. Apparently Foster thought the islands could be annexed to the United States if the queen were offered a substantial monetary award for relinquishing her homeland. In mid-November Archibald Hopkins, a representative of the Annexation Club in Washington, reported to annexationists in Honolulu an offer by United States government to "pay to Queen Liliuokalani, and those connected with her, the sum of two hundred and fifty thousand dollars, for the assignment to the United States of the Sovereignty of Hawaii."[14] However, members of the Annexation Club and Minister Stevens did not favor the plan,[15] and when no progress towards annexation had been made by late December, Foster advised Hopkins that it would be "useless to attempt to bring matters to a head during the short time which remains to this administration." Foster informed the annexationists that the incoming Cleveland administration would be "if not aggressive, at least positive and active" on the Hawaiian matter.[16] While he was eager for annexation, Foster did not expect to see the issue arise during his last weeks in office.

Foster was wrong. Overthrow of the queen and establishment of a provisional government in January 1894 dramatically and unexpectedly brought the question of annexation before the administration and the American public.[17] On January 14, the queen indicated that she intended to promulgate by executive decree a new constitution more favorable to native Hawaiians. Prominent whites reacted by forming a committee of public safety to protect their privileges and interests against the sovereign's actions. Following a mass meeting staged by the Annexation Club on January 16, marines from the U.S.S. *Boston* marched ashore at the orders of Minister Stevens "for the protection of the United States Legation and the United States Consulate, and [to] secure the safety of American citizens."[18] Strategically placed around all important government buildings in Honolulu, the troops quickly brought about the fall of the Hawaiian monarchy. Helpless in the face of American troops, the queen surrendered to superior force, and Minister Stevens immediately extended recognition to the de facto provisional government, which held power with the support of the troops from the *Boston*.[19] Stevens telegraphed news of the revolution to Foster on January 18, and the following day he reported that the new government in Hawaii had dispatched a special commission to Washington, headed by Lorrin Thurston and representing "a large preponderating proportion of the property holders and commercial interests of these islands."[20]

In Washington, Foster reacted to the events in Hawaii by taking steps to help insure immediate annexation. On January 28, he telegraphed instructions approving Stevens' recognition of the de facto government and informing him that he was to continue to keep in close communication with naval forces in Honolulu "with a view to acting, if need be, for the protection of the interests and property of American citizens and aiding in the preservation of good order under the changed conditions reported." Foster also hoped Hawaii's new leaders would "tend to draw closer the intimate ties of amity and common interests which so conspicuously and increasingly link them with the United States."[21]

Foster was fully aware of the international implications of annexation, and he made a systematic effort to collect information regarding the attitudes of foreign powers on the developments in Hawaii. In a lengthy memo, he reported on the attitudes expressed by the foreign ministers in Washington, and he concluded that most favored United States annexation. The Japanese minister had some concern about the treatment of the fifteen thousand Japanese in Hawaii but seemed satisfied that the interests of Japanese subjects in Hawaii would be respected by the United States. The Japanese minister reiterated his government's opposition to the annexation of the islands by any European power and asked to be kept informed of the activities of the Hawaiian commissioners arriving in Washington. The minister from France also demonstrated an interest in the Hawaiian commissioners but did not feel his government would look upon annexation of Hawaii by the United States with any disfavor.

The German and Russian ministers were friendly to American annexation. According to Foster, the German minister "had always considered the relation of the Hawaiian Islands to the United States as one of *quasi* protectorate—the King and Royalty being virtually under the predominating influence of the United States, and if those puppets were to pass away, he anticipated that the Sovereignty of the Islands would be transferred to the United States." The Russian minister to Washington was even more encouraging and suggested that his government would applaud annexation by the Americans. Claiming to have secret information, the Russian diplomat claimed Britain was hostile to American plans in Hawaii and warned that the British would soon interpose obstacles in the way of annexation.[22]

Foster was most concerned about British reaction to American policy in the Pacific. On February 1, he instructed Minister Robert Todd Lincoln in London, "recent events have made our paramount concern [in Hawaii] more evident. You will carefully note and fully report by cable any governmental action adverse to our confirming our position."[23] Lincoln responded by taking a careful reading of British public opinion. He found no great concern in Britain over the future of Hawaii,[24] and the British government made no official statement on the Hawaiian émeute.[25] Meanwhile, the British minister in Washington appeared totally unconcerned about American designs in Hawaii.[26]

While foreign powers seemed to view Hawaii's union with the United States as inevitable, the Harrison administration encountered strong domestic opposition to annexation. Much of this resistance resulted from popular outrage at aggressive and injudicious actions taken by Stevens in Honolulu. On the morning of February 1, the minister declared a United States protectorate over Hawaii and ordered Captain G. C. Wiltse of the *Boston* to take military action to insure the preservation of the provisional government.[27] Having raised the United States flag over Honolulu, Stevens believed he had saved the provisional government from the evil designs of the "hoodlum foreigners and more vicious natives." He now feared only British imperialism if the United States failed to act decisively. Stevens therefore advised the secretary of state that the "Hawaiian pear is now fully ripe, and this is the golden hour for the United States to pluck it."[28]

The revolution in Hawaii was itself a controversial event, and Stevens' declaration of an American protectorate just as negotiations were about to begin with the Hawaiian commissioners put the administration's diplomacy in an awkward position. The minister's activities intensified a furious debate over events in Hawaii[29] and diminished the credibility of Foster's claims that Stevens had not acted in cooperation with the revolutionists.[30] The high-handed methods employed in Hawaii provoked Carl Schurz to write that if the administration sought to annex Hawaii through dubious diplomacy, it would "commit an act utterly inconsistent with the true spirit of democratic government."[31] Although many newspapers and journals advocated acceptance of an imperial diplomacy in Hawaii, the administration's plans for annexation were damaged by the extent to which public opinion had been polarized by the questionable activities of Minister Stevens and the maneuvers in the State Department.

Ultimately Foster felt compelled to disavow Stevens' declaration of a protectorate in Hawaii, but the secretary of state carefully worded his instructions so as not to denounce the minister's continued cooperation and support for the provisional government. On February 14, Foster informed Stevens by telegram that the administration in Washington interpreted his actions solely as cooperation with the provisional government and in no way "tantamount to the assumption of a protectorate over those islands on behalf of the United States, with all the rights and obligations which the term implies." Foster continued:

So far as your course accords the de facto Sovereign Government, the material cooperation of the United States for the maintenance of good order and protection of life and property from apprehended disorders, it is commended; but so far as it may appear to overstep that limit by setting the authority of the United States above that of the Hawaiian Government in the capacity of protector or to impair the independent sovereignty of that Government by substituting the flag of the United States, it is disavowed.[32]

Stevens did not interpret Foster's telegram as disapproval of his conduct and maintained that his "understanding of the spirit and terms of our temporary protectorate is in entire accord with the spirit and terms of the Secretary of State's dispatch."[33] At no time did Stevens believe his course of action was being questioned or disavowed by Foster;[34] and no matter what Foster's intentions might have been in his dispatch of February 14, the United States flag therefore continued to fly over Honolulu while annexation was being negotiated.

Secretary of State Foster was well aware of political opposition to annexation; nevertheless, when the Hawaiian commissioners arrived in Washington he applied his considerable diplomatic skills to preparing a treaty that might win Senate confirmation in spite of the obstacles. Negotiations for a treaty to annex Hawaii to the United States began on the morning of

February 4, when Hawaiian Minister J. Mott Smith introduced the commissioners to Foster. The representatives from Honolulu described the uprising in Hawaii and the events leading to the formation of the provisional government.[35] Foster informed the Hawaiian representatives that President Harrison had just received a letter of protest from the deposed queen, requesting that no action be taken by the United States until she had been granted an opportunity to present her side of the issue. Foster asked the commissioners to prepare a written reply to the queen's charges that Stevens aided those who had plotted her downfall and established the provisional government.[36] The secretary of state then announced that the president had directed him to receive proposals from the commissioners. The Hawaiians offered to write a formal statement[37] and later that same day set forth in detail their conditions for a treaty of annexation. Foster accepted the document and asked the commissioners to allow him time for study.[38]

As a lawyer acquainted with international law and a presidential advisor familiar with political realities, Foster found several problem areas in the commissioners' proposal, and he knew these would delay Senate approval. Foster and Harrison were both anxious for annexation now that the opportunity had arisen, even though Foster doubted that Senate approval could be won before Grover Cleveland's inauguration on March 4.[39] To gain ratification, the secretary of state knew that an agreement had to be reached that appeared to be free of controversial articles. On February 7, Foster announced that he had been authorized by the president to enter final stages of negotiations and bluntly stated that several points presented "some serious embarrassments" to the administration; it was "difficult to reconcile them to the Constitution and laws of the United States, and our existing system."[40]

In an attempt to eliminate all provisions delaying Senate ratification, Foster rejected the commissioners' plan of incorporating into a treaty any agreement to lay a cable to Honolulu. The secretary also disapproved of incorporating into the treaty a provision that the United States should open and improve Pearl Harbor and establish a naval station at that location within a specified period of time. Further, the secretary of state informed the Hawaiians that the exceptions to the Chinese exclusion law they wanted for their contract labor could not be allowed. Foster advised the commissioners to eliminate from consideration in the treaty the question of a bounty on sugar, as this would be one of the most serious obstacles to the passage. The question of whether or not all federal government appointments in Hawaii could be made from among persons like the commissioners who had lived on the islands for at least five years was discussed, and on this issue the secretary insisted that no guarantee could be made.[41]

On February 9, Foster provided Lorrin Thurston, the spokesman for the commissioners, with a tentative draft for a treaty of annexation. The document had been prepared by the secretary following a conference with members of the Senate Committee on Foreign Relations. Foster made it clear that the draft was as far as the administration could go, and he indicated that the proposed text left out the questions of bounty and tariff in order to avoid partisan opposition to the treaty.[42] The following day Thurston reported that his colleagues were reluctant to accept the terms offered in Foster's draft. Stating that the commissioners were unwilling to accept Foster's proposal unless they found that these were the best terms they could hope to obtain, Thurston informed the secretary that he and his associates would discuss the matter further before reaching a conclusion. Thurston said he hoped to be able to give the commissioners' decision to the secretary before the day ended.[43]

Late in the afternoon the commissioners met privately at Wormley's Hotel in Washington. Present besides the commission members were Hawaiian Minister J. Mott Smith, Archibald Hopkins, an ardent annexationist, and Charles R. Bishop, a wealthy Hawaiian banker. Thurston argued that the secretary of state had been an advocate for the annexationists' cause within the administration, and Thurston urged the commission members to accept the Foster treaty draft. Thurston echoed the secretary's view that the terms were the best possible and pointed out that Foster had rejected some of the commission's proposals only because he wanted the treaty to receive approval in the foreign relations committee. After some discussion, Thurston put to his fellow commissioners the question of whether to accept the treaty in its present form or return to Honolulu with nothing. The commissioners voted to accept Foster's terms.[44]

Immediately following the meeting at Wormley's Hotel, the commissioners informed Foster that they had decided to accept his treaty draft; they still desired certain modifications, however. These included: 1) a time limit for final and complete commercial union with the United States; 2) retention of the Hawaiian flag as a local banner to gratify the native population; 3) permission for the provisional government to remove its officers until Congress legislated a permanent form of government; 4) provision for the registration of Hawaiian merchant ships; 5) the right of Chinese lawfully domiciled, but absent from the islands, to return, and no permanent prohibition to immigration from China; 6) a clause canceling the treaty should Congress fail to eliminate duties on imports from Hawaii within a definite period. Foster believed the final point would meet with disfavor in the Senate and suggested instead a clause guaranteeing such legislation within a year of ratification of the treaty. With regard to other points, the secretary agreed that the registry of vessels might safely be left to Congress, and he offered his assurances that Chinese already domiciled in Hawaii could be allowed to return. Foster's statements satisfied the commissioners, and he promised to take all remaining points under consideration for the next conference including the subject of citizenship and provision for the Hawaiian royal family.[45]

The following day, February 11, Foster informed the commissioners of his decisions. The secretary announced that it would be best for political reasons to strike out all references to the question of Hawaiian citizenship, leaving the issue for Congress to decide at a later time. Regarding the use of the Hawaiian flag as a local emblem, Foster eliminated reference to the question from the treaty but assured the commissioners that the flag could be kept for the native population. The article dealing with Chinese immigration was reconstructed in such a way as to make it clear that prohibition of the entry of Chinese laborers into the islands would not necessarily be perpetual, and an article providing for the royal family was modified so as to stipulate an annuity of $20,000 for the queen and a simple payment of $150,000 to the princess. The commissioners agreed to all the modifications Foster proposed. After some "slight liberal corrections" had been made, the treaty was signed on February 14 and was submitted to the Senate within twenty-four hours.[46]

Annexation appeared to have considerable support in Congress. While negotiations between Foster and the Hawaiian commissioners were proceeding, petitions favoring annexation arrived in Washington from the state legislatures of Oregon, California, Colorado, Pennsylvania, Illinois, and New York, as well as from several chambers of commerce. Four resolutions calling for immediate annexation were introduced in Congress.[47] Foster personally contacted Democratic Congressman James H. Blount, the chairman of the House Committee on Foreign Affairs, seeking Democratic support for annexation. Blount, who planned to retire from Congress within weeks, appeared unconcerned with the Hawaiian situation, but he did promise to forward the confidential information entrusted to him by the secretary to influential committee members such as Robert R. Hitt and James B. McCreary.[48]

While the treaty awaited Senate action, Foster instructed Stevens to maintain close contact with United States naval authorities in Honolulu. Just days before he was to resign as secretary of state, Foster informed Stevens that the treaty was still pending in the Senate and instructed him to act "in cooperation with the naval authorities, to support the Provisional Government in the maintenance of security to life and property and good order, until action shall be had upon the treaty."[49] Apparently, whether or not the Senate approved the treaty of annexation, Foster was prepared to have the United States continue indefinitely a quasi protectorate over the provisional government.

Despite Foster's efforts to bring about quick approval of the treaty, complications arose. One factor complicating ratification was the arrival in Washington of Paul Neumann, a lawyer representing the deposed queen.[50]

Reports of the Hawaiian revolution had created some sympathy for Liliuokalani, and indications that a treaty would be concluded before a meeting with the queen's delegate aroused public suspicion.[51] Upon his arrival from Honolulu, Neumann had wired the secretary of state from San Francisco, expressing the hope "that no action [would] be taken by the President in relation to the affairs of the Hawaiian Islands until my arrival."[52] Foster was not anxious to meet with Neumann, since he was already negotiating with the representatives of the provisional government. Furthermore, the secretary had been forewarned by Stevens of the nature of Neumann's mission. The minister claimed that Neumann was a "good natured and politic lawyer" who had won money at card games from the late Hawaiian king and was also a man of "unsavory reputation." While Neumann was ostensibly being sent to Washington to advocate the restoration of the queen, Stevens suspected Neumann's real mission might be to arrange a good cash settlement for the queen.[53]

After stalling until the treaty was negotiated, Foster met with Neumann on February 21. Neumann presented a statement that denounced the provisional government and the actions of Minister Stevens. Neumann requested that the document be placed before the Senate.[54] The secretary of state agreed to forward the message to the president, but he made no promises about the course of action the president might take. After careful questioning by Foster, the queen's representative was forced to admit that he was acting in the capacity of a private individual. Neumann claimed that a referendum would show that only one in ten of the island residents favored annexation under the provisional government, and he stated that he would agree to the restoration of the queen under a United States protectorate. Foster asked if he would accept annexation without the restoration of the queen, provided provision was made for her financial security. Neumann made it clear that he would accept annexation only if the present government were ousted and Congress allowed to determine Hawaii's form of government. "Your opposition then . . . ," replied Foster, "is not so much to annexation as it is to the Provisional Government that now exists." Neumann alluded to the long and friendly relationship between Hawaii and the United States and suggested that the queen herself would welcome a United States protectorate because she did not want the islands taken over "by some other foreign power." Foster concluded the meeting, promising to put Neumann's message before the president.[55]

Neumann's activities put the administration in an embarrassing position. Foster's refusal to listen to the queen's protests before negotiating with the Hawaiian commissioners raised public suspicion on the annexation issue. The *San Francisco Morning Call* criticized the haste with which Foster had negotiated with the commissioners: "It was unjust and indecent. The care taken to suppress the queen's side of the story in order that the treaty might be made irrevocable before public opinion could judge the facts is more than suspicious. If the statements of Mr. Neumann are true the treaty ought not be confirmed at all, and Minister Stevens should be dismissed in disgrace from the diplomatic service. Let us have all the facts before we act upon them."[56] In spite of such public criticism, Foster believed he had assurances from congressional leaders that the treaty had sufficient votes for ratification.[57]

But the treaty failed to win quick Senate approval, and once the Democratic administration was installed, the prospects for annexation lessened. Within a week after his inauguration, Grover Cleveland withdrew the treaty from the Senate for reexamination.[58] Several days later former Congressman Blount was appointed special commissioner to visit Hawaii and investigate the political situation on the island. Blount was also given "paramount" authority in all matters pertaining to the provisional government.[59] Meanwhile, the Hawaiian commissioners sensed an unexpected turn in United States policy. Provisional government caused the commissioners to regret that they had not made greater efforts to press their case before President-elect Cleveland.[60]

During the final days of Harrison's administration, Foster sensed the change in the attitude of Democrats, and he believed it resulted from a decision made by Cleveland and his principal cabinet appointees while in a conference on February 22 at Lakewood, New Jersey. Attending this meeting were Walter Q. Gresham, secretary of state-designate, John G. Carlisle, a former senator and prospective secretary of treasury, and two other cabinet appointees.[61] Following the meeting Carlisle went directly to Washington where he was observed lobbying among Democratic senators for delay on the pending treaty. Foster knew Gresham well, and he was well aware of Gresham's personal dislike for Harrison, a long-time political rival. Foster believed that Gresham had influenced Cleveland's decision to block the annexation of Hawaii, since Cleveland had seemed friendly to annexation before the Lakewood meeting. Knowing that Gresham had an intense hatred for Harrison, Foster considered the abrupt and unexpected action of the new administration to be entirely the result of Gresham's personal vendetta.[62]

Whether or not Gresham sought to embarrass Harrison by investigating and exposing irregularities in the Hawaiian annexation effort, the ultimate consequence of withdrawing the treaty was the frustration of the annexation movement. Commissioner Blount arrived in Hawaii in late March and immediately hauled down the United States flag, ending the protectorate.[63] After conducting extensive interviews for several months with various participants, Blount authored a report concluding that annexationists had acted only after receiving assurances of support from United States Minister Stevens, that Stevens had given recognition to the provisional government before the queen's forces had been asked to surrender, and that most of the Hawaiian people supported the queen and opposed the provisional government.[64] Gresham and Cleveland agreed with Blount's views. On

December 18, 1893, President Cleveland announced that the United States would not annex Hawaii and expressed a hope for restoration of the queen and amnesty for the revolutionists.[65] The declaration of Cleveland's position created great consternation in political circles in the United States and Hawaii.[66]

Restoring the deposed queen presented a dilemma that Cleveland and Gresham were unable to solve. Albert S. Willis of Kentucky was appointed minister and dispatched to Hawaii to urge Liliuokalani to adopt a conciliatory course of action if returned to power and "to pursue a wise and humane policy."[67] The queen resisted Willis' counsel, insisting on beheading the leaders of the provisional government as soon as she regained her throne; when Willis finally convinced the ill-advised queen to grant amnesty, Sanford B. Dole, president of the provisional government, politely refused to leave office.[68] Faced with the prospect of having to intervene with force in Hawaii to restore a monarchy, the Democratic administration did nothing. The provisional government remained in control and eventually established the Hawaiian Republic on July 4, 1894.[69]

The failure to bring about annexation appears to have intensified Foster's resolve, and he remained active in annexationist schemes throughout the Cleveland years. In 1895 he was involved in a plot to secure annexation by joint congressional resolution, thereby avoiding the necessity of obtaining a two-thirds vote in the Senate. When this venture collapsed, Foster associated himself with the Pacific Cable Company of New Jersey and the colorful entrepreneur Colonel Z. S. Spaulding. As Spaulding's representative, Foster visited Honolulu in an unproductive effort to win a contract from the Hawaiian government, and while his business dealings were not successful, he found the trip an excellent opportunity to renew his contacts in the annexation movement.[70] Following his return from the islands, Foster appeared publicly as a forceful spokesman for annexation.[71] Well seasoned in Hawaiian matters by the time McKinley took office, Foster met with the new president shortly after his inauguration to outline steps for another annexation attempt. Foster was working quietly within the State Department in an unofficial capacity when war with Spain suddenly created an urgency about the Hawaiian annexation question. In June 1898, Foster, acting for the enfeebled secretary of state, John Sherman, easily secured the passage of a joint congressional resolution that made the Pacific islands possessions of the United States.[72] Despite Foster's tireless efforts, annexation would have been unlikely in 1898, had not the war with Spain provided a stimulus to the expansionists' cause.

Throughout the struggle for annexation Foster displayed a dogged persistence and harsh realism. Like Harrison and Blaine, Foster saw the acquisition of Hawaii as a fulfillment of American destiny. He viewed the question as a national rather than a partisan issue and was caught by surprise when the Cleveland administration failed to carry out the annexation procedures initiated in early 1893. Perhaps Foster's successor, Walter Gresham, held legitimate reservations about the proprieties of annexation following the coup, but his policies demonstrated little understanding of the hard political realities in Hawaii. While Gresham may have been genuinely concerned for the plight of the deposed queen and the feelings of the native Hawaiians, he was never prepared to see Liliuokalani restored to the throne on her own terms.[73] Although Foster's hasty attempt to secure annexation in 1893 was unwise politically, subsequent events proved that the revolution in Hawaii left the United States no reasonable alternative but to recognize the de facto government in Honolulu.

The frustrated attempt in 1893 served to facilitate ultimate annexation in 1898. Events in 1893 drew the islands' American-born leaders closer to the United States, and in the years following the defeat of Foster's treaty, the retired secretary served as an important link between annexationists in Honolulu and the foreign policy makers in Washington. Foster was the only United States official intimately involved in the negotiations from the time of the coup against Liliuokalani to the annexation five years later. Ironically, the war with Spain over issues not at all related to Hawaii provided the needed catalyst for the annexationists, and within a few months after the passage of the joint resolution, the acquisition of Hawaii was overshadowed by the sudden addition of Puerto Rico and the Philippines to the emerging insular empire.

Shimonoseki

It was ironic that Foster's single most important diplomatic adventure occurred at a time when he held no government position. Yet, no single event in John W. Foster's long career in diplomacy held more drama or greater importance than the peace conference at Shimonoseki, Japan in the early months of 1895. Foster's participation in the conferences as counsel and advisor to the Chinese plenipotentiary Li Hung-chang influenced the final terms of the settlement that ended the Sino-Japanese war. Meanwhile, during this six-month assignment in the service of the Chinese government, Foster found himself in the middle of a plot formulated by Americans with economic interests in China to overthrow the ruling dynasty, place Li Hung-chang on the throne, and thereby open the Chinese empire to American economic penetration. While the plot failed to materialize, it was nevertheless significant because the men involved in the scheme, including Foster, remained committed to furthering United States influence in China.

The Sino-Japanese war of 1894–1895 grew out of a conflict over the control of the Korean peninsula, a conflict that threatened a delicate balance of power in Asia as the Chinese armies collapsed before Japanese offensives.[1] The United States government viewed this situation as dangerous to American interests, and since the U.S. was on friendly terms with both China and Japan, American officials held to a policy of strict neutrality throughout the conflict and rejected several requests to intervene, including a proposal by the British that the United States participate in a joint effort with the European powers to impose a peace.[2] In November 1894 Secretary of State Walter Q. Gresham made cautious moves toward assisting in the creation of a settlement. In messages to Ministers Charles Denby in Peking and Edwin Dun in Tokyo, Gresham announced that President Grover Cleveland was willing to use his "good offices" in the interests of peace.[3] By the time the United States government made the offer, the Chinese government was ready to end the war, recognize the independence of Korea from Chinese control, and pay an indemnity to Japan.[4] Therefore, the Chinese immediately accepted Cleveland's offer to mediate, but the Japanese, enjoying military success on all fronts, objected to ending the hostilities.[5]

While Secretary of State Gresham did not believe the war directly endangered any policy of the United States in Asia, he worried that excessive military success by Japan would cause the European powers to intervene. In Washington Gresham advised Japanese Minister Kurino, "Japan should bring the war to a conclusion. If she continues to knock China to pieces, the powers, England, France, Germany and Russia, under the guise of preserving order, will partition China."[6] Whether moved by Gresham's warnings or by other developments, the Japanese government began to communicate with the Chinese through the United States ministers in Tokyo and Peking, and by mid-December tentative arrangements had been made for the commencement of peace negotiations.[7]

As legal counsel to the Chinese legation in Washington, Foster followed these developments closely. Concerned about the course of the war, he kept himself well informed of events in China through sources within the Chinese legation and by personal contact with expansionist-minded Americans. Foremost among these American associates was James Harrison Wilson, an ambitious railroad builder who dreamed of the unlimited possibilities for United States investors in the Orient. Since 1884, when he first contacted the Chinese legation about railroad concessions, Wilson had maintained a close friendship with Foster, and in the closing months of 1894 the entrepreneur schemed to involve Foster in an incredible plot to end the rule of the reactionary Manchu dynasty and install in China a new leadership favorable to American business interests.[8]

Wilson was in communication with Denby in Peking, and the United States' minister shared Wilson's desire to see American businessmen dominate the China market. Like Wilson, Denby believed that modernization and Westernization would come slowly as long as the autocratic and xenophobic Manchus ruled China. Now, in the wake of the disastrous Sino-Japanese war, Denby and Wilson believed they saw an opportunity to replace the ancient Manchu dynasty with the elderly Chinese statesman Li Hung-chang or his Western-educated adopted son, Li Ching-fong.[9] Wilson informed Foster of the plan, probably hoping that his friend's connections with Chinese officials would smooth the way for future railroad concessions.

During the first months of the war, an American soldier of fortune named William Pethick was, by coincidence, in the United States promoting railroad investment in China. A Civil War veteran, Pethick was a master of foreign languages and served as Li Hung-chang's private secretary.[10] Pethick had known Wilson since 1885, when the railroad builder toured China in search of business ventures. From that time on the two men continued a close correspondence.[11] In September 1894 Pethick presented Wilson with a memorandum on conditions in China. Believing that the Manchu dynasty would not survive a defeat by the Japanese, Pethick concluded that his employer, Li Hung-chang, was clearly best suited to emerge from the chaos as ruler of China.[12] Knowing of Wilson's close friendship with Foster, Pethick expressed concern that the emperor's agents in the Chinese legation might learn of the plot from Foster "in a moment of confidence." In a confidential letter to Wilson, Pethick urged that Foster not be informed of their plans. So concerned was Pethick about secrecy that he signed his message "Man in the Moon," and added as a postscript an unheeded instruction: "Please burn this."[13]

Wilson knew that an experienced diplomat like Foster could keep a secret, and he urged Pethick to visit Foster in Washington. Pethick agreed to do so, talking at length with Foster and finding him to be in agreement about the need for new leadership in China. "It was a relief to pass from the insanity of the Legation to the bright intelligence of your friend," Pethick wrote; "he himself said it would be better to change the dynasty and put Li in power." Pethick optimistically concluded, "your great scheme, General—the changing of the dynasty . . . [and the placing of] your friend [Li] on the throne—is becoming more feasible with every day's fresh news from China."[14] Within a few weeks of his meeting with Foster, Pethick was en route back to China, convinced that the collapse of the dynasty was imminent and that Li Hung-chang would rule China.[15]

Meanwhile, Foster maintained a correspondence with the United States minister in Peking, with whom he had enjoyed a long friendship dating back to the days when both men practiced law in Evansville. Foster and Denby agreed that the Chinese leaders needed American guidance, and following his talk with Pethick, Foster suggested to Denby that a Japanese victory over China might produce some favorable results if the Manchu dynasty were overthrown as a consequence.[16] Denby wrote from Peking of the hopelessness of the Chinese war effort and the need in Peking for the diplomatic aid of the United States. "Instinctively the Chinese turn to us," Denby stated. "The members of the Yamen [Tsungli Yamen or Foreign Office] are great school boys looking for a teacher. . . . They know the United States have no axe to grind."[17]

Remarkably, within days of receiving these words from Denby, a messenger arrived at Foster's Washington residence with a telegram in cipher from the Tsungli Yamen, requesting Foster's "wise counsel" in assisting a Chinese commission appointed to negotiate a peace with Japan. Foster was of course well known to Chinese officials because of his work for the legation in Washington, where he had established a solid friendship with Minister Chang Yin-hoon, who was appointed to lead the peace mission. Also, Foster and his family had visited China in 1894 while on their world tour and had met with government leaders and the diplomatic community in Peking.[18] Although he had been in contact with the Chinese legation for years, Foster claimed that the petition for his services at the peace conferences came as a surprise. It seems highly probable, however, that either Denby, Pethick, or Foster himself urged the appointment upon the Chinese officials.

Foster received the telegram from the Tsungli Yamen on December 22, and he immediately prepared for his new assignment. Within a few hours Foster arrived at the State Department and called upon Walter Gresham, his old personal friend and political crony, who had abandoned the Republican party after 1888 and supported Cleveland over Benjamin Harrison in 1892. Gresham now seemed to feel uneasy and out of place as secretary of state, and Foster offered his assurances that as advisor to the Chinese negotiators he would act as a private citizen, making it clear to all that he did not in any way represent the United States government. Gresham seemed to view Foster's mission, while unofficial in nature, as potentially in conflict with the American government's policy of neutrality in the Far East.[19] Apparently Gresham feared the Japanese would be offended by the former secretary of state's involvement with the Chinese side, and he went to great lengths to announce publicly that Foster would not be representing the United States government while in the service of China. Furthermore, the idealistic Gresham was irked at what he considered meddling for profit in East Asian diplomacy. "You can readily see that if Foster is not already a very rich man, his prospects of becoming a millionaire are flattering," Gresham wrote to Minister Thomas Bayard in London.[20]

Upon leaving Gresham's office, Foster went directly to the Japanese legation in Washington. Proud of his close friendship with the Japanese in Washington, Foster had for some years advocated the abolishing of extraterritoriality in Japan and had thereby earned a measure of goodwill for himself. Foster was pleased when the Japanese minister responded favorably to the news that the American diplomat would be assisting the Chinese peace commissioners.[21] He was even more delighted when the Japanese in Tokyo appeared to appreciate his role as advisor to China. Upon his arrival in Japan he reported to his wife, "the Japanese government is disposed to give me much consideration," and enclosed a copy of a complimentary press release issued by Japanese Minister of Foreign Affairs Mutsu Munemitsu that Foster suggested might be given to some friendly reporters with the Washington *Post* or *Star*, adding "I should like to have it appear in full in Washington under Gresham's nose."[22] Obviously the old friendship between Foster and Gresham was deteriorating rapidly.

Foster arrived at Kobe at the Bay of Yokohama on January 21, 1895, his three-week journey having taken him by rail through the vast Canadian wilderness in the dead of winter and by steamer from Vancouver across rough waters in the Northern Pacific. In Tokyo Foster was to meet with a Chinese delegation headed by Chang Yin-hoon and Shao Yu-lien, a former governor of Taiwan.[23] However, the Chinese delegates remained in Hiroshima and delayed coming to Kobe to meet with Foster, claiming illness, which the American diagnosed as a reluctance to begin the unpleasant business of negotiating a treaty that the defeated Chinese would find difficult to bear. While delayed in Kobe, Foster seized the opportunity to meet with Minister Dun, whom he found attentive and cordial, although Dun had recently been warned by Gresham to be suspicious of Foster. Foster also found the time to make a hurried trip to Tokyo to call upon the ministers of Great Britain, Russia, and France. Following these meetings Foster observed, "every person seems quite impressed with the important position I am to occupy during the negotiations."[24]

During the three weeks Foster had been in transit from Washington the situation for the Chinese government had worsened dramatically as a result of military defeats. As the man responsible for fortifying Port Arthur and developing the modernized navy destroyed by the Japanese, Li Hung-chang became the object of harsh criticism in Peking. Many of Li's former supporters deserted him in his public disgrace.[25] Perhaps Li's long political career would have ended ignominiously at this point if the Japanese had not demanded a man of his stature and prestige to negotiate a peace settlement in place of relatively low-ranking Commissioners Chang and Shao, who had arrived in Japan without proper credentials.[26]

At their urgent request Foster accompanied Chang and Shao on their return to China, where he learned that Li Hung-chang had been appointed peace commissioner and that the viceroy wanted the American advisor to remain. Before meeting with Li, Foster had several meetings in Shanghai with Denby, who was now unhappy with Gresham's conduct of the State Department. From Denby and British diplomats with whom he talked, Foster became convinced that the appointment of Li to handle the peace negotiations would be "for the best," although he became annoyed at the long delay in starting the negotiations.[27] Finally, Foster met for two hours with Li in Tientsin, and found the venerable statesman gracious, alert, and well informed.[28] Presumably, Foster also met with Pethick and Denby during this period, although there is no record of any such conversations.

Since his return to China in early December, Pethick's mind had been anything but idle. While Li brooded about the fate of China and his own uncertain future, Pethick tried to encourage his dejected employer but stopped short of informing him of the plans he, Wilson, Denby, and Foster were developing. In a letter to Wilson, Pethick outlined what he viewed as the two acts necessary for the success of American business interests in China. The first, as Pethick viewed it, was the rapid conclusion of the current hostilities; the second was to be the division of the Chinese Empire into two "spheres of influence." In Pethick's scheme, the southern region would be controlled by Britain, because of its proximity to India, and the northern sphere would be under the influence of the United States, thus forming a buffer area between British imperial holdings and "our friends," the Russians. Military advisors from the United States and Britain would then, in Pethick's view, "give China a good navy, superior to the Japs." Pethick believed that the United States was particularly well suited for the role of guardian in China because Americans had "no political or territorial aims to serve." Pethick concluded that a more aggressive American minister was needed to put the plan into action. "Denby endorses this scheme," Pethick wrote, "but his position will prevent him from actively pushing it."[29]

On March 15 Foster and Pethick accompanied Li Hung-chang, his son Li Ching-fong, and an entourage of 130 as a new peace mission departed for Shimonoseki, where negotiations were to be held.[30] Two days before leaving for Japan, Pethick found time to dispatch a progress report to Wilson in which the writer evaluated the prospects for the success of their scheme as "about even." Again Pethick denounced Denby as "the weakest minister we have out here" and suggested that Wilson himself seek the post in Peking once a Republican administration was restored. Warning that rival commercial syndicates had already appeared on the scene, Pethick predicted a rush of European competition once peace returned, and he urged Wilson to attempt to "concentrate American influence in one powerful China Improvement Co. instead of scattering it among several weaker concerns." Promising to send further reports in code as events unfolded, Pethick assured his reader that he and Foster would be close to Li throughout the negotiations in Japan. As he prepared to embark for the peace conference in Japan, Pethick concluded, "Act 1 over—now for Act 2."[31]

Within twenty-four hours of their arrival in Shimonoseki, the Chinese viceroy and his American counsel met with the Japanese negotiators, Marquis Ito Hirobumi and Viscount Mutsu. At the first conference session held March 20, Li Hung-chang presented a proposal for an armistice calling for the immediate suspension of combat.[32] Alluding to the common cultural heritage of the two nations, Li tried to impress upon the Japanese the argument that prolonged hostilities would only injure China without benefiting Japan.[33] Ito replied the following day, demanding that the cities of Taku, Shanhaikuan, and Tientsin (Li's city of residence) be surrendered to the Japanese army prior to any armistice. The Japanese negotiator also insisted on Japanese control of the railroad between Tientsin and Shanhaikuan and an indemnity. Li answered that these harsh terms had to be submitted to Peking for consideration, as he could not take the responsibility of agreeing to them. The following day, Li informed the Japanese that he had received telegrammed instructions to reject the Japanese armistice plan. With the prospects for a ceasefire gone, the Chinese plenipotentiary then asked the Japanese to outline their conditions for peace, and with this request the meeting was adjourned until the following morning.[34]

Throughout their first three meetings, the Chinese had been negotiating from the weakest possible position. Recently the Japanese Imperial Diet had voted unanimously to grant any amount of money necessary to accomplish Japanese war aims, and Ito had announced at the close of the third meeting that a Japanese fleet was preparing to attack Formosa momentarily. Li ineffectually warned the Japanese that in an era of Western imperialism in Asia, great Oriental peoples should not seek to exploit one another. However, as the third day of conferences drew to a close on the afternoon of March 24, it appeared that the Japanese were completely unmoved by the words of the Chinese viceroy.[35]

Suddenly, a dramatic incident changed the course of the negotiations. As the Chinese plenipotentiary and his party left the conference hall at the end of the third day to return to their quarters, a Japanese fanatic emerged from a crowd of onlookers, drew a pistol, and fired a shot into the face of the aged viceroy, hitting him in the cheekbone. Although in great pain, Li heroically maintained his composure and remained seated on the sedan chair upon which he was being carried. Bleeding profusely, Li somehow managed to get up and walk to his apartment, holding a handkerchief over his wound. In his quarters Li remained conscious, though in great agony, as surgeons probed for the deeply imbedded bullet.[36]

Understandably, the Japanese were horrified and humiliated by the shooting incident. Ito and Mutsu both made visits to Li's bedside, and the emperor of Japan ordered three of his personal physicians and two special nurses to serve the Chinese statesman. As was customary, the chief of police in Shimonoseki and the governor of the province were immediately removed from office. Li received messages of regret and sympathy from embarrassed Japanese officials at all levels, and presents of poultry, fruits, and vegetables poured into the Chinese quarters in Shimonoseki.[37]

Li's American advisor immediately prepared to make the most out of what he considered an unexpected opportunity. On March 28, a few days after the shooting, news reached Shimonoseki that the emperor of Japan had ordered his ambassadors to agree to an immediate and unconditional armistice.[38] Foster viewed this development as an important step toward a peace settlement and believed the viceroy's misfortune to be "the most effective shedding of blood on the Chinese side during the entire war, as it brought the sympathies of the whole world, and made the Japanese plenipotentiaries more considerate of him, if not less exacting in the terms of peace."[39] Although it brought about a cease-fire, the shooting incident did little to lessen the severity of the Japanese demands, which were modified only after difficult negotiating sessions.

The memorandum detailing the Japanese terms arrived on March 30, and the conditions stated were extremely harsh. Still, Foster believed that because of their desire to maintain the respect of Western nations, the Japanese could be forced to make significant modifications. Since his arrival from the United States and his first meetings with Japanese and American officials during the previous month in Tokyo, Foster had anticipated harsh initial demands by the Japanese; therefore, he had been preparing material to counter them.[40] The initial Japanese draft demanded independence for Korea and the cession of the southern part of Shengking province (Liaotung Peninsula), Taiwan (referred to as Formosa), and the Pescadores. The Japanese also called for an indemnity of three hundred million Kuping taels and the opening to Japanese commerce of seven major cities, including Peking, Chungking, and Hangchow. Foster prepared a lengthy reply to the Japanese demands that expressed a willingness to grant the independence of Korea but attempted to seek a compromise on the other points. During the subsequent negotiations Foster based the Chinese argument on Western historical and legal precedents of which he had expert knowledge. He noted in his reply that the Japanese were insisting on cession by the Chinese of territories not taken by the Japanese in battle, demanding an indemnity more than twice the cost of the war, and seeking commercial privilege unwarranted and unusual under the existing circumstances.[41]

In the Japanese reply on April 10, Marquis Ito informed the Chinese that Japan would reduce its territorial demands to Taiwan and the Pescadores and the Liao-tung Peninsula. The indemnity request was cut by 100 million taels and the number of open cities lowered from seven to four, with Peking among those excluded. The Japanese also gave up their insistence on holding Mukden until the Chinese paid the full indemnity.[42] The Chinese asked for further reduction of the indemnity and balked at surrendering the Liaotung area, but Ito insisted that the Japanese terms were "final (and) no longer open to discussion."[43] At the final negotiating session on April 15, Ito rejected Li's last desperate pleas for a reduction in the territorial demands and the indemnity figure. The formal signing of the peace treaty took place in Shimonoseki on April 17, with ratifications scheduled to be exchanged at Chefoo, China within a month.[44]

The Treaty of Shimonoseki provided for the recognition by China of Korean independence, the cessation of Taiwan, the Pescadores, and the Liaotung Peninsula to Japan, the opening of Chungking, Soochow, Hangchow and Sha-shih as treaty ports, guarantees for Japanese citizens to open factories and engage in manufacturing in China and an indemnity of two hundred million taels.[45] Foster considered the terms of the treaty to be severe, although not entirely unreasonable in light of terms negotiated at the conclusion of European wars in past decades. However, he suspected that the Japanese demands for the Liaotung Peninsula were made against the wishes of Marquis Ito, who, the American advisor believed, recognized the danger of intervention by the European powers against a Japanese attempt to gain a foothold on the Asian continent.[46]

During the negotiations of Shimonoseki, Li had taken great care to make sure that the European powers were informed of the details under discussion. Li was hopeful that the Russians or Germans, who were concerned about Japanese expansion in Korea and the Liaotung area, would intervene on behalf of China.[47] In fact, Russia and Germany had been pressuring Japan to leave China with the Liaotung Peninsula, and on April 23 representatives of Russia, Germany, and France jointly called on the Japanese to abandon their efforts to acquire the Chinese territory.[48] In spite of assurances by the German minister to China that there would be intervention against Japan, Li appears to have signed the treaty without certain knowledge that Germany or Russia or both would act to force the Japanese to relinquish their claim to the Liaotung Peninsula.[49]

After meeting with the ministers of all European nations, Foster traveled to Peking, where he urged ratification of the treaty before the Tsungli Yamen on behalf of Li Hung-chang.[50] Foster then returned to Tientsin, where he again met with Li. The viceroy now informed him that Russia, Germany, and France were prepared to force the Japanese to retreat on the issue of the Liaotung Peninsula. Because of the action by the three European powers, Foster decided to remain in China until the Shimonoseki agreement was signed, feeling that his personal prestige and reputation were at stake. Finally, on May 8, Foster witnessed the signing of the treaty at Chefoo amid a great show of force by the German, French, and Russian naval forces.[51] The Japanese, faced with the overwhelming presence of three European powers, were left with no alternative but to give up their ambitions in the Liaotung Peninsula, at least temporarily.

One final issue remained to be settled before Foster could conclude his mission; the difficult matter of transferring Taiwan to the Japanese. In late May the people on the island had declared their independence, establishing the Republic of Taiwan, and it now appeared that the Japanese would have to fight to gain control of their new possession.[52] Li Hung-chang saw this development as an opportunity for the Chinese to renegotiate the Shimonoseki agreement, especially since the Liaotung Peninsula matter had been voided; concerned about the principles of international law and his own reputation, however, Foster urged the viceroy to adhere to the treaty. Meanwhile, Ito refused to consider any further discussion of the Taiwan question and demanded that the Chinese government appoint a commission to handle the orderly transfer of the island to Japan. Much to the Chinese viceroy's consternation, the Tsungli Yamen assigned his son Li Ching-fong to the dangerous and unpopular task of transferring Taiwan to Japanese authorities. Li was now convinced that the government was attempting to place on his family all the blame for the disastrous war and the odious treaty, and fearing for his son's safety, he begged his American advisor to accompany him to Taiwan. Agreeing to perform this final service, Foster joined Lord Li at Shanghai and the two sailed together to meet a Japanese naval fleet anchored near the island. Following a brief meeting with Japanese officials on June 2 on board a man-of-war, the transfer was completed, and Foster and Lord Li quickly returned to the mainland without ever setting foot on Taiwanese soil.[53]

Before leaving China to return home, Foster declined an offer to remain in China as a permanent advisor to Li Hung-chang on foreign policy matters. When the American cited his lucrative business interests as the reason for turning down the viceroy's request, Li responded that China was prepared to pay more than any sum Foster might earn in Washington. Foster then told of the summer fishing trip he had promised his young grandson and name-sake, John Foster Dulles, and said that he did not want to disappoint the lad. The powerful viceroy noted that it would be no problem to bring the boy as well as the entire Foster family to China, but he accepted Foster's polite refusal to stay on in China.[54] While the fishing holiday was probably a true commitment, Foster had more serious reasons for rejecting the position as advisor to Li that he was too discreet to mention. He believed the Chinese government was hopelessly corrupt and incapable of making the reforms necessary to strengthen its foreign policies. Since Li himself had proved loyal to the declining Manchu dynasty and had appeared uninterested in taking the throne for himself, Foster viewed the prospects for political reform and economic modernization as unlikely.[55] However, while he chose not to accept the post as Li's advisor, Foster did remain legal counsel to the Chinese legation in Washington and continued a warm friendship with the viceroy, for whom he held great admiration.

Meanwhile, almost totally obscured by the tumultuous events surrounding the negotiating sessions, the business ventures of Wilson, Denby, and Pethick failed to materialize. Li Hung-chang emphatically refused to consider any involvement in a plot to overthrow the Manchu dynasty. Following the total failure of their scheme, a dejected Pethick wrote to Wilson: "Here we are at the old stand. We started here last Spring; took a big climb; got to the top, and then—tumbled back again to (the) original starting point."[56] Furthermore, by forcing Japan to relinquish its claim to the Liaotung Peninsula, Russia had gained enormous prestige with the Chinese officials, who looked increasingly to Russia for financial aid and military support.[57] The neutral position of the United States government throughout the war and the reluctance of the Cleveland administration to promote American investment schemes actively left entrepreneurs like Wilson and Calvin Brice of Ohio at an insurmountable disadvantage in seeking opportunities in China.[58]

The failure of Wilson and other American businessmen to find opportunities in the China market at the close of the Sino-Japanese war did not stifle the ambitions of promoters and investors in the United States. After 1895 the United States government took a more positive role in support of American investors as the international rivalry for concessions in China intensified.[59] Both Wilson and Denby remained active in the prospects for railroad building in China;[60] as legal counsel for the Chinese legation in Washington, Foster continued to act as a middleman between the Chinese government and American investors. To help counter Russian influence in China and to assist American investors, Foster arranged for Li Hung-chang to visit the United States in February 1896 on his return from the coronation of Nicholas II in Russia. In Washington and New York Foster arranged for Li to meet with prominent businessmen interested in commercial relations with China. The ancient viceroy, still carrying in his cheekbone the bullet he took at Shimonoseki, enjoyed a warm and enthusiastic reception.[61]

Of the principal American figures involved in the events surrounding the Shimonoseki negotiations, only Foster continued to be a prominent and influential national figure in the following decades. Foster emerged as a recognized expert on United States diplomacy in East Asia, and the Chinese government continued to retain Foster as their legal counsel in Washington. Apparently Foster's clients were completely satisfied with their counsel's ability to represent their interests in international negotiations and tribunals.[62] At the same time he provided advice to State Department officials, consistently urging that the United States support China's territorial integrity while seeking to keep the empire open to American merchandise, investment, and missionary activity. Furthermore, Foster's years of diplomatic experience and close personal knowledge of Chinese, Japanese, European, and American leaders enabled him to write with considerable authority about East Asian affairs. Within the period of a few years he produced a widely read book, *American Diplomacy in the Orient*, and many articles on Far Eastern affairs in the nation's most prestigious journals.[63]

Foster viewed Japan as the leading Asian power, necessary for checking Russian expansion and useful as a model for other Asian nations in their efforts to adapt to Western thought and technology. He saw no reason why China, given proper leadership, could not also emerge as a modern, progressive nation. By 1904 Foster foresaw the coming of the Russo-Japanese war, and when that conflict erupted, he wrote to his old friend Wilson, "I prefer to see the triumph of the spirit of government animating Japan than that which controls Russia—autocracy and depotism. . . . I hope Russia will be soundly thrashed by Japan."[64] Foster's assessment of Far Eastern affairs was generally shared by contemporary policy makers in the State Department, with whom Foster had close contacts.[65] It was not until 1917, when Foster himself had come to be disillusioned with Japanese expansionist policies, that American relations with the Tokyo government became strained over the issue of Japanese demands upon China. About the same time that his son-in-law, Robert Lansing, was reaching an understanding with Japanese leaders over their expansionist activities in China during the World War I (known as the Lansing-Ishii Agreement), Foster wrote to his old friend Wilson and observed that recent Japanese activity in China "distinctly lowers my confidence in the good judgment of her leading people."[66]

During the twentieth century United States diplomacy in China would be characterized by a self-righteous, paternalistic mentality.[67] That a few Americans seriously contemplated a coup d'état in 1895 indicates that an attitude of moral superiority had already infected American policies regarding the Chinese. The involvement of Americans in the plot to organize a coup at the close of the Sino-Japanese war demonstrated a naive belief that simple overthrow of the decrepit Manchu dynasty would lead to governmental changes necessary for economic progress in China. While the plotters considered the establishment of new leadership in China potentially beneficial to both Chinese and Americans, Foster, Wilson, Denby, and Pethick were mistaken in believing that such leadership could provide a vehicle for the modernization of China. They were also blind to the new forces of nationalism emerging within the empire.

VIII

The "Handy Man"

During two and a half productive decades following his departure from the office of secretary of state, John W. Foster pursued several careers. He maintained a highly successful international legal practice in Washington, lectured at George Washington University (then called Columbia), wrote several important books, including his memoirs, held office in several prestigious national organizations such as the Carnegie Endowment for International Peace and the American Red Cross, and found many opportunities to vacation with his children and grandchildren at their rustic Lake Ontario retreat at Henderson Harbor, New York. He also remained actively involved in the formulation of United States foreign policies. Because the former secretary of state took on tasks and assignments requiring a broad background and offered advice on diverse problems, one prominent contemporary referred to Foster as the "handy man" of the State Department.[1] His many diplomatic services, both official and otherwise, indicated that he enjoyed the confidence of national leaders and was widely recognized as an expert on a variety of subjects. A series of presidents and secretaries of state employed Foster's talent for negotiation, knowledge of Far Eastern affairs, and expertise in the handling of sensitive diplomatic problems. In every administration from Benjamin Harrison's through Woodrow Wilson's, Foster never strayed far from the vortex of foreign policy decision making. He enjoyed ready access to key policy makers in the Department of State who were either long-time acquaintances and colleagues, political allies or, in the case of Robert Lansing, a member of the family and junior law partner. Foster moved easily through the halls of the State Department,

86

corporate board rooms, and the offices of foreign legations in Washington. At times it proved difficult to distinguish his public service from his private practice, a matter that did not cause Foster any noticeable concern.

The most persistent diplomatic problems to which Foster applied himself in his long years of semiretirement from public life concerned United States relations with Canada and therefore with Great Britain. Early in 1892, several months before his appointment as secretary of state, Foster's Washington-based law firm had been employed to act as the agent for the United States on the international legal dispute arising from the desire of the United States government to protect the Alaskan fur seals from pelagic sealing in the area surrounding the Pribilof Islands. This form of hunting threatened the very survival of the herds and was practiced by Canadians outside United States territorial waters. Following agreement to a modus vivendi in 1891, Britain and the United States signed a treaty of arbitration in February 1892 and submitted the question to an international tribunal. Foster, then engaged in private practice, accepted an appointment by President Benjamin Harrison to act as the agent for the government in organizing and presenting the United States' case.[2]

Foster based his government's argument on the doubtful premise that the Russians, before selling Alaska to the United States, had held the Bering Sea as a *mare clausum*, that the British had recognized this Russian claim, and that matters affecting the fur seals were, therefore, now under the jurisdiction of the United States. The State Department possessed many Russian documents on Alaska, and to bolster the American contention, Foster hired a Russian scholar, Ivan Petroff, to translate those passages that supported the United States' position.[3]

Unfortunately, the overly zealous Petroff knowingly wrote into his translations fraudulent statements justifying the American argument. An alert State Department clerk discovered the discrepancies and informed Foster, but only after the bogus translations had been made available to the British negotiators.[4] The United States' case was further embarrassed when the Russian government, seeking to bolster its own interests in the Bering Sea, signed an agreement with Great Britain respecting sealing that completely contradicted the American position. The British managed to conclude this arrangement with Russia in June 1893 as the international tribunal was meeting in Paris hearing arguments, and reading of the agreement into the arbitral proceedings damaged the United States' case.[5] When the tribunal rendered its decision in August, it entirely rejected the United States claim of jurisdiction over the fur seal rookeries; however, the judges did establish regulations aimed at protecting the seals from pelagic killing and possible extermination.[6]

The judgment of the tribunal did not end the controversy; a suitable arrangement for effective execution of the provisions of the tribunal's award remained to be established. Foster's son-in-law and junior member of his legal firm, Robert Lansing, who worked on the preparation of the case, expressed doubts about the willingness of the British to restrain Canadians involved in pelagic sealing soon after the tribunal had rendered its decision. Since Foster had embarked upon a world tour following the conclusion of the proceedings in Paris, Lansing was concerned that there would be no strong voice in Washington to urge the Cleveland administration and Congress to demand British adherence to the tribunal's decision.[7] Actually, Secretary of State Walter Q. Gresham had already become aware of the problems involved in enforcing compliance to the sealing restrictions and had written to Foster, stating: "If Great Britain is willing to cooperate with us the seal industry may be preserved, but I must say I cannot get rid of the impression that various pretexts may be restored for delay on the part of that Government."[8] Gresham's doubts about a lack of Anglo-American goodwill in this matter would prove well founded. Throughout the remainder of the Cleveland administration the fur seal matter and several lesser disputes regarding Atlantic fisheries, reciprocal trade, and the Alaskan boundary remained unresolved.[9]

While the actual matters concerned in these disputes between the United States and Great Britain appeared trivial on the surface, public opinion and domestic political pressure for a firm stand against British "arrogance" gave the issues increased significance.[10] Profitably occupied with his legal practice, world travels, and the peace negotiations at Shimonoseki, Foster was not actively involved with State Department operations in the Cleveland administration after 1893 and the conclusion of the Paris tribunal. But the election of a Republican president in 1896 brought the former secretary of state back into the diplomatic service, and following the inauguration of William McKinley Foster was again asked to turn his attention to the lingering disagreements in Anglo-American relations.

In the spring of 1897 Foster was called upon to advise State Department officials on the Bering Sea situation.[11] After giving the question careful study, he recommended to the administration that a four-power conference including the United States, Great Britain, Russia, and Japan be held in Washington during the final months of 1897.[12] Foster's proposal was accepted, and he was given a special appointment with the rank of ambassador to travel to St. Petersburg and London to discuss prospects for the international conference.[13] Leaving for the European capitals in May, Foster found a cordial acceptance of his plans for a conference and considered his trip most satisfactory. Therefore, with great optimism, Foster arranged a meeting in October.[14] A few weeks before the formal sessions were to begin, however, the British abruptly decided not to participate. The British were possibly concerned about the publication in the New York *Tribune* of Secretary of State John Sherman's harshly worded note of May 10, 1892 to the British Foreign Office. Drafted by Foster, the note criticized the British for their failure to halt pelagic sealing and for deliberately delaying the printing of a report which the United States negotiators needed to prepare their case. At Foster's urging, Sherman instructed United States Minister John Hay to present the note to the British, a task Hay found distasteful.[15] Whether the British declined to attend the Washington Conference as a delayed reaction to the note of May 10, from pique at the note's publication, or for some other reason, their refusal to join in the four-power meeting doomed the gathering from the start, and in spite of Foster's efforts and aspirations, the International Fur Seal Conference of 1897 ended without a settlement on any of the pending matters.[16]

In the spring of 1898 Foster participated in a series of meetings in Washington at which both the American and British sides agreed to establish a joint high commission to resolve all outstanding differences between the United States and Canada.[17] In August the United States commissioners led by Foster met with their counterparts in Quebec. Although the deliberation of the United States and British Joint High Commission for the Adjustment of Canadian Questions dragged on for eighteen weeks in Quebec and later in Washington, the conferences ended without a settlement.[18] The commission broke up over the question of the Alaskan boundary, an increasingly emotional issue since the discovery of gold in the Klondike River region in 1897. Recently, the Canadians had vigorously asserted that the boundary of the Alaskan panhandle extended inland about thirty miles from the outermost islands off the Pacific coast rather than from the shore of the mainland. The Canadian claim would have given that country control of saltwater inlets previously regarded as wholly within United States territory. The Canadians could not be induced to accept the separation of the Alaskan boundary dispute from the other issues to be negotiated by the joint commission and refused to proceed on the fur seal question until an agreement was reached on the border problem.[19]

A modus vivendi was agreed upon in October 1899. After several years of refusing to submit the question to arbitration, Secretary of State John Hay signed a treaty in Washington on January 24, 1903 calling for a panel of six "impartial jurists of repute"—three chosen by the president and three by the British monarch—to study the whole question and define the boundary.[20] President Roosevelt selected for the American members his personal friend, Senator Henry Cabot Lodge, his secretary of war, Elihu Root, and an outspoken advocate of the United States boundary claim in Alaska, Senator George Turner of Washington. Foster was named legal counsel to prepare the arguments for the United States position and to act as a spokesman for the administration.[21]

When the Alaskan Boundary Tribunal convened in London in September, Foster, who had labored long hours over the United States case, presented a detailed document of more than six hundred pages, including maps and charts.[22] The British, aware of the weakness of the Canadian boundary claim and President Roosevelt's uncompromising attitude regarding the matter, decided to accept a judgment wholly favorable to the United States. Roosevelt's appointment of Lodge, Turner, and Root, all ardent nationalists committed to Roosevelt's foreign policies, indicated that the United States would agree to no compromise on the boundary question; the British recognized this political reality and acted accordingly. By a four-to-two vote, with the two Canadian jurists dissenting, the United States was awarded a strip of land continuous around all the inlets from the Portland Canal north to Mount Elias, thus excluding Canada from contact with the sea. The Canadians felt that for the sake of improved Anglo-American relations, the British had betrayed their claim for an outlet to the Pacific.[23] Indeed, the judgment reached in October 1903 was clearly diplomatic rather than judicial.

Foster's efforts before the Alaskan Boundary Tribunal ended for him ten years of sporadic involvement in United States relations with Great Britain. During this time Foster had gained considerable recognition and notoriety for his diplomatic labors. He was known to the Americans, British, and Canadians as a tough, stubborn negotiator who mastered every detail of both the fur seal and Alaskan boundary controversies. Despite the punctilious preparation of his presentation, he was probably more effective in back room bargaining than in formal negotiating sessions, particularly since his rough, country-lawyer approach to argumentation in the courtroom sometimes ruffled sophisticated English opponents—they occasionally viewed him as unmannerly and boorish.[24] Of his reputation as a fierce, tenacious negotiator, John Hay once remarked, "Foster's worst enemy would never accuse him of any tendency to mercy or tenderness to an opponent."[25] While Foster's blunt and candid speech delighted the secretary of state in private and provided an amusing topic of conversation in Washington society,[26] Hay was probably correct in noting that Foster's unyielding manner did not seem to facilitate a spirit of compromise leading to expeditious settlements.

Throughout his diplomatic career Foster viewed Great Britain as a commercial rival and potential economic and military threat to United States interests. While secretary of state, Foster had dealt with the problems of the joint occupation of Samoa, British encroachment along the Mosquito Coast in Central America, and various disputes concerning Canada.[27] Finally, with the settlement of the Alaskan boundary question to the satisfaction of the United States, only the persistent fur seal problem, reciprocity, and a controversy over North Atlantic fisheries remained to endanger American relations with Great Britain.[28] Foster sensed that a new era of Anglo-American understanding and cooperation was emerging. He was proud of the record established by the two Anglo-Saxon peoples in the judicial settlement of their international disagreements, and he saw no reason why the progress demonstrated in the negotiations between Britain and the United States could not be duplicated elsewhere. He felt that the negotiations in which he participated had a deeper significance than the mundane task of reaching a settlement on a specific issue. To Foster, who simultaneously was involved in a number of organizations promoting international peace through arbitration, the disputes over the fur seals and Alaskan boundary offered a chance to demonstrate moral leadership. He viewed the manner in which the Alaskan boundary dispute ended as far more important than the actual terms of the settlement, because it demonstrated the highly advanced civilization known to the Anglo-Saxon peoples.[29]

Foster's diplomatic dexterity proved invaluable in the first years of the McKinley administration in areas other than Anglo-American relations. Not wanting to separate himself from his family for long periods of time by an extended overseas residence, the former secretary of state graciously declined the president's offers of ambassadorships to Peking, Madrid, or Constantinople.[30] Instead, Foster accepted several short-term assignments such as the work for the Alaskan Boundary Tribunal and remained in Washington where he had the opportunity to practice law and render advice on specific problems as an unofficial advisor.

During the McKinley administration the State Department turned to Foster often, as the president's initial appointments to the office of secretary of state proved to be people inadequately suited for the job. In choosing John Sherman of Ohio to head the State Department, McKinley acted with great reluctance and under political pressure from party boss Mark Hanna, who wanted for himself Sherman's seat in the United States Senate. An elderly Republican warhorse enfeebled after his many years of public services, the once powerful Sherman was unable to comprehend the complexities of foreign policy. For assistant secretary of state the president selected Judge William R. Day, a personal friend and confidant from Canton, Ohio and an able and competent individual but a man utterly lacking in experience with regard to foreign policy.[31] Both Sherman and Day, who succeeded to the post of secretary of state in April 1898 and held that job for only four months, looked to the knowledgeable Foster for counsel on matters with which the senior diplomat was familiar.[32] With the outbreak of war with Spain, the renewed drive for the annexation of Hawaii became Foster's special charge.[33] His involvement in that work along with the preparation of matters dealing with the fur seals and Alaskan boundary made Foster a leading character within the diplomatic establishment, and when the able and articulate John Hay became secretary of state in September 1898, Foster's role in policy making was in no way diminished. Their relationship was exceptionally cordial, and while Hay held his cabinet post, the two men corresponded frequently on varied topics.[34]

Shortly after being named secretary of state, Hay asked Foster to visit the

State Department and discuss foreign policy, adding humbly, "you know what the place requires better than I do."[35] Hay solicited and received informal counsel from the former secretary of state on matters concerning relations with the Congress, affairs in Samoa and Latin America, American missionary activities in Turkey, and the selection of diplomatic appointments.[36] However, Foster's most important advisory service was rendered in regard to United States diplomacy in the Far East during the issuing of the Open Door notes and thereafter.[37]

Hay sought Foster's opinion on the nature of the Boxer Rebellion, as Foster was close to the officials in the Chinese legation. A few weeks before dispatching his second circular note proclaiming the American desire to safeguard the principle of equal and impartial trade with all parts of China, Hay confided to Foster his anger at being accused in the press of pro-British sympathies because his stand against the partition of China was similar to that of Great Britain. "How can we make bricks without straw?" asked Hay, meaning that American policy needed British support. "That we should be compelled to refuse the assistance of the greatest power in the world, *in carrying out our own policy*, because all Irishmen are Democrats and some Germans are fools—is enough to drive a man mad. Yet we shall do what we can."[38] The extent to which Hay's actions during the Boxer Rebellion were influenced by Foster is impossible to discern, but the two men did share a desire to see Chinese territorial integrity preserved and Russian expansion in Manchuria checked.[39]

While advising the State Department on Far Eastern affairs, Foster was constantly in the employment of the Chinese legation in Washington as legal counsel. In this position Foster served as a middleman between the Chinese foreign office and the United States government, represented the interests of China and Chinese in the United States and also served as a mediator between the Chinese government and American investors. While this work was extremely lucrative and brought Foster recognition as an expert on China and Oriental affairs, the job often placed him in the position of having to take stands unpopular with the United States government and the American public and subject to criticism from those who questioned how a man could effectively represent the interest of a foreign government and at the same time advise State Department officials.

The long fight against Chinese exclusion by the United States government involved Foster in the greatest controversy brought about by his legal work with the Chinese legation. Having vehemently argued against the Scott Bill of 1888, which sought to prohibit all Chinese except officials, students, and travelers from entering the United States, he assisted in the negotiation of a compromise agreement between China and the United States in 1894 to prohibit absolutely the importation of Chinese laborers for a period of ten years. After a few years, however, United States immigration officials began to restrict all Chinese from entry into the country except for a few special classes mentioned in the 1894 agreement, and in 1902 representatives from West Coast states, with the strong encouragement and support of Samuel Gompers and organized labor as well as the approval of the Roosevelt administration, presented legislation aimed at permanently excluding from the United States all Chinese immigrants, not just laborers, while at the same time excluding Chinese from entering the territories of Hawaii and the Philippines. Both the House and Senate held hearings on proposed legislation (known as the Mitchell-Kahn Bill) opposed by the powerful American China Development Company, which listed among its stockholders J. P. Morgan, Levi Morton, Andrew Carnegie, Edward Harriman, John D. Rockefeller and Cornelius Vanderbilt, as well as the Pacific Mail and Steamship Company, represented by attorney Maxwell Evarts, the son of the former secretary of state.[40] Representing the interests of the Chinese government at the hearings, Foster joined the American business interests in arguing that the legislation would be a threat to the American China trade. Citing the potential for enormous trade with China, Foster asked committee members, "what will that avail us, if, by our own rush legislation and injustice, we ourselves close this door to our manufacturers, farmers and merchants?"[41] When questioned by a committee member, Foster stated that he was "not opposed to the general policy of exclusion"; rather he believed that while some exclusion of labors might be beneficial, United States treaty obligations had to be upheld.[42] He argued that any law passed by Congress to extend exclusion beyond 1904 would have no validity in international law, that no exclusion laws should include newly acquired insular possessions in the Pacific, and that existing laws were in violation of treaty obligations.[43] Eventually the legislation was set aside in favor of an amended bill offered by Senator Orville Platt that extended the terms of the 1888 legislation until 1904. Both extreme exclusionists and the Chinese were unhappy with this compromise measure, but it was really more of a defeat for the Chinese, who wanted some improvement in the status quo. So disturbed was the Chinese legation at the passage of the compromise bill that a note from the Chinese minister, most likely drafted by Foster, was dispatched to President Roosevelt asking for a veto. The note argued that the new legislation, which altered a treaty between the two countries, was illegal because "it is not in conformity with international law and the comity of nations to include in the operations of a treaty numbers of people and a great extent of territory [Hawaii and the Philippines] which were in no respect the subject of the treaty." The administration claimed that the note arrived at the White House after the president had signed the bill.[44] However, it seems doubtful that the legal arguments would have persuaded the president to veto a bill that had great popularity.

During his appearances before the congressional hearings, Foster was criticized for representing a foreign government; the San Francisco *Chronicle* saw Foster as "a Hessian in law and diplomacy . . . willing to give his services to the highest bidder," and Republican Boies Penrose claimed Foster's testimony should not be considered, since he was "the representative of the Chinese Empire and not a disinterested witness or writer."[45] But such accusations meant little to Foster, who found in the Chinese exclusion matter a situation in which his own personal convictions were in complete harmony with those of his client. A strict legalist, Foster believed that treaty agreements should be adhered to; a pragmatist, he also understood that the open door to China would be closed if there were shortsighted policies that discriminated against the Chinese.

About the same time that the question of Chinese exclusion was being debated in Congress, Foster once again found himself in opposition to the State Department and the Roosevelt administration as he represented his Chinese clients in a dispute concerning the construction of a railroad between Canton and Hankow by the American China Development Company, which had violated its agreement with the Chinese by attempting to sell its stock to Belgian interests including the imperialistic King Leopold II. Alarmed that the Americans were allowing this vital rail line to fall into the hands of European investors and concerned that only ten miles of a proposed 850-mile line had been completed after almost three years, the Chinese formally revoked the Canton-Hankow railroad concession in December 1904.[46] Meanwhile, the Chinese legation in Washington, working through Foster, offered to compensate the company for its efforts and settled for a compromise payment of $6,750,000 after the company's attorneys, Elihu Root and George W. Ingraham, had demanded more than eighteen million. The Chinese offer was accepted at the company's stockholders meeting, and it seemed a liberal settlement in light of the firm's duplicity and incompetence.[47]

President Roosevelt was not satisfied, however; he saw the issue as one in which lowly Chinese were pushing American businessmen around and were thereby damaging the prestige of the United States. Urging Morgan, who was now the company's principal investor, to retain the concession, the president promised to back the company in any disputes with the Chinese. After a brief deliberation, Morgan decided to accept the Chinese offer, as the construction of the railroad no longer seemed worth the effort.[48] To the Chinese, the payment of more than six million dollars to buy back a concession from a company that had broken its agreement may have seemed unjust, but it must also have appeared to be a small price to pay to avoid a diplomatic confrontation, considering that the company's attorneys had originally demanded almost three times the amount of the actual settlement.

In addition to his political contacts in the foreign policy establishment, Foster remained close to the inner workings of the State Department through a close relationship with the younger members of his family, whose diplomatic careers he had launched with considerable care. Because of frail health, through the closing years of his long life he became increasingly secluded and drew closer to his immediate family. Although Foster's legal business, teaching, and occasional service in the State Department kept him in Washington, he and his wife spent ever longer periods of time in the family's summer home at Henderson Harbor, New York. There Foster's younger daughter Eleanor met and married Robert Lansing, a young lawyer in nearby Watertown, in January 1891. A few years later, the Reverend Allen Dulles, who had married Eleanor's sister, Edith, succeeded his father as the pastor of First Presbyterian Church in Watertown and returned to New York from Detroit to settle his family permanently in the small town. The grandparents began to divide their time between Washington and their home on Lake Ontario. A proud and doting grandfather, Foster devoted extraordinary attention to his grandchildren, particularly the sons of his elder daughter Edith and her husband, a pious, scholarly, and liberal Presbyterian minister. Foster enjoyed fishing in the picturesque area around Lake Ontario with his precocious grandsons, John Foster and Allen, as well as their younger sister, Eleanor. The old man demonstrated a profound affection for his grandchildren and his constant companionship with them clearly influenced their development. On many fishing expeditions at the lake and during regular visits to their grandparents' home on Eighteenth Street in Washington, the Dulles children were endlessly enthralled by their grandfather's stories of faraway places. They were enchanted by the constant presence of prominent statesmen, foreign missionaries, and Chinese officials in their grandparents' home, which had become a gathering place for those involved in the world of foreign affairs.[49] From an early age the children expressed a fascination with world affairs, and their proud grandfather encouraged their study of history, geography, and foreign affairs.[50] Perhaps because he had never had a son, the old gentleman had a particular affection for his grandsons, and his companionship markedly influenced their decisions to pursue careers in international affairs.

Interested in the education of all his grandchildren, the family patriarch helped his son-in-law, a poorly paid minister, to finance a college education for his children. In the case of his eldest and favorite grandson, John Foster, money was also made available to assist the youthful recipient of Princeton University's "Prize for Mental Science" when he sought to pursue his studies in philosophy at the Sorbonne in Paris under Henri Bergson; and, at his grandfather's request, the nineteen-year-old student was named secretary for the Chinese delegation to the Second Hague Conference in 1907, an experience that provided the future secretary of state with his initiation into the world of international diplomacy.[51]

When the grandson decided to pursue a career in international affairs instead of the ministry, a decision that did not please his parents, he chose

George Washington University for his law studies so that he could be near his grandfather. During his two years in Washington, the young law student lived with his grandparents, became familiar with leading figures in the capital, and socialized with the sons of President William Howard Taft, establishing a friendship with young Bob Taft that would last for many decades as both rose to positions of leadership in the Republican party.[52] Upon completing his studies but not the residency requirement necessary for a degree, the aspiring attorney found difficulty in attaining a suitable position with any of the major Wall Street law firms. Again the family patriarch assisted, asking William N. Cromwell of the prestigious firm of Sullivan and Cromwell, whose cofounder had been a pre–Civil War acquaintance of the grandfather in Cincinnati, if "the memory of an old association. . . [was not] enough to give this young man a chance."[53] The letter from his influential grandfather started the young, inexperienced, and degree-less lawyer on a career that would ultimately lead to his appointment as secretary of state.

Foster's concern for his grandson's career did not end, once a suitable position had been secured with a major Wall Street firm. Foster encouraged his grandson's early efforts at writing on diplomatic topics, brought him into contact with prominent figures in such associations as the American Society of International Law and, when the young attorney planned a trip abroad, provided letters of introduction to diplomats in London and Paris.[54] When the monotony of routine assignments brought the ambitious youngster to the verge of quitting, his grandfather was ready with sage advice, gentle encouragement, and an offer to speak to the boss. Reflecting upon his own days as a struggling young lawyer, Foster wrote:

. . . received your letters from New York giving an account of your daily occupations in the office, which was quite interesting to me. You are evidently making yourself quite useful to the firm and that is the important thing to-wards your success. You must not allow yourself to tire of the drudgery of the office—that's what new clerks have to go through, I suppose. But your work of that kind is not as bad as what I had to go through in my first year in a law office—I was janitor and charwoman, having to open the office in the morning, swept the rooms and got everything in shape for the days work. When the real business reconvenes after the summer vacations, I shall hope to hear that you have some real legal work to do in the way of briefs and such like. Next will be a meeting of the Executive Committee of the Carnegie Peace Endowment Oct. 26, when your grandma and I expect to be in New York for two or three days, and I hope for an opportunity to go down to your office and see the members of your firm, and may be able to say a word of benefit for you. But it is steady good, hard work that is to determine your advancement.[55]

While he accepted his grandfather's advice and remained with Sullivan and Cromwell, young Dulles was not happy and after several years of boredom in routine assignments, he was prepared to leave the firm and enter business. Once again his grandfather provided the encouragement that kept the future secretary of state from leaving the legal profession in the summer of 1914. "You have now spent several years fitting yourself for the law," Foster wrote, "and you should not allow business to tempt you away from your chosen work."[56] Following his grandfather's advice once again, Dulles remained with the firm, and he soon found the challenges he desired. They did not necessarily come from within his firm but more as a result of the outbreak of war in Europe and the young man's assignment as a special agent with the State Department, where Robert Lansing, his "Uncle Bert," had become, with Foster's assistance, a figure of rising stature.

John W. Foster's influence on the diplomatic career of Robert Lansing was profound. Throughout his early career in international law and diplomacy, Lansing was under Foster's guidance, and the elder statesman's views on diplomatic issues greatly influenced Lansing's thinking on foreign policy questions. Lansing was an industrious, hardworking small-town attorney when he married Eleanor Foster, and this association rescued him from an uninteresting and ordinary legal career. For a few years after his marriage, Lansing continued a modest law practice with his invalid father in Watertown. But following his father's death, Bert and his wife moved to Washington, where they took up residence with Eleanor's parents. Lansing was immediately brought into his father-in-law's sphere of contacts in government and business. In 1892 Foster secured an appointment for his son-in-law as associate counsel for the United States in the Bering Sea case, providing Lansing with an introduction into the specialized world of international law, and with the former secretary of state's backing, he quickly found additional opportunities. Associated with his father-in-law's law firm in Washington, Lansing served as counsel to the Mexican and Chinese legations, and in 1903 he received an appointment to be counselor for the United States before the Alaskan Boundary Tribunal. In addition to offering employment opportunities, Foster interested Lansing in the international arbitration movement; in 1907 both were involved in founding of the American Society of International Law.[57] When Lansing, a Democrat, came under consideration for the position of counselor in the State Department in the Woodrow Wilson administration, Foster arranged for his friend Elihu Root to recommend his son-in-law for the post.[58]

Because President Wilson found Lansing's views on diplomatic matters, particularly with regard to European affairs, more compatible with his own than the absolute noninterventionist posture of Secretary of State William Bryan, the State Department's legal counsel enjoyed considerable influence; and in June 1915, when Bryan quit the administration abruptly in protest against Wilson's policies favoring the Allies in the European war, Wilson not surprisingly appointed Lansing to the cabinet post. Impressed with Lansing's schooling in diplomacy and his work in the movement for peace through international arbitration, the president also appeared to feel that the continued influence of Foster would have a beneficial effect on his new secretary of state.[59] Whatever his true feeling and the motivations surrounding Lansing's appointment, the president's decision would bring into the administration, formally or informally, three generations of diplomats from the same family, all living in the same Washington household where, it can be assumed, international relations dominated the conversation.

Foster held no position within the Wilson administration, but he was quick to submit advice. Shortly after Lansing's appointment as counselor in the State Department, he wrote to offer assistance,[60] and as the United States moved closer to entering the war in Europe, Foster and his son-in-law, now secretary of state, found themselves in agreement that the war could not be settled satisfactorily through unrealistic attempts, like those of the president, to end hostilities through mediation. Believing that "the power of Germany must first be broken," Foster informed Lansing, "I agree with you that the allies will not agree to any peace negotiations until Germany is beaten so thoroughly that she cannot again be the disturber of the peace of the world."[61] Despite their extensive involvement in the peace movement, both men agreed that the German empire presented an unacceptable threat to European civilization and the Western democracies, and they believed that the United States should be willing to enter the fight to restore peace and order. In February 1917 Foster was prepared to see the United States enter the war. He wrote to his grandson, John Foster Dulles, then working under Lansing on a special State Department assignment:

In a large sense I think the Entente Allies are fighting our battle. Suppose Germany should be victorious in the war, and the influence of Great Britain overthrown throughout the world. In what condition would mankind be left? I agree that to take up arms against Germany one must have a casus belli, *but these have already not been wanting.*[62]

For Foster such a view was consistent with both his Christian principles and his desire for peace through nonviolent means. He was never a pacifist and considered warfare a justifiable method of pursuing a righteous cause. Just as he had known in his heart the rightness of his involvement in the war to end slavery half a century earlier, Foster viewed the coming of war with Germany in 1917 as a struggle against the forces of an evil that threatened American democracy and the progress of all mankind.

While Foster, Lansing, and Dulles were sharing views on world affairs, several younger members of the family were beginning their diplomatic careers. Lansing had tried to lure his nephew, John Foster, into the State Department as a special counsel for the United States on arbitration matters during the first weeks of the Wilson administration. Although the temporary post would have offered excellent experience in international affairs, Dulles declined, as it would have required a year in Washington and his firm did not look favorably upon an extended leave for a new employee.[63] After Lansing became secretary of state and the United States entered the world war, however, Dulles readily accepted the special assignments in the State Department and visited Cuba and Central America as a special agent. Meanwhile, Allen and Eleanor Dulles entered the Foreign Service and were assigned overseas.[64]

During his final months John W. Foster, now eighty-one, watched the progress of the war and the momentous developments in world affairs with keen interest, although his declining health prevented him from leaving his Washington residence. He must have known the end was coming; he put his worldly affairs in order, rewrote his will, and named his son-in-law and eldest grandson executors of his considerable estate valued at nearly a half-million dollars.[65] When the end came on November 15, 1917, following an extended illness, there was little time for mourning. The younger family members were in Paris and Switzerland on diplomatic missions, and Secretary of State Lansing, who accompanied the body to the Oak Hill Cemetery in Evansville, was required by his pressing wartime duties to return immediately to Washington following abbreviated services held on Sunday afternoon to accommodate the secretary of state's demanding schedule.[66]

The nature of Foster's relationships with the men formulating foreign policies in the twenty-year period following his resignation as secretary of state in 1893 indicates that Foster held a unique place in the development of American foreign policy during an era of American expansionist diplomacy and increased overseas involvements. The slight, bewhiskered figure of the former secretary of state was a common sight in the halls of the State Department. Truly a "handy man," Foster served as a convenient, reliable, and thoroughly professional consultant to the diplomatic service during a period of unparalleled transition in American foreign policy.

The role Foster had played as a negotiator, facilitator, advisor, confidant, and middleman had not escaped public attention. Although he had held no official appointment during the decade prior to his death, his continuing influence among policy makers was widely recognized. He was cited as the nation's "first professional diplomat" because of his long career in foreign affairs and international law, and speculation arose as to just how much influence Foster had wielded behind the scenes in the many administrations in which he had maneuvered.[67] Foster was the first of many American diplomats who would move in and out of diplomatic assignments to teach at one of the universities in the Washington area, engage in lucrative legal work for foreign governments, and involve themselves in foreign policy associations or sit on the boards of international corporations. Clearly he had established a career pattern that would be followed by those pursuing a diplomatic career as the United States entered its imperial years.

IX

The American Mission

It was the greatest crowd the city of Indianapolis had ever known, more than
one hundred thousand crushed together in a giant sea of humanity, all hoping
to get a glimpse of the celebrities at the foot of the giant "Soldiers and Sailors"
monument that was to be dedicated on this bright spring morning in 1902.
Fifteen hundred Civil War veterans paraded past the reviewing stand while a
band played John Philip Sousa's "Messiah of Nations." Two thousand young
men who had fought in the recent war with Spain joined the march, while to
the side of the platform proudly stood nearly a hundred white-bearded,
ancient survivors of the war with Mexico, fought more than half a century
earlier. In the background flew more than a hundred Indiana battle flags,
many tattered and bloodstained, while on the speaker's platform, almost
hidden behind the bunting, Governor Winfield T. Durbin and a handful of
Indiana's leading citizens looked on with approval. The dedication program
was presided over by General Lew Wallace, one of the state's favorite Civil
War heroes and the author of the novel *Ben Hur*. Indiana's popular poet,
James Whitcomb Riley, read one of his works, and a chorus of three hundred
voices filled the circular plaza surrounding the monument with inspirational
sounds. Finally, it was time for the principal address, to be delivered by
Indiana's most prominent elder statesman, John W. Foster. The slight,
bewhiskered figure, glancing out over the largest gathering he would ever
address, talked of patriotism and duty, of the need to end corruption in
government and the necessity of Civil Service reform. He reviewed the
glorious events of Indiana's history and recalled the heroic deeds of George
Rogers Clark, Oliver P. Morton and the Harrisons. And he spoke of the Civil

War and Indiana's participation in that great struggle. "Right humanity and progress were on the side of the union armies," he stated, "and it was chiefly for this reason we have raised this noble pile of bronze and marble."[1]

It was not an address to be remembered for its dynamic presentation or inspirational message. The speaker was not a spellbinder; it was not his way to excite his listeners. Rather, his presentation was direct, precise, and almost scholarly, and his message, here and on numerous other occasions, was to remind his audience of the lessons of the past and to urge an adherence to those traditional values that had seen the nation survive the Civil War, expand across the continent, and enter the twentieth century as a leader among the nations of the world.

The role of elder statesman came easily to Foster, and he played the part for more than two decades, during which he devoted himself to teaching (at George Washington University), lecturing about the United States in world affairs, and writing books and articles on American foreign policy. He also became involved with prestigious organizations advancing the acceptance of international law and arbitration. In these endeavors he displayed a complex mixture of simple American idealism and cold political pragmatism. With many of his contemporaries Foster maintained the belief that the United States had a civilizing and Christianizing mission in the world; this mission could be performed successfully and peacefully, he believed, but he was prepared to call for the use of force when more pacific measures failed. Foster believed the United States to be on the threshold of world power and therefore called upon to play an ever-increasing role in world affairs, and he hoped that his writings would fill the need, created by expanded international commitments, for an increased study of American foreign policy.

Foster believed that his diplomatic experiences would provide practical lessons for future diplomats and policy makers. In the preface of his first book, *A Century of American Diplomacy*, published in 1900, Foster stated his desire that by studying his review of the nation's diplomatic conduct, "the young men of the country may have their patriotism quickened, and be inspired with a new zeal to assist in maintaining the honorable position of our government in its foreign relations." Foster held that the study of United States foreign policy provided necessary information to aid in solving future problems in the expanded political and commercial relations of the United States.[2] Believing that past American foreign policy had consistently and continually been one of enlightenment and reason, Foster saw in United States diplomatic history from 1776 to 1876 numerous valuable lessons. From an examination of the historical record, he concluded that the United States "had a marked influence in shaping and improving international law. Its influence in elevating the diplomatic intercourse of nations has been scarcely less conspicuous."[3] Foster found few actions by American diplomats deserving of censure and reasoned that a nation that possessed such a history must be destined for even more benevolent policies in the century ahead. Furthermore, he implied that other nations would be in error not to recognize an American claim to world leadership based upon the exemplary conduct of past diplomatic relations.

Nationalistic and partisan throughout, Foster's first historical monograph met an enthusiastic reception with American readers both in the intellectual community and in the diplomatic service.[4] The highly complimentary reviews and correspondence Foster received concerning his initial project as an author and historian must have encouraged him to elaborate on his central theme: that American diplomatic history, because of its generally exemplary nature, was worthy of further study and emulation because it provided lessons that would lead to the betterment of international relations and progress, stability, and order in a civilized world.

In 1904 Foster published his most significant contribution to the study of United States foreign policy, *American Diplomacy in the Orient*. Writing on an area in which he had been personally involved for many years, he interpreted United States policies in the Far East as characterized by "a spirit of justice, forebearance, and magnanimity." Foster argued that American "intercourse with China, Japan, and Korea has been that of a friend interested in their welfare, ready to aid them in their efforts to attain an honorable peace among nations, and willing to recognize the embarrassment which attend those efforts." Foster was uncomfortable about the United States acquisition of the Philippines because the control of this Oriental real estate left the United States no longer a disinterested, noncolonial Western state. Nevertheless, he believed that an inescapable consequence of the Spanish-American War was the establishment of the United States as an Asian power. As a nation with new responsibilities in the Far East, Foster maintained that future American policies in Asia should strive towards "giving the world a freer market, and the inhabitants of the Orient the blessings of Christian Civilization."[5]

Despite the departure from tradition that resulted in the taking of the Philippines, Foster held that Americans harbored "no scheme of territorial aggrandizement" in Asia, and he characterized United States interests as limited to securing "mutual benefit from the establishment of trade" and the promotion of Christianizing activities among native populations.[6] Like expansionist-minded Theodore Roosevelt, Brooks Adams, and Alfred T. Mahan,[7] Foster considered the Orient to be the next great theater of American commercial and economic activity, and he acknowledged that expanded American production would meet stiff competition in the China market from Britain, Russia, and Japan. Foster saw Japan as the most serious threat to United States ambitions in China, and he correctly prophesied that the problem of enlarging American commercial interest in China without antagonizing Japan would present a serious challenge to the United States in coming decades.[8]

Although eager to witness the conversion of the Chinese to Christianity, Foster demonstrated a sympathy and understanding of the Chinese people that was unusual for his era. Long active in the fight against Chinese exclusion, Foster argued forcefully in *American Diplomacy in the Orient* that racial prejudice and extremism in American public opinion had caused the United States to violate its own set of high principles in the unjust treatment of Chinese in the United States and by refusing to trade with Chinese on equal terms.[9] In describing the causes of the recent Boxer Rebellion, Foster stated that with few exceptions anti-foreign feelings existed in all parts of China and throughout the entire population. As factors leading to the Boxer uprising Foster properly listed the opium trade, railroad and steamship lines which put Chinese out of work, the destruction of the Chinese clothing industry by the introduction of American and British cotton goods, the upsetting of burial grounds by railroad lines, and the opening of the interior of China to further inroads of foreign commerce following the defeat in the war with Japan.[10] Viewing contemporary speculations about a "yellow peril" as no exaggeration, Foster warned his American readers of Sir Robert Hart's prediction, "Four hundred millions, sturdy and passionately devoted to their ancient customs, might in time, under the influence of an all-prevailing race hatred, be changed from a peace-loving community into a warlike people, bent upon avenging their wrongs."[11] Foster believed the China market essential to American economic progress and felt that American commercial interests in China would ultimately be as beneficial to the Chinese as to the Americans if they were conducted on the basis of equality and reciprocity.[12]

While he approved of an enlarged American presence abroad, Foster opposed the acquisition of territory, and although as secretary of state he had advocated annexation of Hawaii, he frequently criticized acquisition of overseas possessions. In his opposition to insular imperialism he shared a belief in common with the anti-imperialists of his era who opposed colonial expansion not for commercial, humanitarian, or religious reasons, but because it ran counter to the traditional American ideal that government should not rule without the consent of the governed. Anti-imperialists formed a diverse group including William Jennings Bryan, Grover Cleveland, Carl Schurz, and David Starr Jordan. Even former president Benjamin Harrison was among the old guard Republicans of the Fremont-Lincoln generation who viewed anti-colonialism as an extension of the antislavery fight.[13] Foster did not participate in the anti-imperialist movement but was sympathetic to its argument. With regard to the question of Cuban annexation, Foster warned against incorporating into the Union an additional Negro population that was also Roman Catholic. "Catholics in the United States are among our most patriotic and useful citizens," Foster wrote in 1906, "but it would not be desirable to have one more of our states composed entirely of them."[14]

Viewing the Philippines, Cuba, and Puerto Rico as territories composed of alien peoples, Foster believed that these territories could be governed only through undemocratic and authoritarian measures, and the early history of United States policy in the former Spanish possessions quickly convinced Foster that the imperialist impulse of 1898 was a mistake.[15] Although he had labored in the 1890s to annex Hawaii, bring Cuba and Puerto Rico into a close economic relationship with the United States, and secure for his government naval stations in the Caribbean and Pacific, Foster's expansionist designs stopped short of advocating the subjugation of foreign peoples into an American colonial system.

Unquestionably Foster made his greatest impact on the reading public through his writing on American policy in East Asia, an area in which he possessed considerable expertise and firsthand experience. Foster's contemporaries largely ignored United States diplomatic history, and those few who ventured into the field concentrated their studies on United States relations with Europe rather than in the Pacific area. Therefore, despite his unprofessional reliance on personal recollections, his failure to make critical analyses of the public papers and documents he used, and his overwhelming prejudices, Foster's historical studies, particularly *American Diplomacy in the Orient*, had immeasurable importance, as they were virtually the only works available on the topics he covered.

Foster's era produced a school of popular historical writers that included Theodore Roosevelt, Henry Adams, James Ford Rhodes, and Alfred T. Mahan. These socially well known amateur historians, prominent among the nation's elite, aligned themselves with successful forces in American history. They sought to inform and instruct their fellow countrymen in the practical lessons of the national experience, which they believed indicated that the United States had been given a world mission.[16] Although Foster could not completely accept the pessimistic social Darwinist doctrines of Roosevelt, Adams, Rhodes, and Mahan, his nationalistic sense of American destiny was in agreement with the general conclusions of the evolutionist historians, and like the more famous and accomplished patrician historians of his time, Foster exhibited a faith in the inevitability of progress, pronounced moral judgments, and explained with certitude to his readers the verdict of history.

Another topic to which Foster addressed himself was the development of professionalism in the United States Foreign Service. Realizing that an expansionist foreign policy would create new and expanded commitments abroad, Foster had as early as the 1890s joined with such keen observers of the international arena as economist Brooks Adams and historian-diplomat Andrew D. White in expressing a concern that growing American influence in world affairs would no longer allow for a diplomatic corps subject to the uncertainties of the old spoils system. While involved in publicizing the increasing importance of foreign affairs, Foster argued for the need to develop a diplomatic system based on merit rather than political favoritism— the means by which he had entered the Foreign Service. Foster enumerated such qualities as even temper, tact, shrewdness, and discretion as requisites for a successful career in diplomacy; he stressed the importance of selecting men with ability, character, and "gentlemanly accomplishments," warning that a "boor in manners, or one disagreeable instead of affable in his demeanor, can hardly expect to make himself popular in social circles or even hope to be successful in the dispatch of the business of his country."[17]

Foster believed that the United States was destined to play an ever-increasing role in world affairs, and he understood that in such a position the United States would necessarily have to abandon its traditional isolation. He wrote, "while the caution which Washington gave his countrymen in his farewell address to avoid entangling alliances has not lost its virtue, the nation has attained such a position among the powers of the earth that it cannot remain a passive spectator of international affairs."[18] Foster reasoned that the United States could best aspire to its lofty calling of world leadership by promoting a wider acceptance of international arbitration as a means of assuring the ideals of peace and justice.

A tireless advocate of the acceptance of international arbitration by all nations, Foster considered the Hague court a reasonable and practical instrument for maintaining order throughout the world. From 1865 to 1900 serious problems between the United States and Great Britain had been submitted to international arbitration with generally favorable results, and diplomats in both countries expressed confidence in the methods and procedures of arbitration.[19] Foster had participated extensively in the negotiation of several of these disputes with the British and possessed a lawyer's fascination for formal pacts and legal contracts. In April 1896 Foster was a prominent figure at the National Arbitration Conference held in Washington and attended by more than three hundred leading Americans, including James Cardinal Gibbons, Chauncey Depew, Carl Schurz, Simeon Baldwin, and United States Supreme Court Justice David J. Brewer. With his interest in peace through arbitration, he understandably viewed the calling of the Hague Peace Conference of 1899 with great enthusiasm, writing of it as "one of the most important events which marked the close of the nineteenth century."[20] Joining with former president Cleveland, former vice president Levi P. Morton, and former secretaries of state Richard Olney, William M. Evarts and William R. Day, Foster signed a petition of the International Law Association urging the Senate to ratify the Hague convention and make the United States an official member of the court.[21] Foster would argue that the United States, by its conspicuous participation at the Hague and the subsequent ratification of the convention, had a right to claim leadership in the cause of world peace.

The nationalistic Foster could not refrain from lavishing praise upon his government for its role in the First Hague Conference.[22] In contrast to less optimistic foreign policy makers of his era, Foster believed the accomplishments of the Hague court to be actual and reasonable rather than illusory and quixotic. In a brief book written in 1904 at the request of the Mohonk Arbitration Conference, Foster, then serving as president of the National Arbitration Conference, wrote of the First Hague Conference in the following terms:

The delegates to that great assembly were practical men. They did not even condemn war as wholly unrighteous. They did not attempt the impossible. They recognized their work as imperfect, but it was the best then attainable. I think it should be the policy of the friends of universal peace to labor to perfect that instrument (the arbitration convention), and to make the Hague court popular with the nations as an effective means of adjusting international differences.[23]

Foster held that a "permanent world's parliament of states" remained in the far distant future and that the Hague court presented a viable method of lessening the threat of war until a more efficient international forum could be invented.[24] On the eve of the calling of the Second Hague Conference Foster presented for public consideration his own proposals for modifying the structure of the court. His suggestions included increased membership from among the Latin American republics, payment of a retainer to attract expert judges, consideration of a means for lessening the expenses of arbiration procedures for smaller countries, and a wider use of English ("now the language most prevalent among the Christian nations") in place of French.[25]

Efforts on behalf of world peace through arbitration led to Foster's involvement in the founding of the American Society of International Law.[26] The idea for establishing such an organization grew out of the discussions at the Eleventh Mohonk Conference on International Arbitration held at the resort hotel of Albert K. Smiley, a prominent Quaker. Those attending this meeting in the quiet surroundings of the New York lake region decided that mere political pressure by peace groups had proven ineffective. These men believed that to meet the complex problems confronting the peace movement, enlarged and coordinated efforts would have to be made in the area of public education. They felt that American citizens were inadequately informed about international rights and obligations, as well as about the nature of arbitration procedures.[27] The American Society of International Law was officially established in January 1906 in the offices of the New York Bar Association, and Elihu Root was made president, with James Brown Scott, a professor of international law at Columbia University, named secretary.

The avowed aim of the new organization was "to foster the study of international law and promote the establishment of international relations on the basis of law and justice." The society proclaimed from its beginnings that membership would not be limited to specialists; however, the method by which the society carried out its functions tended to limit participation to a close circle of elite professionals. Professor Scott set up the society's offices in his home and accepted no compensation for his services; contributions to the organization's official publication, the *American Journal of International Law*, were always gratuitous.[28] Foster, accompanied by his son-in-law and junior law partner, Robert Lansing, attended both the Eleventh Mohonk Conference and the later meeting in which the society was established, and contributed generously to the first issues of the journal.[29]

The determined stand Foster took with respect to arbitration brought him into direct conflict with President Theodore Roosevelt and Secretary of State John Hay. Lobbying in Washington in early 1905 in support of ratification of ten bilateral arbitration agreements that Hay had negotiated, Foster urged the administration to accept the limitation of Senate amendments.[30] Roosevelt and Hay felt that the Senate's refusal to surrender the power of defining arbitration to the president made the treaties meaningless, since the Senate would have to approve every special agreement by redefining the questions at issue in each arbitration.[31] The president discussed the controversy personally with Foster and explained his position that the Senate amendments were unconstitutional and made the treaties a "farce."[32] Nevertheless, Foster was not convinced by Roosevelt's arguments, much to the frustration of the president. In his private correspondence, Roosevelt wrote that "the people who have exasperated me more than any others are those, like John W. Foster, Andrew Carnegie and Wayne McVeagh, who, partly from jealousy of John Hay and partly from that curious vanity which makes men desire to cover up defeat, have insisted that we ought to take, on the half-loaf principle, a measure which is not a half a loaf at all, but a distinct, though slight, step backwards."[33]

In spite of all difficulties, Foster continued his work in the cause of international peace without any apparent discouragement. As the president of the Twelfth Annual Mohonk Conference, held in the summer of 1906, he urged that the United States, in cooperation with Great Britain, lead the world powers in a campaign to limit armaments. Foster also expressed the hope that the United States would assume a leading role at the coming Second Hague Conference by attempting to bring about a reduction or limitation in weaponry. With Foster presiding, the Mohonk conference adopted a resolution calling for international action for arms limitation and petitioned President Roosevelt to instruct the delegates to the Hague conference to urge that international group to consider a plan for the restriction of armaments.[34] Although Roosevelt was sympathetic to the idea of the Hague court, he viewed with alarm proposals for disarmament as presented by those he believed to be "the preposterous apostles of peace of the type of ex-Secretary of State Foster. . . ."[35]

Disapproval from the White House, however, did not lessen Foster's participation in the activities of the peace movement. In May 1907 the former secretary of state, his wife, and their grandson, John Foster Dulles, a nineteen-year-old student at Princeton, departed for Europe to attend the Second Hague Conference on what was to be the elderly diplomat's final trip abroad.[36] Foster viewed the conference with great optimism because of the expanded representation, which included many Latin American countries, and the expressed intention of the conference to give all nations equal respect and treatment. The fact that millions of subjected colonial peoples were not included among the forty-four states recognized at the conference did not seem to bother Foster. In his *Memoirs* he proclaimed the Second Hague Conference to be "in some respects the most important event in the history of the human race. It was the first time that the political representatives of all the nations of the earth had met together."[37]

Foster's principal contribution to the work of the conference was a brief speech in support of the United States delegation's proposal on the inviolability of private property at sea during time of war. In his presentation Foster stated: "I foresee the day when the right of search will be abolished, when the suppression of contraband will be permitted only in the territorial waters of the belligerents, and when the high seas will be open to the peaceful commerce of the whole world and protected from the vexatious proceedings of warring powers."[38] The American position met with no success due to the opposition of the German and British delegations.[39] However, despite this failure and the general skepticism expressed by many critics of the Hague conference, Foster sustained a firm belief in the ultimate success of the Hague movement.[40]

In 1910 Foster accepted a prestigious position on the board of the Carnegie Endowment for International Peace, created by the founder of the United States Steel Corporation with a gift of ten million dollars. The endowment, like other peace organizations with which Foster associated himself, was conservative and legalistic, emphasizing scholarly research and intellectual rhetoric.[41] Foster was not disturbed by the obvious elitism of the peace movement and continued his involvement in various peace societies until the outbreak of World War I brought to the surface the ineffectiveness of the peace movement. During this period his statements on the question of armaments became more pronounced and determined. He denounced popular historians and politicians who claimed that war was inevitable, and he charged that all foreign wars in which the American people had engaged had been brought about by United States aggression and jingoism. Foster argued that the Roman Empire fell not because it became soft but because it weakened itself through constant warfare. Theodore Roosevelt, ambitious naval commanders, and proponents of an expanded navy, became particular targets of Foster's attacks.[42]

Participation in the peace movement was not necessarily a popular activity, and Foster was on occasion unjustly accused of being unpatriotic because of his critical statements regarding United States foreign policies.[43] In February

1909, President Roosevelt, who unlike Foster viewed the Japanese as a genuine threat to American interests in the Pacific,[44] privately expressed his displeasure with Foster to Philander C. Knox: "The minute we arrange matters so that for the moment everything is smooth and pleasant, the more foolish peace societies, led by men like ex-Secretary of State Foster and ex-Secretary of the Navy [John D.] Long, clamor for a stoppage in the building up of the navy."[45] That John W. Foster, the same man who two decades earlier had participated in the "spirited diplomacy" of the Harrison administration, could now criticize an aggressive foreign policy, obviously left the president confused as well as infuriated. In actuality, however, Foster's concept of American mission was not opposed to the president's. Both believed that the United States should aspire to a role of world leadership; their differences centered over the tactics to be employed in achieving this goal. Whereas Roosevelt considered armed force necessary to execute strategy, Foster held that the American mission could be carried out through moral leadership.

Men like Foster believed world peace through international law to be in the American interest. The various organizations promoting international peace through law, arbitration, and disarmament in which Foster participated combined a new sense of United States power and world leadership with a desire to create a world of harmonious order. These apostles of peace believed that the American destiny was one of moral leadership and that their nation should use its strength to bestow on the earth's less fortunate peoples the blessings of American democracy and progress. Those peace societies concentrating on the wider acceptance of international law tended to be generally conservative and legalistic in orientation, preferring stability over change and striving to preserve the contemporary distribution of power among national states.[46] At times Foster must have been uncomfortable in the presence of the diverse assortment of romantic idealists, zealous pacifists, and isolationistic anti-imperialists who joined the various elements comprising the peace movement. Foster was a consummately pragmatic individual, and in spite of his own moralistic rhetoric, he never lost sight of the harsh realities of international diplomacy.

In his private correspondence Foster displayed a sense of political expediency and opportunism that never surfaced in his pious and bombastic speeches and pamphlets extolling the virtues of peace. Writing privately to his close friend General James Harrison Wilson in November 1903, Foster expressed complete agreement with President Roosevelt's bold and decisive actions regarding the recognition of Panama's independence from Colombia, which followed a revolt inspired by the United States:

The action of the government does look a bit premature, and un-intelligent criticism is apt to be applied to it. Neither you nor I want to see our country in the attitude of a land-grabber or reckless of its international obligations, but it has assumed a great obligation respecting an inter-oceanic canal, and it must discharge that duty. . . . It was our duty to make it an American—that is a United States enterprise . . . the United States should have exclusive police control and sovereignty over it. Columbia should not be permitted to stand in the way of such a great, world work.

Foster disagreed with Wilson's contention that the United States should have taken Panama outright from the uncooperative Colombians. Instead, the former secretary of state defended the more sophisticated approach of employing a native coup d'état, a method he himself had employed unsuccessfully in an attempt to annex Hawaii in 1893,

. . . a better way is opened through the Panama revolt. However that was brought about it is now a de-facto government and the president would be unfaithful to this great duty assumed by us, if he did not embrace the opportunity. Hawaii is a precedent for such action, to say nothing of others.[47]

Foster never embraced nonviolence. He viewed war as an unfortunate necessity which, under certain circumstances, was entirely justified. He considered war a positive good if waged for the cause of moral progress. The Civil War, in which he had fought, served for him as an example of a just and righteous conflict waged against forces of an unacceptable evil. In an address delivered in 1902 at the dedication of Soldiers' Monument in Indianapolis, Foster proudly told his audience, "Never in the history of human warfare has there been a triumph more significant of blessing to mankind. . . ."[48] When in 1914 the peace movement failed to avert world war, Foster again saw a classic struggle between the righteous and those who would threaten democracy and Christian civilization. "I am not well enough to write you my views on the war situation," a dying Foster confided in his last letter to General Wilson, "Though a pacifist after a fashion, I am so bitter with Germany I rather hope we will get into the scrimmage."[49]

A dilemma confronting those like Foster who believed in the inevitability of expanded American influence abroad was that at the same time they hoped to see this eventuality achieved, if possible, without violence. For many like Foster the solution appeared to be in the worldwide acceptance of Christianity.[50] A deeply religious man, Foster had been involved in missionary work his entire life and had served on the Presbyterian Board of Foreign Missions.[51] A conservative, inflexible, fundamentalist Presbyterian, he contributed generously of his fortune and energies to further missionary efforts in the Far East and Turkey.[52] Foster viewed Christianity as a real force in the world, destined ultimately to encompass all the peoples of the world in a common system of ethical principles and values.

Foster's views on the coming millennium of Christian civilization were clearly expressed in an address delivered before the Presbyterian Ministerial

Association meeting in Philadelphia in 1899. Not in the least reluctant to state his opinions on theology before the ministers of his church, the distinguished layman described the nineteenth century as one of enormous Christian accomplishment and pronounced the coming era to be one that would witness the complete conversion of the world to Christianity.[53] The inherent superiority of Christian ethics, Western civilization, and American values appeared obvious to Foster. Observing that only the true faith had "made Christian nations the powerful nations of the earth," he added, "What but the influence of Christ's gospel has made the home in our land so different from that in Asia or Africa?"[54] From extensive world travels Foster believed one could readily distinguish the benefits the Almighty bestowed on the chosen:

. . . *no one but he who has visited the lands of the rival systems today, of Mohammedanism, of Bramanism, and Buddhism, can fully appreciate the superiority of the civilization of Christ and the marked difference in system; and when one sees [to] what blind superstition, and what depths of immorality these have led their adherents, it is inconceivable that any one who lives under the light and blessings of the gospel can make any comparison favorable to them.*[55]

Foster believed that Americans, given the gift of Christian faith, were thereby charged with the duty of spreading the "Civilization of Christ." The elder American statesman summarized his understanding of American mission with the statement: "God sent forth his son to give man a system of life which would satisfy the longings of his soul, and enable him to establish a civilization destined to rule the world and abide forever."[56] Thus, Foster believed, by the acceptance of fundamentalist Christianity, the American mission in the world would be fulfilled, and peace and order could be maintained under the ideals he so fondly cherished.

Foster's belief that Christian principles would soon be given the world's nations was misplaced. The twentieth century did not witness the coming of the "Civilization of Christ," based on fundamentalist Protestant theology, and in fact, as the century progressed, the spread of the Christian faith in the developing regions of what came to be known as the "Third World" was almost negligible. Furthermore, the failure of Christians to make many converts among non-Christian peoples and the outright rejection of all forms of Christian faith by secular governments coming to power after the two world wars provided Americans with a shattering experience. The optimistic and self-righteous faith that Foster professed and shared with many contemporary American policy makers, as well as those of the next generations, hindered United States efforts to deal reasonably with the harsh realities of nationalism, communism and anti-Americanism. Rather than accepting an American form of Christianity, new nations emerging from colonial rule and decaying monarchies turned to materialistic philosophies.

This development created among Americans a sense of indignation and rejection and caused policy makers to seek ways of supporting any governments that seemed to adhere to American values, while isolating and containing the cancerous spread of regimes espousing philosophies that were anathema to Christian values as they were expressed by the leaders of the United States.

The missionary diplomacy advocated by Foster and others of his time combined theology with foreign policy and expressed an overbearing attitude of moral superiority and self-righteousness. Foster naively expected non-Christian people to accept readily the simple faith that he held responsible for his personal material successes as well as those of his nation. The final decades of the nineteenth century had been years of prosperity, economic growth, continental expansion, and success in war. These material blessings led to an overly optimistic assessment of the readiness of colonial peoples to accept Christianity and Western values, and ventures in moralistic diplomacy would invariably lead to frustration and rejection. Further, at times the nation would find itself unable to adhere to its own lofty rhetoric, and the result would be a sense of disillusionment and self-doubt.

Although the peace movement with its obvious organizational weaknesses and misplaced emphasis on rationality and legalistics failed to bring about a tranquil world, there were nevertheless noticeable positive results, and the work of the pre-World War I peace advocates laid a foundation for a later generation of internationalists. The early movement encouraged the development of arbitration and international law, urged the acceptance of treaties and international agreements, and educated public leaders to the benefits of world order.[57] Despite the failure of the early peace movement to recognize the rising tide of nationalism among colonial peoples and its neglect of economic and political realities, Foster and his more famous colleagues in the peace movement created precedents for use by future advocates of international arbitration and left examples that could be studied and improved upon. Bringing the United States into full participation with international bodies seeking to maintain world order would be a long and painful process, but the creation of the League of Nations and the ultimate entry of the United States into the United Nations both had their origins in the peace movement that began in the 1890s.

The Legacy

His demand on life from callow youth to ripe old age was not for a brilliant career, but for an honorable mission, a place where he might be able to do something for the world.

> Reverend Charles Wood,
> memorial sermon delivered
> at the Church of the Covenant,
> Washington, December 2, 1917.

Forty years after his death, the words of John W. Foster were still a guiding force within the Department of State. During the height of the Cold War, Foster's grandson and namesake, John Foster Dulles, held the office of secretary of state and mapped the strategy of "brinksmanship" in the same rooms of the old Executive Office Building that his grandfather had once occupied. Meanwhile, another grandson, Allen W. Dulles, the brother of the secretary of state, headed the Central Intelligence Agency—the largest intelligence-gathering organization the world had ever known. Those few upper-echelon State Department officials who occasionally joined John Foster Dulles in his office must occasionally have had peculiar feelings. They learned not to be surprised when the secretary interrupted a key discussion on diplomatic strategy and, with his awkward smile, remarked, "My grandfather had something to say on that subject." The secretary of state would then reach for the worn old books, always placed near his desk, turn quickly to the exact page in the appropriate volume, and read aloud to his staff members.[1]

To assess adequately the influence of any individual upon historical developments without overstatement is at best a hazardous task. This is particularly the case with regard to an enigmatic figure such as John W. Foster, whose career spans four decades and includes involvement in a wide range of endeavors. Perhaps no other diplomat of his era had a career as diverse; but although he appeared repeatedly in crucial situations throughout the diplomatic record of the late nineteenth century, he remained almost always behind the scenes, a relatively obscure figure, yet one of importance in his time. He did much to shape the foreign policies of his era, and while he was not a public leader who moved the populace, his views, as expressed in his published writings, reached a wide audience and reflected the political and intellectual milieu of his time.

Considered by his contemporaries to be America's first professional diplomat, Foster made important contributions to the development of diplomatic tactics and strategies. Despite his pious, moralistic rhetoric, Foster in action was consistently pragmatic, opportunistic, and nationalistic. He participated in the scheme to withhold recognition of the Díaz government in Mexico until American interests were served and the new leadership expressed a sympathy for American economic ventures. He recognized the coup by white planters in Hawaii as an opportunity for bringing about annexation without direct United States involvement in the overthrow of a native government. Finally, he was a tough and forceful negotiator and led United States delegations in international arbitrations that set precedents for the twentieth century.

Foster was an early exponent of what came to be known as the open door policy. Throughout his years in the diplomatic service Foster expressed an interest in increasing United States foreign trade and displayed a particular interest in the possibility of reciprocity agreements as a device by which the Latin American market could be safely secured for his fellow countrymen. In the Far East, where United States hegemony was impossible, he argued for trade on equal terms for all nations seeking commerce in the Orient. Assuming that in open competition American products and principles would triumph, Foster advocated an open door wherever United States influence was not already dominant.

Possibly the leading international lawyer of his era, Foster demonstrated in his career the interplay between personal moral convictions, legal traditions, and the economic and political ethics of the times. He was a central figure in the Washington legal establishment that grew with the national government and expanded United States interests abroad. Combining a keen legal mind with a wide range of important contacts, he was able to offer his clients two significant government-related specialties, a knowledge of the law and a familiarity with the corridors of power. His career set a pattern for countless lawyer-diplomats who would fill the ranks of the foreign policy establishment and move easily from corporate board rooms to desks in the State Department.

International organizations promoting peace through arbitration and law appealed to Foster's sense of Christian morality and his feel for legal formalities. These groups likewise offered a vehicle for the dispersement of Western civilization. Foster's extensive participation in the peace movement and his efforts to establish an international organization to maintain peace through law and negotiation indicated a desire to see a world order preserved under Anglo-Saxon standards. To a great degree, his confidence in international arbitration resulted from his work in negotiating disputes between the United States and Great Britain over relatively minor problems. He failed to realize that the successful settlement of insignificant differences between two countries, both preoccupied with imperial expansion around the globe, was no reason to expect arbitral proceedings to solve vital political and military problems between hostile nations—especially if those nations held different philosophies and values. The optimism Foster so frequently expressed about the possibilities for the future of world peace organizations appears naive when one considers that the nature of arbitrations in which he was personally involved concerned only mundane problems between two nations already in basic agreement about fundamental issues.

Because of his own experience in the Civil War and his Christian education, Foster looked upon warfare as disgusting and uncivilized. He was not a pacifist, however, and he could tolerate violence if physical force appeared necessary as a means for achieving what he considered a just and beneficial result. Thus, the threat of war was proper when employed to teach Chileans respect for the American flag, a coup in Hawaii became acceptable because it facilitated annexation, and United States involvement in World War I made that holocaust a crusade to save Western civilization. In Foster's mind, force, while distasteful, was a perfectly acceptable political and diplomatic tool if employed in pursuit of the right goal. Fortunately for his conscience, Foster always found himself allied with the just.

Foster enthusiastically approved of the rise of the United States to a status of world power. He considered continental expansion to be his nation's "manifest destiny"; and, in his various roles within the foreign policy establishment, he labored to enlarge the scope of American influence abroad. However, Foster never accepted the rationale of the imperialists of 1898. While he advocated and sought to promote increased foreign trade, tried to secure naval outposts in the Caribbean and Pacific, and called for increased United States presence around the world, he nevertheless viewed the insular imperialism that accompanied the war with Spain as a break with traditional United States foreign policy, since it meant the acquisition of colonies and the incorporation of masses of nonwhite peoples into an American empire. Ironically, the imperial impulse of 1898 was in large measure a result of the "spirited diplomacy" of the Harrison administration, in which Foster played a key role. Furthermore, his rhetoric calling for the United States to acquire Hawaii, which he believed to be the logical limit of continental expansion, and his pleas for the government in Washington to accept a mission of moral leadership among the races of the earth, both contributed to the emergence of his nation as an imperial power. In effect, Foster was an unwitting harbinger of American insular imperialism.

Foster and his contemporaries in the foreign policy establishment were men who had fought on the victorious side in the Civil War, gained powerful positions in the Republican Party, and acquired great wealth. Confident of their moral superiority, they believed that their adherence to Christian principles had accounted for the personal successes they enjoyed. They were also convinced that their nation, by following similar righteous principles, could not help but assume a role of world leadership. Several succeeding generations of American policymakers agreed with the philosophy of Foster's era.

The story of John W. Foster's diplomatic record provides a means for gaining an understanding of a transitional period in American history—the gradual evolution of an inward-looking emergent nation concentrating on continental expansion to the position of a world power with imperial ambitions abroad. Perhaps Foster's unique contribution to American diplomacy was his transmission of nineteenth-century idealism, nationalism, and a sense of world mission to men like Robert Lansing, John Foster, and Allen W. Dulles, who were to form and implement foreign policy in the twentieth century.

With its entry into the First World War, the United States moved irreversibly into the arena of international diplomacy. Calls for a return to "normalcy" and the lingering isolationist sentiment could not alter the policy towards a new internationalism along the lines Foster and others had advocated in the 1890s. From World War I through the Cold War era and the American involvement in Vietnam, American diplomacy was formulated by self-righteous men who believed in an American destiny of world leadership; and the new foreign policy was implemented by an emerging class of professional diplomats who, like Foster, moved easily in and out of the nation's great law firms, preferred stability over social change, and understood the dynamics of international business. They were certain that they knew what was best for the world and were prepared to use force not only in the defense of real American interests but also in the furtherance of American influence.

Foster knew that a major phase of American history had matured in his lifetime. His era witnessed the settlement of the western lands, the trauma of the Civil War, the growth of an industrial economy and the development of modern communication and transportation networks. He lived to see the

United States enter the world war in 1917 as an undisputed leader among the world's major powers. During his final years he must certainly have been comforted to know that the nation's destiny would be shaped by a generation of diplomatic leaders who accepted his ideals and values as well as his vision of American mission.

Notes

CHAPTER I

1. An added problem for Republicans in Indiana was the removal of Schyler Colfax from the ticket as the vice-presidential candidate. Foster had attended the party convention and worked for Colfax. Colfax to Foster (telegram), June 6, 1872, Foster Paper. For an account of the campaign of 1872, see William D. Foulke, *Oliver P. Morton*, vol. 2, 255–269; *A History of the Republican Party of Indiana*, vol. 1 ed. by Russell M. Seeds, 43–45. Also see Matthew Josephson, *The Politicos, 1865–1896*, 142–165.
2. Morton to Foster, March 15, 1872 and April 2, 1872, Foster Papers.
3. Morton to E. D. Morgan, Aug. 12, 1878, in Josephson, *The Politicos*, 168. Also see the Evansville *Daily Journal* (Oct. 11, 1872). Foster also sought help from the neighboring state of Ohio. Inviting the popular Governor Rutherford B. Hayes to give a series of talks in Indiana, Foster wrote, "We are closely pursued by our opponents and the campaign will be the most stoutly contested in years. We will need all the help our friends can give us." Foster to Hayes, June 28, 1872, Hayes Papers.
4. Evansville *Daily Journal* (Oct. 12 and Nov. 5, 1872).
5. Blaine to Foster, Nov. 10, 1872, Foster Papers. Foster, *Diplomatic Memoirs*, vol. 1, 10–11.
6. *Memoirs*, vol. 1, 3–4. Grant was informed by the Hoosier politicos that Foster's appointment to Mexico would be most satisfactory to the Republican party of Indiana. Oliver P. Morton and others to Grant, Jan. 23, 1873, Rutherford B. Hayes Papers.
7. Edward White, ed., *Evansville and Its Men of Mark*, 72–73. Information regarding family background is found in John W. Foster's biography of his father, which he had printed for family members, *Biographical Sketch of Matthew W. Foster*, and in Ruth Miley McClehan, "*The Pike County Indiana Ancestors of John Foster Dulles*," an unpublished manuscript in the Indiana

Historical Library. Also see the Evansville *Courier* (Nov. 17, 1917); Evansville *Journal (Nov. 20, 1851)*.

8. Foster, *Biographical Sketch of Matthew Foster*, 38, 57, 61; Foster, "From Reminiscences of John W. Foster," in John E. Iglehart, ed., *An Account of Vandenburg County From Its Organization*, vol. 3, 178–180. Also see *History of Vandenburg County, From Earliest Times to The Present*, 149–150.

9. Foster, *Memoirs*, vol. 1, 8; Foster, *Biographical Sketch*, 59–60; *Indiana University Bulletin*, 1905, vol. 3, nos. 4, 8; Evansville *Enquirer* (April 24, 1857). Also see William R. Castle, "John Watson Foster," *American Secretaries of State and Their Diplomacy*, vol. 8, 188; James A. Woodburn, *A History of Indiana University, 1890–1902*, 131.

10. The McFerson family also operated the Glendale Female Seminary in Glendale, Ohio, where the marriage of Mary Parke took place. Evansville *Enquirer* (Sept. 3, 1859); Evansville *Courier*, Nov. 17, 1917; Iglehart, ed., *Vandenburg County*, vol. 3, 238–241.

11. Evansville *Daily Journal* (Dec. 31, 1857).

12. Foster, *Memoirs*, vol. 1, 9. Located on the Ohio River, Evansville was a hotbed of pro-southern sentiment and racial tension where slave raiding was common. For an interesting contemporary description of ante bellum Evansville, see Frank M. Gilbert, *History of the City of Evansville*, vol. 1, 164–177. Also see Kenneth Stampp, *Indiana Politics During the Civil War*, 11–13.

13. Foster, *Memoirs*, vol. 1, 9; Foster, *War Stories for My Grandchildren*, 2–3, 177. Foster's personal recollection of his military career as stated in *War Stories* includes numerous excerpts from private correspondence. The letters cited here were given by Mrs. Foster to her granddaughter and are now held in the Eleanor Lansing Dulles Papers in the Dwight D. Eisenhower Library in Abilene, Kansas. *War Stories* was printed privately in limited numbers by his grandchildren, who as youngsters had never tired of hearing his reminiscences.

14. Foster, *War Stories*, 2, 177. Foster's wartime recollections, written in the final year of his life, are published in Iglehart, ed., *Vandenburg County*, vol. 3, 227–234. Also see Seeds, ed., *History of the Republican Party*, 362.

15. Report of Col. James Veatch, Feb. 18, 1862, *The War of Rebellion: A Compilation of the Official Records of the Union and Confederate Armies*, series 1, vol. 7, 228. (Hereinafter referred to as *Official Records*).

16. Foster to Veatch, April 11, 1862, *Official Records*, series 1, vol. 10, part 1, 230. Also see pp. 222 and 223 and Foster, *War Stories*, 61–67. Foster wrote a description of the Battle of Shiloh in a letter to his father, who had it published in the New York *Tribune* (April 22, 1863). The young officer was unhappy about his father's action and did not appreciate the notoriety it brought him. *War Stories*, 78.

17. *The Papers of Ulysses S. Grant*, ed. by John Y. Simon, vo. 5, 400, vol. 6, 438; *Indiana in the War of Rebellion: Report of the Adjutant General*, 189.

18. Foster to General Boyle, Jan. 5, 1863, Robert Todd Lincoln Papers.

19. President Lincoln to General Boyle, Feb. 1, 1863, *Collected Works of Abraham Lincoln*, vol. 6, 85–86. Senator Powell to President Lincoln, Jan. 31, 1863, Robert Todd Lincoln Papers. Senator Daniel W. Voorhees of Indiana

denounced Foster as the dictator of Kentucky, *Congressional Globe*, 38th Cong., 1st Sess., 1863–1864, part 3, 2536.

20. Foster to Boyle, Feb. 16, 1863, Robert Todd Lincoln Papers, 103; General Boyle to President Lincoln, Feb. 11, 20, 1863, *Collected Works of Abraham Lincoln*, vol. 6, 87.

21. Foster, *War Stories*, 116. Foster's actions in Kentucky remained a source of bitter feelings for many years. In 1893 an angry citizen raised the issue of Foster's confiscations in Kentucky to protest his appointment to be the agent for the United States government before the Paris Tribunal. See Blanton Luncan to Secretaries Gresham and Carlisle, March 31, 1893, Walter Q. Gresham Papers.

22. Foster to Mrs. Foster, Sept. 2, 12, and 16, 1863, in *War Stories*, 123, 130–135.

23. Foster to Burnside, Sept. 22, 1863, *Official Records*, series I, vol. 30, part 2, 592–593; General Halleck to Stanton, Nov. 15, 1863, 545–546, 548, 550–551, 567–568, 570, 578–599, 641.

24. Foster, *War Stories*, 19, 20, 57, 116, 177; *Memoirs*, vol. 1, 9.

25. Foster, *War Stories*, 9–10, 33, 34, 38, 53, 167–168.

26. Foster to Mrs. Foster, Aug. 7, 1864; *War Stories*, 174.

27. A complete résumé of Foster's military career is found in the "Statement of Military Service of John W. Foster" as provided by the adjutant general's office of the War Department, printed in *War Stories*, 191–192.

28. *War Stories*, 191–192. *Indiana in the War of Rebellion*, 565, 575; Seeds, ed., *History of the Republican Party*, 362.

29. Morton to Foster, Nov. 18, 1866 and Dec. 3, 1866, Morton Letterbook No. 4, Indiana Historical Library.

30. Foster to Baker, Jan. 27, Feb. 1 (telegram), Feb. 11, 17, March 31, and May 26, 1868, Conrad Baker Papers.

31. Foster to Baker (private), Jan. 26, 1869, Conrad Baker Papers; Seeds, ed., *History of the Republican Party*, 362.

32. Evansville *Daily Journal*, Nov. 12, 1872.

33. After having risen to the office of secretary of state, Foster became involved in efforts to reform the Foreign Service. He proposed that secretaries of legations enter the service through competitive exams, but he doubted the wisdom of appointing ministers and ambassadors from the ranks of the secretaries. He believed that the United States had been well served by the practice of appointing ministers with diverse backgrounds and a sense for domestic politics. See Foster's *The Practice of Diplomacy*, 7–14; *Memoirs*, vol. 1, 12–13; also Warren F. Ilchman, *Professional Diplomacy in the United States, 1799–1939*, 63, 88.

CHAPTER II

1. Henry Bamford Parkes, *A History of Mexico*, 3rd ed. 281–283; Herbert Howe Bancroft, *History of Mexico*, vol. 6, 390–407.

2. Foster's instructions indicated the major issues of concern to be implementation of the Conventions of 1868 and 1872 regarding claims of United States citizens against Mexico for property losses. Foster was also instructed to afford as much protection as possible to United States citizens residing in Mexico. Fish to

Foster, April 26, June 25, 1873, USDS Instructions, Mexico, vols. 18, 19. The condition of U.S.–Mexican relations in 1873 is discussed in James M. Callahan, *American Foreign Policy in Mexican Relations*, 341–349.

3. Foster to R. S. Chew, chief clerk of the State Department, March 29, 1875, National Archives, USDS Despatches, Mexico, vol. 47.

4. *New York Times* (May 18, 1873).

5. George M. Robeson, secretary of the navy, to Foster, May 1, 1873, Foster Papers; Foster to R. S. Chew, May 17, 1873; Foster to Fish, May 19, 1873, USDS Despatches, Mexico, vol. 48.

6. Foster to Fish, July 10, 1873, with newspaper clippings, USDS Despatches, Mexico, vol. 49; Foster *Memoirs*, vol. 1, 19.

7. Foster to Fish, August 27, with enclosure of press clippings from *The Two Republics* (Aug. 23, 1873) and *Estralla de Occidente* (July 11, 1873), USDS Despatches, Mexico, vol. 49.

8. Foster to Fish, Dec. 31, 1873, USDS Despatches, Mexico, vol. 50. The rebellion by the fiercely independent natives of primitive Yucatan was the resumption of a long struggle against federal authority. Lerdo's inability to put down the revolt or settle for a compromise weakened his administration. See Bancroft, *History of Mexico*, vol. 6, 408–418.

9. Fish to Foster, Jan. 16, 1874, USDS Instructions, Mexico, vol. 19. This order probably resulted from comments by Foster that appeared in the New York *Tribune* (Jan. 15, 1874).

10. This observation came from Foster and appeared in the New York *Tribune* (Jan. 15, 1874).

11. Foster to Fish, March 2, 4 and May 23, 1875, USDS, *Foreign Relations, 1875*, 885–887, 913, 922.

12. Foster to Fish, July 28, Sept. 23 and 27, 1875, USDS, *Foreign Relations, 1875*, 947–948, 950, 951.

13. Foster to Fish, Feb. 2 and April 22, 1876, USDS, *Foreign Relations, 1876*, 392, 396–398; Foster to Fish (unofficial), March 14, 1876, Hamilton Fish Papers.

14. Foster to Fish, Nov. 28, 1876, USDS Despatches, Mexico, vol. 57.

15. F. W. Seward to Foster, May 16, 1877, USDS Instructions, Mexico, vol. 19; *Report of the Committee on Foreign Affairs on Relations of the United States with Mexico*, House Report No. 701, 45th Cong., 2nd Sess., Appendix G, 447.

16. "Plan de Tuxtepec Reformado en Palo Blanco", March 21, 1876, *Archivo de General Díaz: Memorias y Documentos*, 97–100. Also see Bancroft, *History of Mexico*, vol. 6, 420–423.

17. The question of whether Díaz was at this point in his career truly a revolutionary or merely a political opportunist has never been resolved. Mexican historian Daniel Casío-Villegas has stated, "Porfirio Díaz in his revolutionary days was what the press today would call a pink: a fierce anticlericalist and a Jacobin Liberal who was both xenophobic and anti-imperialist." Casío-Villegas bases this assessment on the fact that Díaz, while seeking to broaden his support in Mexico, threatened to void all contracts made by Lerdo with foreign governments. *The United States versus Porfirio Díaz*, trans. by Nettie Lee Benson, xi. Also see Robert D. Gregg, *The Influence of Border Troubles on Relations between the United States and Mexico, 1876–1910*, 17–18.

18. Foster to Fish (personal), Nov. 18 and 28, 1876, Fish Papers. The payment resulted from a decision of the Claims Commission Convention of 1868. Díaz negotiated a loan of $500,000 in Mexico City for the purpose of making the January payment. See Stuart A. MacCorkle *American Policy of Recognition towards Mexico*, 68.

19. Foster to Fish, Jan. 20, 1877, Fish Papers.

20. Fish to Foster, Jan. 19, 1877, USDS Instructions, Mexico, vol. 19; Foster had established in the meantime a procedure whereby the Díaz government would make the January payment through Lerdo's minister in Washington, thus putting aside temporarily the issue of recognition. MacCorkle, *American Policy of Recognition*, 70–71; Casío Villegas, *The United States versus Porfirio Díaz*, 22–26.

21. Callahan, *American Foreign Policy*, 371; MacCorkle, *American Policy of Recognition*, 72–73; Gregg, *Border Troubles*, 26–27.

22. Foster to Evarts (private and unofficial), April 28, 1877, USDS Despatches, Mexico, vol. 59; Foster, *Memoirs*, vol. 1, 87–88. Early in the Hayes administration it was rumored that Foster would be replaced as minister to Mexico, but Senator Morton urged Hayes to keep Foster in Mexico, as he had learned the language and was doing a good job. Foster's work in Mexico City had been severely criticized by Julius A. Kelton, who had served as counsel general in Mexico City. Foster informed Hayes that he would resign if any of Kelton's claims could be proved. Morton to Hayes, March 15, 1877; W. Dennison to Hayes, March 1, 1878; Foster to Hayes (unofficial and personal), Aug. 17, 1878; Rutherford B. Hayes Papers. Foster to Halloway, May 5 and May 8, 1877, William Halloway Papers.

23. Foster to Evarts, July 30, 1877, USDS, *Foreign Relations, 1877*, 426; Foster to Evarts (unofficial), Nov. 13, 1877, USDS Despatches, Mexico, vol. 60.

24. Documents relating to border problems between the United States and Mexico are contained in *Report of the Committee on Foreign Affairs on the Relations of the United States with Mexico*, 45th Cong., 2nd Sess., *House Report* No. 701. For a thorough discussion of the political pressures on Hayes to end the border problems before granting recognition, see Gregg, *Border Troubles*, 31–34.

25. Evarts to Foster, May 16 and Aug. 2, 1877, USDS Instructions, Mexico, vol. 19; MacCorkle, *American Policy of Recognition*, 74–77; Pauline S. Relyea, *Diplomatic Relations between the United States and Mexico under Porfirio Díaz, 1876–1910*, 29.

26. Foster to Evarts (confidential), October 6, 1877, USDS Despatches, Mexico, vol. 60; Foster, *Memoirs*, vol. 1, 92–94. A compilation of press clippings questioning U.S. government involvement in a plot to seize northern Mexico in General Frisbie's scheme is found in *Hayes Administration Scrap Book, Mexico and China, 1877–1881*, vol. 106, Rutherford B. Hayes Papers. Also see Callahan, *Policy in Mexican Relations*, 379–381, 400; Chester L. Barrows, *William M. Evarts*, 355.

27. W. C. Stuart to President Hayes, April 23, 1877; W. H. Estell to Hayes, Aug. 7, 1877. Rutherford B. Hayes Papers.

28. For rumors in the press of a plan for a war with Mexico, see *Hayes Administration Scrap Book, Mexico and China*, Rutherford B. Hayes Papers,

vol. 106, 4–5, 7, 11–19. Also see W. R. Lewis, "The Hayes Administration and Mexico", *Southwestern Historical Quarterly* 24 (Oct. 1920), 140–153; Callahan, *Policy in Mexican Relations* 355–357, 374–375, 390.

29. Foster, *Memoirs*, 1, 92. President Hayes seems to have given the possibility of war with Mexico little serious consideration and saw the recognition of Díaz as the only viable alternative, recording in his diary, "Should Díaz be recognized as President of Mexico, shall we determine it now or let Mexico hang by the eyelids during August. There is no good reason why we should not recognize M. when we are ready." *Hayes: The Diary of a President, 1875–1881*, 92.

30. Evarts to Foster, June 4, 1877, enclosure of secretary of war to General Sherman, June 1, 1877, House Executive Document No. 13, 45th Cong., 1st Sess., 14–15.

31. Foster to Evarts, June 22, 1877, with enclosures, USDS Despatches, Mexico, vol. 59; Foster to Evarts, June 28, 1877, and enclosure from *Diario Official* (June 21, 1877), 28, 53; Gregg, *Border Troubles*, 51–54; Pauline S. Relyea, *Diplomatic Relations between the United States and Mexico*, 41–42.

32. Memo to the Mexican Foreign Office, June 23, 1877, *Mexican Border Troubles*, 45th Cong., 1st Sess., House Executive Document No. 13, 104–105. The excited state of the Mexican capital over the Ord incident frustrated Foster, and at one point he remarked unkindly that the Mexican authorities exhibited a "volatile and childish character." Foster to Evarts (confidential), June 30, 1877, USDS Despatches, Mexico, vol. 59.

33. Foster to Evarts (personal) Sept. 10, 1877, USDS Despatches, Mexico, vol. 60; Evarts to Foster (unofficial) Oct. 5, 1877, USDS Instructions, Mexico, vol. 19. Foster, *Memoirs*, vol. 1, 94. Although Evarts had denied Foster's request to return to Washington, Foster did not abandon his efforts to convince the president to pursue a moderate policy towards Mexico. Bypassing Evarts, Foster wrote directly to the president. Commenting on his annual message to Congress, Foster stated, "Your reference to the Mexican question is temperate and judicious, and cannot fail to have a favorable reception here where a more severe treatment of the matter was faced." Foster to R. B. Hayes (personal), Dec. 24, 1877, Rutherford B. Hayes Papers.

34. Gregg, *Border Troubles*, 78–79; Charles W. Hackett, "The Recognition of the Díaz Government by the United States", *Southwestern Historical Quarterly* 28 (July 1924), 53.

35. Substance of remarks made by Mr. John W. Foster, the minister to Mexico, before the Subcommittee of the Committee on Foreign Affairs to Investigate the Mexican Question, on Saturday, Feb. 9, 1878, at the Department of State. USDS Despatches, Mexico, vol. 61.

36. Report of the remarks on Feb. 16, 1878 of Mr. Evarts, the secretary of state, and Mr. Foster, the minister to Mexico, before the Subcommittee of the Committee on Foreign Affairs appointed to examine into the Mexican question. USDS Despatches, Mexico, vol. 61.

37. Evarts to Foster, March 23, 1878, USDS, *Foreign Relations, 1878*, 543–544.

38. Foster, *Memoirs*, vol. 1, 95, vol. 2, 262–263; Foster to Vallarta, April 9, 1878, enclosure no. 1, USDS Despatches, Mexico, vol. 61. Evarts designated much of the responsibility for Mexican affairs as Seward's. See F. W. Seward, *Reminiscences of a War-Time Statesman and Diplomat*, 435.

39. Foster to Avila, Nov. 21, 1878, enclosure, USDS, *Foreign Relations, 1879*, 735; also see 730–734; Foster to Evarts (telegram), July 20, 1878, USDS Despatches, Mexico, vol. 62; Foster to Evarts, July 17, 1880, USDS *Foreign Relations, 1880–1881*, 724–725.
40. Avila to Foster, Nov. 25, 1878, enclosure no. 3, USDS, *Foreign Relations, 1879*, 739.
41. Evarts to Foster, March 1, 1880, with enclosure, Alex Ramsey, secretary of war, to Evarts, Feb. 29, 1879, USDS, *Foreign Relations, 1880–1881*, 735.
42. *Treaties and Conventions between the United States of America and Other Powers*, ed. by William M. Malloy, vol. 1 (Washington D.C.: USGPO, 1910), 1144–1145; Gregg, *Border Troubles*, 152–155; Relyea, *Diplomatic Relations between the United States and Mexico*, 45.
43. Foster, *Memoirs*, vol. 1, 109. While in Mexico the industrious Foster made a study of the coffee industry, and his report was published by the Department of Agriculture. "The Cultivation of Coffee in Mexico," *Monthly Report of the Department of Agriculture*, 14 (July 1876).
44. Foster to Evarts (private and unofficial), April 28, 1877, USDS Despatches, Mexico, vol. 59.
45. Report of Remarks on Feb. 16, 1878 of Mr. Evarts and Mr. Foster before the Subcommittee of the Committee on Foreign Affairs. Feb. 16, 1878, USDS Despatches, Mexico, vol. 61.
46. Foster to Fish, Jan. 17, 1875, Fish Papers. Foster to Arias, acting minister of foreign affairs, Jan. 29, 1876, USDS Despatches, Mexico, vol. 58.
47. Foster to Fish, Jan. 16, 1875, USDS, *Foreign Relations, 1875*.
48. See the article by Matias Romero of July 7, 1876 in *El Correo del Comercio*, USDS Despatches, Mexico, vol. 55.
49. Foster had an interesting correspondence with Senator John Tyler Morgan regarding reciprocity with Mexico. Morgan to Foster, Sept. 27, 1878, Foster Papers; Foster to Morgan, July 2, 1878, Morgan Papers. Also see David Pletcher, *The Awkward Years: American Foreign Relations under Garfield and Arthur*, 181.
50. Foster to Evarts, Dec. 27, 1879, USDS, *Foreign Relations, 1880–1881*, 726. Foster, *Memoirs*, vol. 1, 160; Gregg, *Border Troubles*, 19–21.
51. Foster, *Memoirs*, vol. 1, 110–111, Foster to Evarts, Jan. 28, 1879, with enclosures, USDS, *Foreign Relations, 1879*, 774–779, 780–795; Foster to Evarts, May 31, 1879, 811–812; Foster to Evarts, Aug. 16, 1879, enclosure, 826–833; Foster to Evarts, Dec. 24, 1879, enclosure, 719–722.
52. *New York Times* (Feb. 13, 1879), 2.
53. Foster to Evarts, Feb. 7, 1879, and Evarts to Foster, Feb. 20, 1879, USDS, *Foreign Relations, 1879*, 796, 799.
54. Foster to Evarts, December 9, 1878, with enclosure of letters from United States citizens complaining of unfair taxation, USDS, *Foreign Relations, 1879*, 416–449.
55. Foster to Carsile Mason, Oct. 9, 1878, USDS, *Foreign Relations, 1877–1878*, 641–649. In this letter Foster cautioned potential investors regarding conditions such as unfair taxation, banditry, and an unstable economy. This candid but generally negative assessment to the spokesman of the Manufacturers

Association of the Northwest brought severe criticism when Mr. Mason sent Foster's letter to Mexican Minister of Finance Matias Romero. Romero denounced Foster's letter in a lengthy and detailed report that attempted to refute all of Foster's charges. *Report of the Minister of Finance of the United States of Mexico on the 15th of January, 1879, on the Actual Condition of Mexico* (New York: Ponce de Léon, 1880). Some U.S. citizens in Mexico thought Foster should be recalled because of his letter to the Manufacturers Association. See Edmund D. Hatton to President Hayes, March 8, 1879, National Archives, USDS General Records, Record Group 59, Appointment Papers. Historian David Pletcher credits Foster with a valid evaluation of the conditions in Mexico, *Rails, Mines and Progress, Seven American Promoters in Mexico, 1867–1911*, 296–297.

56. Foster, *Memoirs*, vol. 2, 282–285.

57. Foster, *Memoirs*, vol. 1, 98–99, 106–107, 240–241; Foster to Frelinghuysen (unofficial) Oct. 20, 1883, USDS Despatches, Spain, vol. 107.

58. Foster to Evarts, Sept. 24, 1879, USDS, *Foreign Relations, 1879*, 837.

59. Daniel Casío-Villegas argued that the *porfiriato* was necessary for Mexico's national development, in "El Porfiriato, era de consolidacion", *Historia Mexicana*, 13 (1966), 76–87. For a more critical evaluation of Díaz and his regime, see Charles C. Cumberland, *Mexican Revolution: Genesis under Madero*, 3–28; Karl M. Schmidt, *Mexico and the United States, 1821–1973*.

60. Foster, *Memoirs*, vol. 1, 116. Foster expressed similar sentiments in "Porfirio Díaz: Soldier and Statesman," "The New Mexico," *National Geographic* 13 (Jan. 1902), 1–24. Foster argued that Latin American nations needed strong executive government because the history and culture of the Latins made the Anglo-Saxon type of constitutional democracy impossible. "The Latin American Constitutions and Revolutions," *National Geographic* 12 (May 1901), 169–175.

61. Statement of United States citizens, March 2, 1880, USDS, *Foreign Relations, 1880–1881*, 738. F. W. Seward, acting secretary of state, to Foster, August 14, 1879; Evarts to Foster, Dec. 5, 1879, USDS Instructions, Mexico, vol. 20. For detailed accounts of Foster's travels into Oaxaca and the interior states of Mexico, see Foster, *Memoirs*, vol. 1, 61–70, 121–136. For evaluations of Foster as a capable, well-informed diplomat with a solid knowledge of the Mexican language and political environment, see: Casío-Villegas, *The United States versus Porfirio Díaz*, 221, 228, 234, 235–236; Louis M. Drago, introduction to José León Suarez, *Mr. John W. Foster*; Gerano Estrada, prologue to "Las Memoias Deplomaticas de Mr. Foster sobre Mexico," *Archivo Historico Diplomatico Mexicana*, no. 29 (Mexico: Publications de la Secretaria de Relaciones Exteriores, 1929); Pletcher, *Rails, Mines and Progress*, 174.

62. USDS, *Foreign Relations, 1880–1881*, 738–739.

63. Evarts to Foster (personal), Feb. 10, 1880, Foster Papers. Foster, *Memoirs*, vol. 1, 137. Foster's nomination was confirmed on Jan. 27, 1880. *Senate Executive Journal*, 46 Cong., 2nd Sess., vol. 12, 171, 198, 205, 208–209.

64. *House Select Committee on Alleged Frauds in the Late Presidential Election* ("Potter Committee"), U.S. House of Representatives, 45th Cong., 3rd Sess., Miscellaneous Document No. 31, vol. 2, 108, 98. Foster to Rutherford B. Hayes, Oct. 14, 1876, Rutherford B. Hayes Papers. Foster informed Hayes that his

return to Indiana brought severe criticism from Democrats who questioned his leaving his diplomatic post to engage in domestic politics. Foster to Benjamin Harrison (telegram), Aug. 5, 1876; Foster to Harrison Aug. 15, 1876, Harrison Papers.

65. Foster's political patron Oliver Morton did not list Foster among those from Indiana recommended for a cabinet post. Instead, he urged that Foster be kept in Mexico. Morton to E. B. Martindale, March 10, 1877, and Morton to R. B. Hayes, March 15, 1877, Rutherford B. Hayes Papers. Also see Dudley W. Foulke, *Life of Oliver P. Morton*, vol. 2, 480.

66. Foster, *Memoirs*, vol. 1, 29, 59.

CHAPTER III

1. David M. Pletcher, *The Awkward Years: American Foreign Relations under Garfield and Arthur*, 11, 348–352. Foster Rhea Dulles, *Prelude to World Power*, 120; Warren F. Ilchman, *Professional Diplomacy in the United States, 1799–1939*, 23–24; Milton Plesur, *America's Outward Thrust: Approaches to Foreign Affairs, 1865–1890*, 35–39.

2. Pletcher, *Awkward Years*, 355.

3. Evarts to Foster, April 14, 1880, USDS, *Foreign Relations, 1880–1881*, 873; Foster, *Memoirs*, vol. 1, 163.

4. Evarts to Foster, June 28, Sept. 4, 1880, USDS, *Foreign Relations, 1880–1881*, 876, 880.

5. Foster to Evarts, Sept. 16, 1880, USDS, *Foreign Relations, 1880–1881*, 881–882; Foster, *Memoirs*, vol. 1 164–166.

6. Foster to Evart, Dec. 30, 1880, USDS, *Foreign Relations, 1881*, 998–999.

7. Evarts to Foster, March 31, 1881, USDS, *Foreign Relations, 1881*, 1007–1008; Foster, *Memoirs*, vol. 1, 166.

8. Evarts to Foster, March 3, 1881, USDS, *Foreign Relations, 1881*, 1007. Foster made a long and careful study of Korean law concerning Jews, found the statutes confusing and vague, and reported his findings to Washington. Foster to Evarts, Dec. 31, 1880, USDS, *Foreign Relations, 1881*, 1005–1006; Foster, *Memoirs*, vol. 1, 166–167.

9. Foster to Evarts, Nov. 18, 1880, USDS, *Foreign Relations, 1880*, 995.

10. Foster to Blaine, March 14, 1881, USDS, *Foreign Relations, 1881*, 1008–1009; Foster, *Memoirs*, vol. 1, 181–184.

11. Foster to Blaine, March 15, 1881 (with enclosure), Blaine to Foster, April 13, 1881, USDS, *Foreign Relations, 1881*, 1009–1010. For a discussion of United States policy and public opinion toward Russia at this time, see Thomas A. Bailey, *America Faces Russia*, 122–124.

12. Foster remained in St. Petersburg during the campaign, although he expressed a "deep interest" in having Garfield elected. Foster to Carl Schurz, Aug. 20, 1880, Indiana Historical Society Library. Harrison to Foster, Dec. 4, 1880, Foster Papers. Foster had encouraged Harrison to seek a seat in the United States Senate a few months earlier. Foster to Harrison, Oct. 23, 1880, Harrison Papers. Also see Harry J. Sievers, *Benjamin Harrison*, vol. 2, 181.

13. Foster to Harrison, Jan. 1, 1881, Harrison Papers.

14. Foster, *Memoirs*, vol. 1, 213–215.
15. Foster viewed the disorders in Russia following the Russo-Japanese war as evidence of the Almighty's displeasure. Foster, *Memoirs*, vol. 1, 167.
16. Foster, *Memoirs*, vol. 1, 213, 239, and vol. 2, 281–282, 301.
17. Foster, *Memoirs*, vol. 1, 240. Foster apparently did not seek the appointment of Spain, nor did Indiana politicians push his nomination upon the administration. It also seemed that Foster stood to take a temporary financial loss by accepting the assignment. *New York Times*, Feb. 25, 1883, Feb. 26, 1883. Foster was appointed envoy extraordinary and minister plenipotentiary to Spain on Feb. 26. *Senate Executive Journal*, 47th Cong., 2nd Sess., vol. 22, 671, 672, 674.
18. Foster, *Memoirs*, vol. 1, 240; Pletcher, *Awkward Years*, 170, 289–290.
19. *New York Times*, Feb. 26, 1883.
20. Foster to Frelinghuysen, June 16, 1883, USDS Despatches, Spain, vol. 106.
21. See the remarks of the Spanish foreign minister before a delegation of the Tariff Reform Society in New York City. *New York Times* (Oct. 21, 1883); Pletcher, *Awkward Years*, 289–290. Foster personally believed that most enlightened Spaniards were reconciled to the eventual loss of Cuba. Foster, *Memoirs*, vol. 1 256.
22. Foster to Frelinghuysen, Oct. 19, 20, 27, 1883, National Archives, USDS Despatches, Spain, vol. 107; Foster, *Memoirs*, vol. 1, 244–246.
23. Foster to Frelinghuysen, Dec. 17, 27, 1883, National Archives, USDS Despatches, Spain, vol. 107, 108; Jan. 3, 4, 1884, USDS, *Foreign Relations, 1884*, 471–472.
24. Foster to Frelinghuysen, Jan. 11, Feb. 28, 1884, National Archives, USDS, Despatches, Spain, vol. 108; Pletcher, *Awkward Years*, 291. For analysis of the reciprocity issue in 1884 see Tom Terrill, *The Tariff, Politics and American Foreign Policy, 1874–1901*, 79.
25. Frelinghuysen to Foster (confidential), March 19, 1884, Frelinghuysen to Foster (cipher telegram), March 28, 1884, USDS, Instructions, Spain, vol. 19.
26. Foster to Gresham, March 30, 1884, Walter Q. Gresham Papers. Regarding his return Foster wrote: "I have not intimated to him [Frelinghuysen] any other interest." According to Matilda Gresham's biography of her husband, the Greshams were very close to the Fosters and lived in the Foster home in Washington while the Fosters were in Spain. *Life of Walter Quintin Gresham, 1832–1895*, 271.
27. Foster to Gresham, Feb. 11, 27 and March 20, 1884, Walter Q. Gresham Papers.
28. Foster to Gresham, Feb. 11, 1884, Gresham Papers. Foster, *Memoirs*, vol. 2, 271, 274.
29. Gresham to Foster, March 20, 1884, and Foster to Gresham (telegram), June 1 and 3, 1884, Gresham Papers. Foster to Noble C. Butler, May 28, 1884, Noble C. Butler Papers.
30. Foster to Gresham (telegram), June 6, 1884; Gresham to Foster (telegram), June 6, 1884; S. P. Thompson to Gresham (private), June 12, 1884, Gresham Papers.
31. Foster to Gresham, Sept. 31 and Dec. 14, 1884, Gresham Papers; Foster, *Memoirs*, vol. 2, 272.
32. Frelinghuysen to Foster, June 7, July 2, Aug. 29, 1884, USDS Instructions, Spain, vol. 19.
33. Foster to Frelinghuysen, Nov. 25, 1884, enclosure, notes of conferences with

minister of state, president of the ministry and Señor Salvador de Albacete, special plenipotentiary, USDS Despatches, Spain, vol. 111.

34. Foster to Gresham, Sept. 31(?), 1884, Gresham Papers. Also see Foster to Gresham, Sept. 28 and Oct. 26, 1884, Gresham Papers.

35. Pletcher, *Awkward Years*, 304, 306–307, 353. The text of the treaty can be found in the *Congressional Record*, 48th Cong., 2nd Sess., vol. 16, part 1, 148–156.

36. *Congressional Record*, 48th Cong., 2nd Sess., vol. 16, part 1, 300, 540, 560, 621, 647, 681.

37. Foster, *Memoirs*, vol. 2, 1. Foster believed that Blaine opposed the treaty largely because he still harbored resentment at having been dropped from the cabinet by Arthur after the death of Garfield. *Memoirs*, vol. 1, 259–260. Also see Pletcher, *Awkward Years*, 348.

38. Foster, *Memoirs*, vol. 1, 1; Denna F. Fleming, *The Treaty Veto of the American Senate*, 73; William S. Holt, *Treaties Defeated by the Senate*, 140–141. The failure of the reciprocity treaty probably hurt the Cuban economy and might even have hastened the independence movement in Cuba. See Herminio Portell Vilá, *Historia de Cuba en sus Relaciones con los Estados Unidos y España*, vol. 3, 39.

39. Foster, *Memoirs*, vol. 1, 296–297; Bayard to Foster, April 15, 18, 1885, USDS Instructions, Spain, vol. 19.

40. Bayard to Foster (telegram), Aug. 4, 1885, USDS Instructions, Spain, vol. 19.

41. *New York Times*, June 30, 1892, July 1, 1892; "Foster's Many Masters," *New York Times*, July 4, 1892.

42. Foster to Gresham, Feb. 26, 1885, and Oct. 18, 1885, Gresham Papers. Foster, *Memoirs*, vol. 2, 300–301.

43. For example, Foster won from the Díaz government a settlement of $15,000 for General Lew Wallace, hero of the American Civil War and the author of *Ben Hur*. Through contacts in Washington and Peking, Foster arranged for a handsome payment to the family of American General Fredrick T. Ward, who had been killed helping the Chinese government suppress the Tai-ping Rebellion. Foster managed to have the payment taken out of the Boxer indemnity fund. Foster, *Memoirs*, vol. 2, 288–289, 296–297.

44. Foster, *Memoirs*, vol. 2, 301. At the time of his appointment as secretary of state, Foster was arguing a claims case for the Mexican government before the U.S. Congress. The case eventually reached the Supreme Court and was decided in favor of Mexico. See *Before the Congress of the United States: The Mexican Fraudulent Claims Argument of John W. Foster before the Committee of Foreign Affairs of the House of Representatives, in Support of Senate Bills No. 539 and 606* (Washington, D.C.: USGPO, 1892). The settlement of this dispute, known as the "Weil and La Abra claims," involved a payment to Mexico by the United States of more than $1 million. Foster presented a complete account of the case, in *The Practice of Diplomacy*, 374–377. Also see John B. Moore, *History and Digest of Arbitrations*, vol. 2, 1344–1348.

45. Foster, *Memoirs*, vol. 1, 155–157. For a discussion of the public careers of the nineteenth-century Chinese diplomats in Washington, see Earl Swisher, "Chinese Representation in the United States," *University of Colorado Studies in History* 5 (Jan. 1967). Swisher's study provides useful background information

on the nature of the Chinese legation.
46. Cheng Tsao-ju to Bayard, Nov. 30, 1885 and Feb. 15, 1886, USDS, *Foreign Relations, 1886*, 101–156; House Report No. 2044 (May, 1886), 49th Cong., 1st Sess., 4–7.
47. Bayard to Cheng Tsao-ju, Feb. 18, 1886, USDS, *Foreign Relations 1886*, 101–156, 159. Charles C. Tansill, *The Foreign Policies of Thomas F. Bayard, 1885–1897*, 142, 148–149.
48. *Congression Record*, 48th Cong., 1st Sess., vol. 17, part 5, 5110–5115, 5184–5190, 5196–5199, 5229–5315; Tansill, *Thomas Bayard*, 149.
49. Foster, *Memoirs*, vol. 2, 287, Also of interest regarding Foster's views on the fair treatment of Chinese people in the U. S. is "The Chinese Boycott," *Atlantic Monthly* 97 (Jan. 1906), 118–127.
50. USDS, *Foreign Relations, 1888*, 393–394.
51. According to John Bassett Moore, the bill for the summary exclusion of the Chinese (known as the Scott Bill) originated in the Democratic National Committee without the Department of State's being consulted. Letter of Moore to C. C. Tansill, June 16, 1939, in Tansill, *Thomas Bayard*, 175.
52. Foster Rhea Dulles, *China and America: The Story of Their Relations since 1784*, 92; S. W. Kung, *The Chinese in American Life*, 63; John A. S. Grenville and George B. Young, *Politics, Strategy and American Diplomacy: Studies in Foreign Policy, 1873–1917*, 59–63.
53. Foster to Gresham, May 4, 1888, Gresham Papers.
54. Memorandum written by John Bassett Moore after a conversation with John W. Foster, Sept. 19, 1888, cited in Tansill, *Thomas Bayard*, 174.
55. In 1904 Foster wrote that the Scott act of 1888 had as its "deliberate purpose to abrogate by indirect legislation the Chinese immigration treaty of 1880. Its impropriety was aggravated by the fact that it was passed while a treaty dealing with the subject was pending ratification." *American Diplomacy in the Orient*, 308. Also see Foster's remarks on Chinese immigration in Senate Report No. 776, 57th Con., 1st Sess., part 2, 53ff. Foster denounced a Supreme Court ruling excluding the reentry of Chinese immigrants; see "A Decision of the Most Profound Importance," *Independent* 58, (June 8, 1905) 1292–1293. Foster's efforts to assist the Chinese government are recorded in Mary Coolidge, *Chinese Immigration*, 219, 246–247, 250.
56. Chinese legation to Foster, June 19, 1906, Foster Papers.
57. H. Wayne Morgan, *From Hayes to McKinley: National Party Politics, 1877–1906*, 286; Josephson, *The Politicos*, 415–416.
58. Foster to Gresham, May 11, Feb.24, and March 16 and 28, 1888, Gresham Papers; Matilda Gresham, *Walter Q. Gresham*, vol. 2, 570–571, 579; Seivers, *Benjamin Harrison*, vol. 2, 251.
59. Matilda Gresham, *Walter Q. Gresham*, vol. 2, 571.
60. Foster to Gresham, June 10, 1888, Gresham Papers. Only two of the Foster's children reached adulthood, Edith and Eleanor.
61. H. W. Morgan, *From Hayes to McKinley*, 277–319; Josephson, *The Politicos*, 417 418.
62. Carl Schurz, *Speeches, Correspondence and Political Papers of Carl Schurz*, vol. 5, 95.

63. Foster to Gresham, June 27, 1888, Gresham Papers.
64. Foster to Gresham, June 27, 1888, Gresham Papers. Foster, *Memoirs*, vol. 2, 272.
65. For Foster's candid evaluations of Harrison, Blaine, and Gresham, see Foster, *Memoirs*, vol. 2, 249–254, 263–264, 267–270, 271–274.
66. The protective tariff was undoubtedly the central issue of the 1888 presidential campaign. Harrison, backed by manufacturers and big business interests, allied himself with the tariff. The question of rights over the fur seals in the Bering Sea emerged as an issue in the northwest, and because it involved negotiations with Great Britain, Americans appeared to want their government to take a strong stand. Sir Lionel Sackville-West, British minister to Washington, became a campaign issue when he foolishly indicated in writing that Cleveland was preferable to Harrison for the improvement of Anglo-American relations. The best account of the election of 1888 and the issues involved is presented in H. W. Morgan, *From Hayes to McKinley*, 277–319.
67. Grenville and Young, *Politics, Strategy and American Diplomacy*, 75–77; Ilchman, *Professional Diplomacy in the United States*, 51.

CHAPTER IV

1. The thesis that the Harrison administration foreshadowed later imperialist diplomatic ventures is advanced in Albert T. Volwiler, "Harrison, Blaine and American Foreign Policy, 1889–1893," *Proceedings of the American Philosophical Society* 79 (1938), 638–639. Also see Foster Rhea Dulles, *The Imperial Years*, 52–53; and *Prelude to World Power, 1860–1900*, 17. Walter La Feber argues that a search for new markets dominated Harrison's administration in its formulation of a policy for building a "new empire," *The New Empire: An Interpretation of American Expansion, 1860–1898*, 102–112, 127–130, 121–127, 137–138. William A. Williams proposes that "Metropolitan Republicans" committed themselves to market expansion at this time to hold the support of midwestern farm-businessmen, *The Roots of the Modern American Empire*, 319–348. John A. S. Grenville and George B. Young suggest that the building of capital ships during the Harrison years enabled the United States to conduct a more aggressive foreign policy, *Politics, Strategy, and American Diplomacy*, vol. 1, 38. For details of the naval building program under Benjamin Tracy, see Walter Herrick, *The American Naval Revolution*, 202–217.
2. Of his relationship with Harrison, Foster stated: "It is to his great credit that he never allowed my attachment to Gresham to interfere with our friendship." Foster, *Memoirs*, vol. 2, 250. Foster was quick to telegram congratulations to Harrison following his election victory; and as the president-elect prepared to come to Washington, Foster offered him the use of his family pew at the New York Avenue Presbyterian Church. Foster to Harrison (telegram), November 9, 1888; Foster to Harrison, Jan. 6, 1889, Harrison Papers.
3. Private memoranda of Harrison on his relations with Blaine, May 22, 1893. *Correspondence between Harrison and Blaine*, coll. and ed. by Albert T. Volwiler, 299–301. For an excellent account of the political factors that led to the selection of Blaine, see H. Wayne Morgan, *From Hayes to McKinley*, 320–322.

Also see J. A. Williams, "Stephen B. Elkins and the Benjamin Harrison Campaign and Cabinet, 1887–1891," *Indiana Magazine of History* 68 (March 1972), 1–8, 12–16.

4. Harrison warned Blaine that as secretary of state he would not have the same independence that he had enjoyed in the Garfield administration. Harrison to Blaine (private), Jan. 17, 1889, 44–45; also see the draft of this letter that more clearly indicates Harrison's true feelings, *Correspondence between Harrison and Blaine*, 45–48, 388–389, 462, 464–465; David S. Muzzey, *James G. Blaine*, 388–391, 462–465; Graham H. Stuart, *The Department of State*, 171–173.

5. See Volwiler's introduction to *Correspondence between Harrison and Blaine* for an account of the personal relationship between Blaine and Harrison, 1–17. Also see Muzzey, *James G. Blaine*, 390–391, 464–465; Alice Felt Tyler, *The Foreign Policies of James G. Blaine*, 367; F. R. Dulles, *The Imperial Years*, 51–52.

6. Stuart, *The Department of State*, 172–173. Walker Blaine was appointed solicitor as a compromise and served as solicitor in the State Department until his death in January 1890. William F. Wharton of Massachusetts was named assistant secretary of state at the suggestion of Senator Henry C. Lodge.

7. Shelby M. Cullom, *Fifty Years in Public Service*, 252–253; Muzzey, *James G. Blaine*, 388–389; May, *Imperial Democracy*, 17.

8. This assessment is made by Volwiler in *Correspondence between Harrison and Blaine*, 2–3; Stuart, *The Department of State*, 177; Grenville and Young, *Politics, Strategy and American Diplomacy*, 89.

9. Private memoranda of Harrison, May 22, 1893, *Correspondence between Harrison and Blaine*, 295.

10. Blaine to Harrison, Aug. 10, 1891, *Correspondence between Harrison and Blaine*, 174. Also see Blaine to Harrison (confidential), Sept. 23, 1891, 174. Muzzey, *Blaine*, 392–394; Wilfred H. Callcott, *The Caribbean Policy of the United States, 1890–1920*, 57–58.

11. Blaine to Harrison, June 19, 1890, Senate Document No. 158, 51st Cong., 1 Sess. Blaine to Harrison, July 24, 1890; Harrison to Blaine, Sept. 10, 1890; Blaine to Harrison (confidential), Sept. 23, 1891, *Correspondence between Harrison and Blaine*, 113, 126, 193–194. For an examination of Blaine's views on reciprocity regarding Latin America, see A. Curtis Wilgus, "James G. Blaine and the Pan-American Movement," *Hispanic American Historical Review* 5 (Nov. 1922), 694–708. For an analysis of reciprocity with Latin America that views the Harrison administration's efforts as a piecemeal program that anticipated the dollar diplomacy of the Taft administration, see David Pletcher, "Reciprocity and Latin America in the Early 1890s: A Foretaste of Dollar Diplomacy," *Pacific Historical Review* 47 (Feb. 1978), 53–89.

12. Foster, *Memoirs*, vol. 2, 2–5; Muzzey, *James G. Blaine*, 442–451; Tyler, *Foreign Policies of Blaine*, 183–187.

13. Foster, *Memoirs*, vol. 1, 329–330; vol. 2, 5–6, 8; memoranda of Harrison, May 22, 1893, *Correspondence between Harrison and Blaine*, 302.

14. Foster, *Memoirs*, vol. 2, 5–9. Memorandum to Dr. Salvador Mendonca (minister from Brazil), Nov. 14, 1890, Foster Papers. The first reciprocal trade agreement Foster arranged was with Brazil, and he felt that this treaty would improve his position in negotiating with Spain. For the text of the treaty with

Brazil, see Senate Executive Document No. 119, 52nd Cong., 1st Sess. Also see Foster's views regarding reciprocity as expressed in *Proceedings of the Banquet of the Spanish-American Commercial Union, New York, May 1, 1889* (New York, 1889), 17–19.

15. Blaine to Ramon O. Williams (confidential), Feb. 6, 1891, facsimile printed in *Memoirs*, vol. 2, 9.

16. Foster, *Memoirs*, vol. 1, 329; vol. 2, 9. H. Portell Vilá, *Historia de Cuba en sus Relaciones con los Estados Unidos y Españia*, vol. 3, 74–77.

17. E. C. Grubb to Blaine, March 4, 1891, USDS Despatches, Spain, vol. 122.

18. Foster to Blaine (telegram), March 31, 1891, Harrison Papers. A complete record of the conference is contained in exhibit no. 1. in Foster to Blaine (confidential), April 17, 1891, USDS Despatches, Spain, vol. 122.

19. Harrison's worries about other nations benefiting from the reciprocity treaty because of most-favored-nation clauses are expressed in handwritten notes on the despatch of Foster to Blaine, March 31, 1891, Harrison Papers. Also see Foster to Blaine (telegram), April 17, 1891, USDS Despatches, Spain, vol. 122. Harrison-Blaine, June 8, 14, 1891, *Correspondence between Harrison and Blaine*, 159, 161.

20. Blaine-Harrison, June 11, 1891, *Correspondence between Harrison and Blaine*, 160. Harrison believed that his secretary of state should have the privilege of signing the document and had the appropriate papers sent to Blaine at his retreat in Maine. Harrison to Blaine, June 21, 1891, 16.

21. Harrison to Blaine, June 25, 1891, *Correspondence between Harrison and Blaine*, 163.

22. While advising the president on foreign affairs, Foster was serving as legal counsel for foreign governments in claims against the United States. During 1891 and 1892 Foster was involved with legal matters concerning claims of the Díaz government over the fraudulent La Arba and Weil mine claims. See Foster, *Memoirs*, vol. 2, 282–285; *Before the Congress of the United States: The Mexican Fraudulent Claims Argument of John W. Foster before the Committee of Foreign Affairs*; John Bassett Moore, *A Digest of International Law*, vol. 7, 68; vol. 20, 114; Fleming, *The Treaty Veto of the Senate*, 57–58.

23. Foster, *Memoirs*, vol. 2, 10. Diplomatic correspondence concerning reciprocity for the British islands in the Caribbean is contained in USDS, *Foreign Relations, 1892, 1893*.

24. Harrison to Blaine, May 28, 1891, *Correspondence between Harrison and Blaine*, 156. For a complete treatment on the pork dispute, arguing that protection of German pork producers rather than possible disease in the American product caused the German restrictions, see L. L. Snyder, "The American-German Pork Dispute, 1879–1891," *Journal of Modern History* 17 (March 1945), 16–28. Also see Jeannette Keim, *Forty Years of German-American Political Relations*, 67–78; John L. Gignillat, "Pigs, Politics and Protection: The European Boycott of American Pork, 1879–1891," *Agricultural History*, 35 (Jan. 1961), 3–12.

25. Harrison to Blaine, May 28 and Aug. 1, 1891, *Correspondence between Harrison and Blaine*, 156, 167–168; Blaine to Harrison, Aug. 22, 1891, 180–181; Foster to Harrison, July 18, 1891, and Foster to Elijah W. Halford (private secretary to the president), Aug. 3, 1891, Harrison Papers.

26. Confidential minutes of interview between Foster and Von Munn at Saratoga, N.Y., Aug. 22, 1891, Harrison Papers; Foster to William W. Phelps, Aug. 23, 1891, Harrison Papers; Von Munn to Blaine, Sept. 3, 1891, USDS *Foreign Relations, 1891*, 528.
27. James M. Callahan, *American Foreign Policy in Canadian Relations*, 413.
28. Foster, *Memoirs*, vol. 2, 176.
29. Foster, *Memoirs*, vol. 2, 179; Callahan, *Policy in Canadian Relations*, 422.
30. Blaine to Harrison, Sept. 23, 1891, and Harrison to Blaine, Sept. 26, 1891, *Correspondence between Harrison and Blaine*, 193–195.
31. Goodwin Smith to Foster, Feb. 16, 1892; J. D. Edgar to Foster, March 23, 1892, Foster Papers. Also see John B. Brebner, *North Atlantic Triangle*, (New Haven, Conn., 1945), 256; Callahan, *Policy in Canadian Relations*, 422–423.
32. Foster to Harrison, June 6, 1892, Senate Executive Document No. 114, 52nd Cong., 1st Sess., 3, 43. Callahan, *Policy in Canadian Relations*, 424–425.
33. Foster to Harrison, June 11, 1892, Harrison Papers; Howard B. Schonberger, *Transportation to the Seaboard*, 153; Callahan, *Policy in Canadian Relations*, 425–426.
34. Harrison to Foster, August 17, 1892, Harrison Papers; *Congressional Record*, 52nd Cong., 1st Sess., 6428, 6680, 6950.
35. Blaine to Foster, June 1, 1892, USDS Instructions, Special Missions, vol. 4. Harrison to E. J. Phelps, March 8, 1892. Harrison confided to Phelps, a former minister to Great Britain, "Blaine has become too ill to even confer with me upon the subject" (Harrison Papers). Blaine to Harrison, May 12, 1892, *Correspondence between Harrison and Blaine*, 281; Foster, *Memoirs*, vol. 2, 20. For the correspondence leading to an agreement to accept a modus vivendi in the Bering Sea and submit the issue to international arbitration, see USDS, *Foreign Relations, 1891*, 524–643.
36. John Bassett Moore, "The Chilean Controversy," *Political Science Quarterly* 8 (1893), 467–468. Moore's article on the Chilean matter is extremely valuable. At the time of the controversy, Moore was third assistant secretary of state, and his writing reflects his empirical knowledge. He also used State Department documents, and his understanding of the legal questions involved makes his study most authoritative. Also important is Osgood Hardy, "The Itata Incident," *Hispanic American Historical Review* 5 (May 22, 1922), 195–226. United States relations with Chile during this period are described in Fredrick Pike, *Chile and the United States, 1808–1962*, 66–85; William R. Sherman, *The Diplomatic and Commercial Relations between the United States and Chile, 1820–1914*, 143–193.
37. Egan to Blaine, April 23 and May 8, 1981, USDS, *Foreign Relations, 1891*, 110, 122; Moore, "Chilean Controversy," 468.
38. Lazcano to Blaine, March 10, 1891, USDS, *Foreign Relations, 1891*, 314.
39. Blaine to Lazcano, March 13, 1891, USDS, *Foreign Relations, 1891*, 314. An important source on the administration's policy during the *Itata* affair is John Bassett Moore, "Some Incidents in the Chilean Controversy," a sixteen-page handwritten memorandum written by the third assistant secretary of state for his personal records, John Bassett Moore Papers, hereafter referred to as "Incidents".
40. Moore, "Incidents."

41. On the morning of May 4, Foster visited Moore in the latter's office to discuss the proceedings of the previous evening. Moore reiterated his position that the purchase of arms by the Congressional forces was legal under the Treaty of Washington, 1871 (Moore, "Incidents").

42. Lazcano to Blaine, March 5, 1891, USDS, *Foreign Relations, 1891*, 316. A detailed description of the escape of the *Itata* from San Diego can be found in Hardy, "Itata Incident," 207–217.

43. Errazuriz to Blaine (telegram), June 5, 1891, USDS, *Foreign Relations, 1891*, 317; Egan to Blaine, June 27, 1891, enclosure of Rear Admiral McCann to Egan, June 12, 1891, USDS, *Foreign Relations, 1891*, 140, 141; Moore, "Chilean Controversy," 469.

44. Moore, "Chilean Controversy," 269.

45. Moore, "Chilean Controversy," 469–473. Minister Thomas Egan, a Midwestern "Blaine Irishman" was considered by his contemporaries to be largely responsible for the deterioration of relations with Chile, especially by antagonizing the British interests in that country. See Sherman, *The United States and Chile*, 145–152. Historian Osgood Hardy finds Egan's performance in Chile at a difficult time to have been highly competent; he views the Chilean crisis as manufactured in Washington, not Santiago. "Was Egan a Blundering Minister?" *Hispanic American Historical Review* 8 (Sept. 1932), 285–292.

46. Moore, "Incidents"; memorandum handed by the Chilean minister to the acting secretary of state (Wharton), June 22, 1891, USDS, *Foreign Relations, 1891*, 317–319.

47. Egan to Blaine, Sept. 1, 1891, and Egan to Wharton, Sept. 7, 1891, Harrison Papers; Egan to Blaine, Sept. 7, 1891, USDS *Foreign Relations, 1891*, 160.

48. Wharton to Egan (telegram), Oct. 1, 1891; Egan to Blaine, Oct. 6 and 13, 1891, USDS, *Foreign Relations, 1891*, 117, 179–184. The legal aspects of the political asylum question are discussed in Moore, "Chilean Controversy," 475–482. Also see Hardy, "Itata Incident," 221–222.

49. The *Baltimore* was one of several ships dispatched to Chilean waters during the early stages of the revolution in response to Egan's request of naval forces for the "protection of United States interests." Egan to Blaine, Jan. 17, 1891, Blaine to Egan, March 23, 1891, USDS, *Foreign Relations, 1891*, 93, 107.

50. Egan to Blaine, Oct. 18 and 10 and Nov. 3, 1891, *Foreign Relations, 1891*, 194–195, 213–217. Also see *Relations with Chile*, 52nd Cong., 1st Sess., House Executive Document No. 91.

51. Message of the president to the Senate and House of Representatives, Dec. 6, 1891, USDS, *Foreign Relations, 1891*, ix; also see Pedro Montt to Blaine, Dec. 11, 1891, 325–326; Montt to Blaine, Dec. 19, 1891, 326–330; Moore, "Chilean Controversy," 490–492.

52. Foster very coolly and candidly wrote in his *Memoirs* that the "revolution which occurred in Chile . . . occasioned the government of the United States much trouble, even bringing it to the brink of war; but it furnished me some professional business." The Congressional government, apparently aware of Foster's great influence within the administration, asked Foster to remain on as counsel to the Chilean legation in Washington, even after Balmaceda was ousted. Foster refused, not wanting to involve himself further with the Chileans in this

controversial situation, *Memoirs*, vol. 2, 289–290.
53. Harrison to Blaine, Oct. 1, 1891, *Correspondence between Harrison and Blaine*, 201.
54. Volwiler, "Harrison-Blaine Foreign Policy," 639; John K. Mahon, "Benjamin Tracy; Secretary of the Navy, 1889–1893," *New York Historical Society Quarterly*, 44 (April 1960), 179–201.
55. Harrison to Blaine, Jan. 2, 1892 and Blaine to Harrison, Jan. 5, 1892, *Correspondence between Harrison and Blaine*, 226, 233.
56. Message of the president to the Senate and House of Representatives, Dec. 6, 1891, USDS, *Foreign Relations, 1891*, ix. In response to Blaine's moderate views, Harrison reportedly erupted in a cabinet meeting and emphatically stated, "Mr. Secretary, that insult was to the uniform of the United States sailors." Volwiler, "Harrison-Blaine Foreign Policy," 640.
57. Blaine to Harrison, Jan. 2, 1892, and Harrison to Blaine, Jan. 4, 1892, *Correspondence between Harrison and Blaine*, 226, 231–232.
58. Foster to Harrison, Jan. 12, 27, 1892, Harrison Papers.
59. Blaine to Egan (telegram), Jan. 21, 1892, USDS, *Foreign Relations, 1891*, 307–308. This message does not reflect Blaine's opinions on the Chilean affair. See Volwiler, "Harrison-Blaine Foreign Policy," 640, 643, 644, 647; Dulles, *The Imperial Years*, 60–61; Muzzey, *James G. Blaine*, 471; LeFeber, *The New Empire*, 134–135.
60. Foster, "Pan-American Diplomacy," *Atlantic Monthly* 89 (April 1903), 485.
61. Foster to Egan, July 15, 1892, USDS, *Foreign Relations, 1892*, 63. Also see Egan to Foster (telegram, confidential), July 11, 1892, enclosure of President Montt's message to Congress, June 1, 1892, Harrison Papers.
62. Quoted in Alexander De Conde, *A History of American Foreign Policy*, 2nd ed. (New York: Charles Scribner's Sons, 1971), 314.

CHAPTER V

1. Blaine to Harrison, June 4, 1892 (12:45 P.M.); Harrison to Blaine, June 4, 1892. Harrison's private secretary, Elijah Halford, delivered the president's letter to Blaine personally at 1:30 P.M. *Correspondence between Harrison and Blaine*, 288.
2. Sidney Smith (Blaine's secretary) to Halford, March 6, (1892) *Correspondence between Harrison and Blaine*, 243; Harrison to E. J. Phelps, March 8, 1892, Harrison Papers; Muzzey, *James G. Blaine*, 467. For an account of the effort to dump Harrison in favor of Blaine, see H. Wayne Morgan, "The Election of 1892" in Arthur Schlesinger, Jr., *The History of American Presidential Election*, 1703–1716.
3. Numerous letters warning Harrison of Blaine's disloyalty and the possibility of an attempt to capture the Republican nomination can be found in the Harrison Papers. Of particular interest is Foster to Halford, June 7, 1892.
4. Regarding the uneasy relationship between Blaine and Harrison during the months prior to Blaine's resignation, Foster wrote, "in my relations with the Department of State during his [Blaine's] incumbency, I had a difficult part to act

in preserving the confidence and esteem of both President Harrison and himself, especially when tension between them became more and more acute." Foster, *Memoirs*, vol. 2, 268. Foster believed that Blaine's illness and the deaths of his sons, Walker and Emmons, led to his resignation, not presidential ambitions, *Memoirs*, vol.2, 267–268.

5. *New York Times*, June 24, 1892.
6. F. G. Shanks, (president of National Press Intelligence Co.) to Tracy, June 11, 1892, Tracy Papers; *New York Times*, June 30, 1892. Chauncey Depew claimed that Harrison actually offered him the post. According to Depew, Harrison said, "it was largely through your efforts that I became president, and I am greatly indebted to you for my nomination." After turning down the job, Depew claimed he had the president's assurance that the position would be waiting for him in a second administration. Chauncey Depew, *My Memories of Eighty Years*, 138–139.
7. Within a week following his appointment as secretary of state, Foster wrote to Blaine that he had never aspired to the post and accepted it only out of loyalty to Harrison. Foster also informed Blaine that he would strive to follow the policy you have marked out in the Department." Foster to Blaine, July 8, 1892, Blaine Papers. Also see *Nation* 55 (July 7, 1892), 1; *New York Times*, June 24, 1892. Harrison sent Foster's nomination to the Senate on June 29, 1892, and it was confirmed without debate.-*Senate Executive Journal*, vol. 18, 52nd Cong., 1st Sess., 253, 254.
8. Donald M. Dozer, "Benjamin Harrison and the Presidential Campaign of 1892," *American Historical Review* 54 (Oct. 1948), 72. In September, 1891, the New York *Mail and Express* had reported a breakfast meeting in a New York Hotel between Foster and leading Gresham backers including Indiana Republicans Charles Fairbanks, Otto Gresham, and the younger Oliver P. Morton. The meeting spurred speculation of a Gresham boom, but Foster told reporters that the meeting was just an accidental encounter. Foster also denied involvement in a Gresham plot in a letter to the president's private secretary. Foster to Halford, Sept. 1, 1891, with enclosure of *Mail and Express* article, Harrison Papers.
9. *Nation* 55 (July 7, 1891), 1.
10. "Not a Proper Appointment," *New York Times*, June 30, 1892.
11. *New York Times*, July 4, 1892.
12. Message of the president, Dec. 6, 1892, USDS, *Foreign Relations, 1892*, vii, ix, xii, vii. Also see Harrison's campaign statements as recorded in Thomas Campbell-Copeland, ed., *Harrison and Reid, Their Lives and Records* (New York, Charles L. Webster 1892), part 1, 29. 30.
13. Foster, *American Diplomacy in the Orient*, 386; George H. Ryden, *The Foreign Policy of the United States in Relation to Samoa*, 532–533.
14. Foster to White, Nov. 5, 21, 1892, USDS, *Foreign Relations, 1892*, 237–239, 245.
15. John Bassett Moore, *Digest of International Law*, vol. 3, 238–241; Callcott, *Caribbean Policy*, 75–76.
16. Foster to Robert T. Lincoln, Oct. 6, 1892, USDS, *Foreign Relations, 1892*, 234–235; Foster to Harrison, Aug. 12, 1892, Harrison Papers.
17. See Callcott, *Caribbean Policy*, 65–66; Sumner Welles, *Naboth's Vineyard*, (New York; Payson and Clark, 1928), vol. 1, 468–495.

18. See Foster to Hicks, Jan. 23, 1893, USDS, Instructions, Peru, vol. 17. Also of interest on the Chimbote matter is Seward Livermore, "American Strategy and Diplomacy in the South Pacific, 1890–1914," *Pacific Historical Review*, 12 (March 1943), 36–37.

19. See Harrison's position on the silver question in Campbell-Copeland, *Harrison and Reid*, part 2, 39–40.

20. Foster to Harrison, Aug. 3, 1892, Harrison Papers.

21. Foster's instructions to the United States delegates to the International Monetary Conference in Brussels, Nov. 10, 1892, found in Henry Russell, *International Monetary Conferences*, 379.

22. Russell, *International Monetary Conferences*, 377–378, 379–382, 408.

23. Foster, *Memoirs*, vol. 2, 250, 270–271; William R. Castle, "John W. Foster," in *American Secretaries of State*, vol. 8, 203; Stuart, *The Department of State*, 178, 179.

24. Arbitrations with Great Britain regarding the Bering Sea fur seal question and other disputes provided Foster with periodic employment for over a decade. Foster describes his role before the Arbitral Tribunal in Paris in his *Memoirs*, vol. 2, 20–50. Also see USDS, *Fur Seal Arbitration: Proceedings of the Tribunal of Arbitration Convened at Paris*; *Report upon the Present Condition of the Fur Seal Rookeries off the Prifilof Islands* (sometimes referred to as the *Elliot Report*) 54th Cong., 1st Sees., House Document No. 175. The historical material on the Fur Seal question is enormous, considering the relative insignificance of the dispute. The most important works include William Williams, "Reminiscences of the Bering Sea Arbitration," *American Journal of International Law*, 38 (Oct. 1943), 562–548; John Bassett Moore, *History and Digest of International Arbitrations*, vol. 1, 755–959; Moore, *Principles of American Diplomacy*, 147–154. For an analysis of the final settlement of the fur seal controversy, see Thomas A. Bailey, "The North Pacfic Seal Convention of 1911," *Pacific Historical Review*, 4 (March 1935), 1–14.

25. Arthur M. Schlesinger, Jr. ed., *History of American Presidential Elections*, 1734–1735.

26. Harrison to Whitelaw Reid, Dec. 5, 1892, in Schlesinger, ed., *History of American Presidential Elections*, 1732.

27. Foster to Gresham, Feb. 16, 1893, Gresham Papers. Foster to Harrison, Feb. 21, 1893, Harrison Papers; *New York Times*, Feb. 23, 1893. Foster resigned before Harrison left office, and Assistant Secretary of State Wharton served as interimsecretary for the final weeks of the administration. Foster left the department a week early to travel to Paris, where the fur seal case was to be presented before an international tribunal.

28. Matilda Gresham, *Walter Q. Gresham*, vol. 2, 744; George Dulebohn, *Principles of Foreign Policy under the Cleveland Administration*, 38.

29. Matilda Gresham, *Walter Q. Gresham*, vol. 2, 717, 727.

30. Dulles, *The Imperial Years*, 71–72; Montgomery Schuyster, "Walter Q. Gresham," in *American Secretaries of State*, vol. 8, 244–248.

31. Foster to Gresham, Feb. 10, 1893. Also pertaining to the New York meeting is Foster to Gresham (confidential) March 3, 1893, Gresham Papers.

32. Greville and Young, *Politics, Strategy and Foreign Policy*, 74–75, 86–87.

33. Volwiler, "Harrison-Blaine Foreign Policy," 648.
34. See A. T. Volwiler's review of Muzzey's *James G. Blaine, American Historical Review*, 41 (April, 1936), 554–557.

CHAPTER VI

1. On United States relations with Hawaii in the decades preceding the Harrison administration, see Sylvester K. Stevens, *American Expansion in Hawaii, 1842–1898*, 1–186; Merze Tate, *The United States and the Hawaiian Kingdom*. Also of value for an examination of expansionist ambitions for Hawaii is Fredrick Merk, *Manifest Destiny and Mission in American History*, 231–236.
2. Blaine to Harrison, Aug. 10, 1891, in *The Correspondence between Benjamin Harrison and James G. Blaine, 1882–1893*, 174. On October 14, 1891, Harrison wrote to Blaine, "The necessity of maintaining and increasing our hold in the Sandwich (Hawaiian) Islands is very apparent and very pressing." (p. 206.)
3. Stevens, *American Expansion in Hawaii*, 188–203; Tate, *The United States and the Hawaiian Kingdom*, 111–115; William A. Russ, "The Role of Sugar in Hawaiian Annexation," *Pacific Historical Review*, 12 (1943), 339–350; Richard D. Weigle, "Sugar and the Hawaiian Revolution," *Pacific Historical Review*, 16 (1947), 41–58.
4. Thurston to Blaine, May 27, 1892, Miscellaneous Letters, 1892, USDS Papers, National Archives; Lorrin A. Thurston, *Memoirs of the Hawaiian Revolution*, ed. by Andrew Farrell, 230–232. Also see Julius Pratt, "The 'Large Policy' of 1898," *Mississippi Valley Historical Review*, 9 (1932), 227.
5. Stevens *American Expansion in Hawaii*, 194–196; Tate, *The United States and the Hawaii Kingdom*, 149–152; Tate, *Hawaii: Reciprocity or Annexation*, 236.
6. Stevens to Foster, Sept. 9 and 14, 1892, USDS, *Foreign Relations, 1894*, app. 2, 360, 361. For C. B. Wilson's role, see Tate, *The United States and the Hawaiian Kingdom*, 113, 115, 125, 162, 169, 171, 184.
7. Stevens to Foster, Oct. 8, 1892, USDS Despatches, Hawaii, 25; Stevens to Foster, Oct. 19, 1892, USDS, *Foreign Relations, 1894*, app. 2, 362.
8. Stevens to Foster, Oct. 31, 1892, USDS *Foreign Relations, 1894*, app. 2, 374.
9. Foster to Stevens, Nov. 8, 1892, USDS, *Foreign Relations, 1894*, 376.
10. Stevens to Foster, Nov. 8, 1893, USDS, *Foreign Relations, 1894*, 376.
11. Stevens to Foster, Nov. 20, 1892, USDS, *Foreign Relations, 1894*, 188–196.
12. See Foster's *Diplomatic Memoirs*, vol. 2, 166–167.
13. See Foster's classic study, *American Diplomacy in the Orient*, 366. United States expansion in Hawaii was justified, wrote Foster, because "the native inhabitants had proved themselves incapable of maintaining a respectable and responsible government, and lacked the energy or the will to improve the advantages which Providence had given them in a fertile soil. They were fast dying out as a race, and their places were being occupied by sturdy laborers from China and Japan. There was presented to the American residents the same problem which confronted their contact with the aborigines of the Atlantic coast." (p. 385.)
14. Hopkins to Thurston, Nov. 15, 1892, in Thurston, *Memoirs*, 233.
15. Thurston to Hopkins, Dec. 14, 1892, in Thurston, *Memoirs*, 235–236.

16. Hopkins to Thurston, Dec. 29, 1892, in Thurston, *Memoirs*, 242–243.
17. For accounts of the revolution, see Tate, *The United States and the Hawaiian Kingdom*, 155–193; Stevens, *American Expansion in Hawaii*, 215–229; W. D. Alexander, *History of the Later Years of the Hawaiian Monarchy and the Revolution of 1893*, 29–71. An exhaustive study of the entire revolution can be found in William A. Russ, *The Hawaii Revolution, 1893–1894*.
18. Stevens to Foster, Jan. 18, 1893, USDS, *Foreign Relations, 1894*, app. 2, 385. Stevens later claimed in testimony before a Senate committee that "the only government was the 1,000 citizens who called the mass meeting and the presence of the ship *Boston* in the harbor. I had got information that I deemed reliable that a government springing out of that condition of things had become a *de facto* government, and by the invariable usage of the word I was bound to recognize it." 53rd Cong. 2nd Sess., Senate Report No. 227 (known as the [John Tyler] Morgan Report), 561–562. Tate believes that Stevens led the queen into a trap by leaving Honolulu on January 4 for a brief trip. In the absence of the minister, the queen took aggressive steps that brought the reaction Stevens had anticipated. Tate, *The United States and the Hawaiian Kingdom*, 129–130.
19. Stevens to Foster, Jan. 18, 1893, USDS, *Foreign Relations, 1894*, app. 2, 387–388, 388–397.
20. Stevens to Foster, Jan. 19, 1893, USDS, *Foreign Relations, 1894*, 398.
21. Foster to Stevens, Jan. 28, 1893, USDS, *Foreign Relations, 1894*, 399.
22. USDS memorandum to the president, Feb. 2, 1893, Benjamin Harrison Papers.
23. Foster to Lincoln Feb. 1, 1893, USDS Instructions, Great Britain, vol. 30.
24. Lincoln to Foster, Feb. 2, 10 and 17, 1893, USDS Despatches, Great Britain, vol. 173. Also, see Merze Tate, "Great Britain and the Sovereignty of Hawaii," *Pacific Historical Review*, 31 (1962), 337–344.
25. Lincoln to Foster, Feb. 10, 1893, USDS Despatches, Great Britain, vol. 173.
26. USDS, memo to the president, Feb. 2, 1893, Harrison Papers.
27. Stevens to Foster, Feb. 1, 1893, in USDS, *Foreign Relations, 1894*, app. 2, 399. Stevens also asked for naval reinforcements as "precautionary measures." For events in Honolulu leading to the establishment of the protectorate, see Tate, *The United States and the Hawaiian Kingdom*, 210–211.
28. Stevens sent two dispatches dated February 1, but these were probably written earlier and dated just before being placed on a steamer departing Honolulu. USDS, *Foreign Relations, 1894*, app. 2, 400–402, 404. Also see Stevens to Captain Wiltse, Feb. 1, 1893, and Provisional Government to Stevens, Jan. 31, 1893, 404, 405. On February 8, Stevens reported with great satisfaction that the "natives showed unexpected regard for the flag of the United States." Stevens to Foster, Feb. 8, 1893, 405.
29. An indication of newspaper opinion read by the administration can be found in the memorandum entitled "Opinion of the Leading Newspapers on the Hawaiian Question," Benjamin Tracy Papers. This report contained editorial comment from thirty-seven prominent papers and found opinion evenly divided without regard to party affiliation or geographic location. Among the most outspoken in opposition to the administration was the St. Louis *Republican*, which demanded the immediate recall of Stevens. For the public debate on Hawaiian annexation, see Tate, *The United States and the Hawaiian Kingdom*, 213–215; Ernest R.

May, *Imperial Democracy*, 13–17; Foster Rhea Dulles, *The Imperial Years* (New York, 1956), 68–70.

30. *New York Times*, Feb. 10, 1893.
31. *Harper's Weekly* 37 (Feb. 25, 1893), 170.
32. Foster to Stevens, Feb. 14, 1893, USDS, *Foreign Relations, 1894*, app. 2, 406–407.
33. Stevens to Foster, Feb. 27, 1893, in USDS, *Foreign Relations, 1894*, 409.
34. In testimony before a Senate committee on affairs in Hawaii, Stevens claimed that he did not understand Foster's instructions to be a renunciation or repeal of the protectorate; rather, he believed his orders were "to sustain the sovereignty of the Provisional Government—that their [the Provisional Government's] sovereignty was threatened under the circumstances." When questioned as to whether or not he had received a dispatch disavowing the protectorate, Stevens replied: "I shall object to the term disavowal; I do not admit there was a disavowal." *Sen. Rept.* 227, 53rd Cong., 2 sess. (1895), 555, 556.
35. "Protocol of the First Conference between the Hawaiian Commissioners and the Secretary of State," Feb. 4, 1893, National Archives, U.S. Department of State, Hawaii, Notes from. The protocols are listed under the date February 4, 1893. The Hawaiian special commissioners to Foster, Feb. 3, 1893, USDS, *Foreign Relations, 1894*, app. 2, 224–233. The protocols, stenographic reports of the conferences, and other pertinent documents can be found in "Negotiations of the Hawaiian Annexation Treaty of 1893," Hawaiian Historical Society, *Annual Report, 1942* (Honolulu, 1943), 6–64.
36. Protocol of the first conference, Feb. 4, 1893, USDS, Hawaii, Notes from. Liliuokalani to Benjamin Harrison, Jan. 18, 1893, USDS, *Foreign Relations, 1894*, app. 2, 219–220.
37. Protocol of the first conference, USDS, 1810, Hawaii, Notes from.
38. Stenographic report of the first conference, Hawaiian Historical Society, *Annual Report, 1942*, 22–24; Hawaiian Special Commissioners to Foster, Feb. 4, 1893, *Foreign Relations, 1894*, app. 2, 235–236.
39. Thurston to Dole, Feb. 9, 1893, Hawaiian Historical Society, *Annual Report, 1942*, 44.
40. Stenographic report of the second conference, Feb. 7, 1893, Hawaiian Historical Society, *Annual Report*, 1942, 26–27.
41. Stenographic report of the second conference, Feb. 7, 1893, *ibid.*, 27–40. Thurston recorded Foster as stating: "our main problem was to secure annexation, and that whether Hawaii should be annexed as a state or a territory was secondary." Thurston, *Memoirs*, 283. For a comprehensive study of the statehood question, see Charles H. Hunter, "Statehood and the Hawaiian Annexation Treaty of 1893," Hawaiian Historical Society, *Annual Report, 1950* (Honolulu, 1951).
42. Protocol of the third conference between the secretary of state and Lorrin Thurston, chairman of the Hawaiian Commission, Feb. 9, 1893; draft of treaty from Secretary of State Foster to Thurston at third conference, Feb. 9, in Hawaiian Historical Society, *Annual Report, 1942*, 47–49.
43. Protocol of the fourth conference between the secretary of state and Thurston, Feb. 18, 1893. USDS, Hawaii, Notes from.

44. Minutes of the meeting held Feb. 10, 1893 at Wormley's Hotel, Washington, D.C., in Hawaiian Historical Society, *Annual Report, 1942*, 50–52.
45. Protocol of the fifth conference between the secretary of state and the Hawaiian commissioners, Feb. 10, 1893 USDS, Hawaii, Notes from; report of the fifth conference, Hawaiian Historical Society, *Annual Report, 1942*, 54–58.
46. Protocol of the sixth conference, Feb. 11, 1893; protocol of the seventh conference, Feb. 14, 1893, USDS, Hawaii, Notes from; the treaty and the accompanying messages of Harrison and Foster are found in USDS, *Foreign Relations, 1894*, app. 2, 197–205.
47. *Congressional Record*, 52 Cong., 2 Sess. (1893), 1027, 1037, 1091, 1170, 1406, 1563, 1605, 2032; *New York Times*, Jan. 30, 1893.
48. "Morgan Report," Senate Report No. 227, 53rd Cong., 2nd Sess., 403–405.
49. Foster to Stevens, Feb. 22, 1893, USDS *Foreign Relations, 1894*, app. 2, 408.
50. Tate, *The United States and the Hawaiian Kingdom*, 214.
51. *Washington Post*, Feb. 10, 1893; *New York Herald*, Feb. 10, 1893.
52. Neumann to Foster, Feb. 9, 1893, Harrison Papers.
53. Stevens to Foster, Jan. 26, 1893, *Foreign Relations, 1894*, app. 2, 398–399; Stevens to Foster, Feb. 1, 1893, 402–403.
54. Neumann to Foster, Feb. 21, 1893, USDS, Hawaii, Notes from, IV.
55. Stenographic notes of an interview between the secretary of state and Paul Neumann at the Department of State, on Tuesday, Feb. 21, 1893, Harrison Papers.
56. San Francisco *Morning Call*, Feb. 24 and 25, 1893, quoted in Tate, *The United States and the Hawaiian Kingdom*, 215.
57. Foster, *Memoirs*, vol. 2, 167–168.
58. Richardson, ed., *Messages and Papers of the Presidents*, (New York: Bureau of National Literature), vol. 9, 393.
59. Gresham to Blount, March 11, 1893, enclosed Cleveland to Date and Gresham to Stevens, March 11, 1893, USDS, *Foreign Relations, 1894*, app. 2, 467–469.
60. Tate, *The United States and the Hawaiian Kingdom*, 231–232; *New York Times*, March 11, 1893.
61. Matilda Gresham, *Walter Q. Gresham*, vol. 2, 168. The letters of the Hawaiian queen to Harrison and Cleveland can be found in USDS, *Foreign Relations, 1894*, app. 2, 219–220, 1278.
62. Foster, *Memoirs*, vol. 2, 168. Senator Shelby Cullom, a powerful Republican from Illinois, believed that the hatred Gresham had for Harrison went beyond reason. Cullom remembered Gresham becoming upset at the mere mention of Harrison's name. Cullom, *Fifty Years of Public Service*, 262.
63. Blount to Gresham, April 6, 1893, in *Report of the Commissioner to the Hawaiian Islands*, 53 Cong. 2 Sess., House Executive Document No. 47 (commonly referred to as the "Blount Report").
64. Blount to Gresham, July 17, 1893, in the Blount Report, House Executive Document No. 47, 118–119, 120, 133.
65. Message of the president, Dec. 18, 1893, in USDS, *Foreign Relations, 1894*, app. 2, 445–458.
66. For a discussion of the angry reaction to Gresham's plan for Hawaii, see Tate, *The United States and the Hawaiian Kingdom*, 238–239; Donald Rowland, "The

Establishment of the Republic of Hawaii, 1893–1894," *Pacific Historical Review*, 4 (1935), 205–206. Within government circles there was considerable apprehension about Gresham's position. John Bassett Moore writing to former secretary of state Thomas Bayard stated: "Mr. Stevens' course was unprincipled, false and indefensible, but it will not be possible to make out that the leaders in the revolutionary movement were equally censurable, nor is there any reason why we should attempt to do so. . . . [It is] specially unfortunate that any ground should have been afforded to our people to suppose that the administration was fatuously pursuing a policy that looked solely to the restoration of the queen." Moore to Bayard, Dec. 13, 1893, quoted in Charles C. Tansill, *The Foreign Policy of Thomas F. Bayard, 1875–1911*, 406. Cabinet member Richard Olney tried to warn Gresham about the danger of attempting to remove the firmly established provisional government, stating: "It must be remembered that the Stevens Government is our government; that it was set up by our Minister by the aid of our naval and military forces and was accorded the protection of our flag; and that whatever be the views of this administration, its predecessor practically sanctioned everything Minister Stevens took upon himself to do." Olney to Gresham, Oct. 9, 1893, in Henry James, *Richard Olney*, 215.

67. Gresham to Willis, Oct. 18, 1893, USDS, *Foreign Relations, 1894*, app. 2, 1191.
68. Dole to Willis, Dec. 23, 1893, USDS, *Foreign Relations, 1894*, app. 2, 1274; Willis to Gresham, Dec. 23, 1893, 1275–1282.
69. For a history of these events, see Donald Rowland, "The Establishment of the Republic of Hawaii, 1893–1894," *Pacific Historical Review*, 4 (1935), 201–220; Russ, *The Hawaiian Republic*, 1–48.
70. Foster, *Memoirs*, vol. 2, 169–170; Russ, *The Hawaiian Republic*, 109–110, 270–272. Probably with some justification Liliuokalani viewed Foster's trip to Honolulu as an agent for the cable company to be merely a cover for annexationist activities. Liliuokalani, *Hawaii's Story*, 330.
71. In an address delivered in March 1897 before the National Geographic Society in Washington, D.C., Foster sought to justify American expansion in Hawaii by stating, "We have a strong equitable claim to the islands. The people of the United States contributed millions of dollars to bring the inhabitants out of [a] wretched state of barbarism and servitude and secure them a place among the civilized peoples of the earth. Americans gave them a written language, taught their kings the principles of government, for a century and a half were the real administrators of public affairs, . . ." *The Annexation of Hawaii: an Address Delivered before the National Geographic Society, March 26, 1897* (Washington, D. C., 1897), 15. This pamphlet was printed as Senate Document 23, 55th Cong., 1st Sess.
72. Foster, *Memoirs*, vol. 2, 272–274; Foster to Robert R. Hitt, June 19, 1898, R. R. Hitt Papers. Congressman Hitt, the chairman of the House Committee on Foreign Affairs, was a close personal friend of Foster; they had been classmates at Indiana University. Also see, Tate, *The United States and the Hawaiian Kingdom*, 270; H. Wayne Morgan, *William McKinley and His America*, 294.
73. John Bassett Moore recorded a conversation with Gresham on May 5, 1894, in which the secretary of state claimed he would have carried out the policy of the Harrison administration in Hawaii had not Minister Willis complicated matters

by upsetting the members of the provisional government. Gresham said he wanted to appoint someone other than Willis to Hawaii. If the members of the provisional government had not been led by Willis to believe that the United States was hostile to them, Gresham suggested to Moore, matters might have proceeded smoothly toward eventual annexation. Memorandum of conversation with Gresham, May 5, 1894, in "Diary," May 9, 1894, John Bassett Moore Papers.

CHAPTER VII

1. For a documentary history of the events leading to the war, see Vladimir (Zerone Volpicelli), *The China-Japan War* (London, 1896), 1–86. Also see Immanuel C. Y. Hsü, *The Rise of Modern China* (London, 1970), Harold M. Vinacke, *A History of the Far East in Modern Times*, 6th ed., 130–136.
2. Charles Denby to Walter Q. Gresham, July 9, 1894; Gresham to Goschen, Oct. 12, 1894, USDS, *Foreign Relations, 1894*, app. 1, 30, 70, 76, 82. Payson Treat, "The Good Offices of the United States during the Sino-Japanese War," *Political Science Quarterly* 47 (1932), 547–563; Jeffery Dorwart, *The Pigtail War: American Involvement in the Sino-Japanese War, 1894–95*, 73–82. Also of interest is the description of American policy during this period presented by Foster in *American Diplomacy in the Orient*, 332–339.
3. Gresham to Denby and Dun, Nov. 6, 1894, USDS, *Foreign Relations, 1894*, app. 1, 76.
4. Tsungli Yamen to Denby, Nov. 3, 1894, USDS, *Foreign Relations, 1894*, 75. Korea was at this point already independent of Chinese control. For the text of the Korean treaty with Japan that was signed on July 25, 1894, see USDS, *Foreign Relations, 1894*, 93–94.
5. Denby to Gresham, Nov. 10, 1894, USDS, *Foreign Relations, 1894*, 76. The U.S. minister to Japan predicted that the government in Tokyo would "drive a hard bargain," Dun to Gresham, Nov. 6, 1894, 79.
6. Quoted in Schyler, "Walter Q. Gresham," in *American Secretaries of State and Their Diplomacy*, vol. 8, 265. Also see Matilda Gresham, *Walter Q. Gresham*, 788, 789, 334.
7. *Foreign Relations*, app. 1, 80 ff.; Charles Denby *China and Her People*, vol. 2, 130–138; Treat "Good Offices of the United States," 564–569; Roy A. Hidemichi, *Japan's Foreign Relations, 1542–1936*, 149–153.
8. Marilyn B. Young, *The Rhetoric of Empire*, 35, 56–57. For a biographical sketch of Wilson, see David Healy, *U.S. Expansionism*, 68–95.
9. Wilson to W. D. Smith (confidential), Sept. 23, 1894, Wilson Papers. Healy, *U.S. Expansionism*, 182–183. Richard Van Alstyne, *The United States and East Asia*, 65–66, 68.
10. Pethick to Wilson, Aug. 31, 1894, Wilson Papers.
11. The correspondence between Wilson and Pethick during the years 1885–1895 is in the Wilson Papers, vol. 18. According to Foster, Pethick journeyed to China following military service in the Civil War and mastered the Chinese language as well as any foreigner. Also fluent in French and German, the American

adventurer found employment as the private secretary for Li Hung-chang, and he assisted the Chinese viceroy in conducting foreign affairs. Regarding Pethick's position Foster stated: "His influence upon that statesman [Li Hung-chang] and upon Chinese politics was very decided, and always in the direction of liberal ideas and progress." Foster, *American Diplomacy in the Orient*, 296; Foster, "The Great Chinese Viceroy and Diplomat," *International Quarterly*, 2 (Nov. 1900), 589.

12. Pethick to Wilson (Sept. 1894), Wilson Papers.
13. "Man in the Moon" (Pethick) to Wilson, September 20(?), 1894, Wilson Papers.
14. Pethick to Wilson, Sept. 28, 1894, Wilson Papers.
15. Pethick to Wilson, Oct. 6, 16, 1894, Wilson Papers. Pethick devised a secret code in order to continue his correspondence with Wilson after returning to China.
16. Foster also informed Denby that he was urging the Chinese to seek a loan from U.S. bankers, advising his clients that U.S. bankers, unlike their European counterparts, were independent of government and were therefore not inclined to threaten Chinese autonomy. Foster to Denby, Sept. 28, 1894, in Wilson Papers; also see Young, *Rhetoric of Empire*, 40, 241.
17. Denby to Foster, Nov. 13, 1894, quoted in Foster, *Memoirs*, vol. 2, 106.
18. Sir Robert Hart of Great Britain met with Foster and recorded "The American ex-sec. Foster and a party are here, and we are to have a week's feasting." Hart, *The I. G. in Peking: Letters of Robert Hart, Chinese Maritime Customs, 1868–1907*, vol. 2, 923. Foster, *Memoirs*, vol. 2, 90–101, 102.
19. Foster, *Memoirs*, vol. 2, 102; Senate Executive Document No. 24, 53rd Cong., 3rd Sess. Matilda Gresham, *Walter Gresham*, vol. 2, 788. In spite of their long friendship, Foster did not consider Gresham a capable secretary of state because he lacked experience in foreign affairs and was overly sensitive to public criticism. Foster frequently met with the secretary of state on matters of official business and stated that "our old time friendship was renewed, but it was not resumed with the unrestrained cordiality of former days. There was an explicable something in his new environment which seemed to chill our intercourse." Foster, *Memoirs*, vol. 2, 273.
20. Gresham to Bayard, Dec. 24, 1894, Gresham Papers.
21. *New York Times*, Dec. 28, 1894. When word of the mission was made public, speculation arose that Foster would be arranging a loan for the Chinese government. In response to rumors, Foster made a statement of doubtful veracity, denying that he had any personal interest in such loan. *New York Times*, Dec. 28, 29, 30, 1894.
22. Foster to Parke (Mrs. J. W. Foster), Jan. 22, 1895. John Foster Dulles Papers.
23. Foster to Parke, Dec. 29, 1874, Jan. 13, 1875, J. F. Dulles Papers. Foster held Chang in very high regard, viewing him as one of the leading modernizers in China. A pleasant and openly friendly man, Chang was famous in Washington for giving elaborate parties at the Chinese legation on DuPont Circle. Chang worked closely with Foster on the Rock Springs, Colorado indemnity case and the question of Chinese exclusion. In 1898 Chang was involved in the "100 Days" reform movement and fell into disfavor with court conservatives and the empress dowager. Exiled to Mongolia, Chang was beheaded as a traitor during the anti-foreign hysteria of the Boxer Rebellion in 1900. See Foster, *American Diplomacy*

in the Orient, 339; A. W. Hummel, ed., *Eminent Chinese of the Ching Period*, vol. 1, 62–63. Earl Swisher, "Chinese Representation in the United States," *University of Colorado Studies Series in History* 5 (Jan. 1967), 21–24.

24. Foster to Parke, Jan. 22, 1894, J. F. Dulles Papers.

25. Foster, *Memoirs*, vol. 2, 110–114. Hosea B. Morse, *The International Relations of the Chinese Empire* (London, Longmans, Green and Co., 1918), vol. 3, 40.

26. Foster informed the Chinese commissioners of the matter of the improper credentials upon first meeting with Shao and Chang, and the American was not surprised when the Japanese refused to accept the commissioner's letters of credence. Foster, "Diary, 1895," handwritten manuscript in J. F. Dulles Papers. Foster to Parke, Feb. 3, 1895, J. F. Dulles Papers. Denby to Gresham, Dec. 1, 8, 20, 1894 and (telegram) Feb. 4, 1895, National Archives, USDS Despatches, China, vol. 98; Denby, *China and Her People*, vol. 2, 134–319. Also see Dun to Gresham, Feb. 4, 15, 1895 in USDS, *Foreign Relations, 1894*, app. 1, 97–103.

27. Foster to Parke, Feb. 17, 1895, J. F. Dulles Papers. Foster believed that every day the Chinese delayed would make the Japanese terms more harsh. Yet, he felt the continued Chinese defeats might have some good results; at one point he wrote "it will be unfortunate if peace is made before Peking is taken, as the mass of the Chinese, including the rulers have not yet been made to see the helplessness and the inefficiency and worthlessness of the government—so I suppose I ought to curb my impatience and let things drift along. But I feel it my duty to do the best I can for my client and can hardly help chafing under the delay." Foster to Parke, Feb. 21, 1895, J. F. Dulles Papers.

28. J. W. Foster to Parke, March 10, 1895, Foster, "Diary, 1895," John F. Dulles Papers.

29. Pethick to Wilson, Jan. 7, 1895, Wilson Papers. Denby had not been entirely neglectful of American business interests in China during this period. He informed Secretary of State Gresham that China would be in great debt at the war's end, and because of China's reluctance to take out loans with foreigners, Denby speculated that the Chinese might instead be willing to sell concessions to various syndicates. Denby concluded, "The present purpose is simply to suggest to American capitalists, railroad men, ship builders, bankers, and merchants to consider the desirability of securing for themselves the great franchises to which I have alluded." Denby asked the secretary of state to be "active" in this matter. Denby to Gresham, Dec. 28, 1894, USDS Despatches, China, vol. 98.

30. Foster to Parke, March 17, 1895, J. F. Dulles Papers; *History of the Peace Negotiations, Documentary and Verbal, between China and Japan, March–April, 1895* (Tientsin, China, 1895), frontispiece, 3; Denby to Gresham, March 15, 1895, *Foreign Relations, 1894*; app. 1, 166; Morse, *International Relations of the Chinese Empire*, vol. 3, 42–43.

31. Pethick to Wilson (private), March 13, 1895, Wilson Papers.

32. Foster, "Diary, 1895"; *History of the Peace Negotiations*, 2–4. All the discussions and written communications at Shimonoseki were in English. The editors of the *History of the Peace Negotiations* claimed, "English seems to have been the clear medium in which both Plenipotentiaries found relief from the vagueness and ambiguity of their languages." (pp. 1–ii.) As Li did not speak English, Foster drafted all his documents. Handwritten drafts of the proposals and counterdrafts

and Foster's diary of the proceedings at Shimonoseki are preserved along with Foster's letters to his wife in the J. F. Dulles Papers. Foster's *Memoirs*, based on his diary and the official notes of the conferences, are also a generally reliable source for the chronology and history of the peace negotiations, in spite of the emphasis Foster placed on his own role.

33. Foster, "Diary, 1895"; Li appeared to be following advice given by Denby. Before the viceroy departed for Shimonoseki, the American minister told Li he should "reason with Japan that if she crippled China her trade and commerce would suffer; that he would use all the arguments drawn from geographical situation, national analogies and commercial interests to induce Japan not to diminish China; and he should strenuously endeavor to save from cession any of the mainland." Denby to Gresham, March 5, 1895. USDS Despatches, China, vol. 98.

34. Foster, "Diary, 1895"; *History of the Peace Negotiations*, 3–4, 9–11.

35. Dun to Gresham, Feb. 5, 1895, *Foreign Relations, 1894*, app. 1, 99; *History of the Peace Negotiations*, 2, 3, 6, 10; Foster, *Memoirs*, vol. 2, 130–131.

36. Foster to Peking government (telegram), March 24, 1895. The message stated in part: "Wound serious but not fatal. Viceroy shows great fortitude, converses freely with clear mind and insists on attending to public business." *History of the Peace Negotiations*, 4; Foster, "Diary, 1895", Foster to Parke, March 25, 1895, J. F. Dulles Papers.

37. Foster, "Diary, 1895"; *History of the Peace Negotiations*, 5–6. Li's assailant was an unemployed laborer and political fanatic who believed Li was responsible for the war. The would-be assassin was tried within a week of the shooting and was sentenced to life imprisonment.

38. Memorandum from Viscount Matsu, March 28, 1895, *History of the Peace Negotiations*, 9. On March 30 the armistice was extended for a period of twenty-one days. The Convention of Armistice, March 30, 1895 is in *History of the Peace Negotiations*, 9–10.

39. Foster, (Diary, 1895) and *Memoirs*, vol. 2 134.

40. Foster, *Memoirs*, vol.2, 137–138. According to Pethick, Foster drafted all documents for the Chinese plenipotentiary, including the detailed reply to Japan's proposals. Pethick wrote that Foster's report "had an excellent effect upon the Japs. . . (and helped) to reduce their demands." Pethick to Wilson, Sept. 17, 1895, Wilson Papers.

41. *History of the Peace Negotiations*, 11–14, 16–21. At this point Li Ching-fong had been appointed plenipotentiary to act in place of his father at negotiating sessions. (p. 6).

42. *History of the Peace Negotiations*, 13, 21–24.

43. *History of the Peace Negotiations*, 14–15, 24–25. Foster, "Diary, 1895."

44. *History of the Peace Negotiations*, 17–29; Foster, "Diary, 1895," 17–29. The treaty of Shimonoseki provided for the following; (1) recognition by China of Korean independence; (2) an indemnity of 200 million taels; (3) cessation of Formosa, the Pescadores, and the Liaotung peninsula to Japan; (4) the opening of Chungking, Soochow, Hangchow, and Sha-shih as treaty ports; and (5) the right of Japanese citizens to open factories and engage in manufacturing in China. In effect, the treaty gave the Japanese rights in China equal to those granted to Western powers (by the most-favored-nation clause) in addition to

sizable territorial gains. (One tael = one ounce of silver. Since a tael is not a minted coin its value in foreign trade varies with the price of silver, perhaps about 50 cents per ounce in 1900.)

45. For an evaluation of the treaty's effects on China and the political situation in the Far East, see Hsu, *The Rise of Modern China*, 410–411; Vinache, *History of the Far East in Modern Times*, 142–144, 146–165.

46. Foster to Parke, April 16, 1895, J. F. Dulles Papers. Foster, *Memoirs*, vol. 2, 138–139, 153; Foster, "Marquis Ito: The Japanese Statesman," *International Quarterly* 9 (June 1904), 270.

47. Denby believed Li was actively seeking assurances of foreign intervention before leaving for the negotiations in Japan. Denby to Gresham, Feb. 26, 1894. USDS, *Foreign Relations, 1894*, pp. 1, 152–153; Morese, *International Relations of the Chinese Empire*, vol. 3, 47; William Langer, *The Diplomacy of Imperialism, 1890–1902*, 179.

48. A. Yarmolinski, ed., *Memoirs of Count Witte*, 83. Morse, *International Relations of the Chinese Empire*, vol. 3, 47; Hidemichi, *Japan's Foreign Relations*, 161–163; Edward Zabriskie, *American-Russian Rivalry in the Far East, 1895–1914*, 27–29.

49. Foster, *Memoirs*, vol. 2, 152–153; Langer, *Diplomacy of Imperialism*, 84.

50. Foster, "Diary, 1895." Pethick to Wilson, Sept. 17, 1895, Wilson Papers. Li was afraid that going to Peking with the treaty might give his enemies in the government an opportunity to demand his execution. Foster believed that Li's fears about going to Peking were justified; see Foster, "Great Chinese Viceroy," 591; Foster, *Memoirs*, vol. 2, 147–150.

51. Foster, "Diary, 1895" and *Memoirs*, vol. 2, 151–152. For the Japanese response to the triple intervention, see Morinosuke Kajima, *The Diplomacy of Japan, 1894–1922*, vol. 1, 15–36.

52. Morse, *International Relations of the Chinses Empire*, vol. 3, 5. Hsü, *Rise of Modern China*, 408.

53. Foster, "Diary, 1895", and *Memoirs*, vol. 2, 154–160.

54. Foster to Park, March 31, 1895, J. F. Dulles Papers. Also see *Memoirs*, vol 2, 156. Foster's fees for his six-month period of service totaled $60,000 plus expenses. Foster to Parke, April 20, 21, 1895.

55. Foster considered Li a great patriot more concerned with the future of China than with his own life and fortune. Foster to Wilson, Jan. 12, 1908, Wilson Papers. Regarding China's political state following the Sino-Japanese War, Foster wrote: "China was shown to be a great helpless giant, having no competent rulers or leaders." "China", *National Geographic* 15 (Dec. 1904), 467.

56. Pethick to Wilson, Sept. 17, 1895, Wilson Papers. Rival American syndicates appeared in China at the war's end and appeared to have better financial backing than Wilson. Foster to Wilson, April 23, 1895, Wilson Papers. For a detailed study of the various speculators and investment schemes, see Young, *Rhetoric of Empire*, 56–73.

57. Hsu, *Rise of Modern China*, 413–415. Zabriskie, *American-Russian Rivalry*, 30–31.

58. Brice, a U.S. senator and corporate lawyer, headed a syndicate that competed with Wilson's. Foster gave some assistance to the Brice group, in the hope that they would open further opportunities for American investors. Still, Foster

warned the Brice people to be serious and even-handed in their negotiations with the Chinese. Foster to Wilson, Aug. 9, Sept. 21, 1896, Wilson Papers. Also see Young, *Rhetoric of Empire*, 249; Van Alstyne, *The United States and East Asia*, 72, 74. C. S. Campbell, *Special Business Interests and the Open Door Policy*, 21–23.

59. Young, *Rhetoric of Empire*, 15, 52–53; McCormick, *China Market*, 70–71.

60. Burnham, Williams, and Co. to Wilson, March 6, 1896, and attached letter of Burnham, Williams, and Co. to Denby, March 6, 1898, Wilson Papers. Denby appeared ready to quit the Foreign Service at this time to work for American railroad builders.

61. Foster, *Memoirs*, vol. 2, 298–299, 309–312; *New York Times*, Feb. 24, 1896; Denby to Olney, April 6, May 25, 1896, USDS, Despatches, China, vol. 101; Van Alstyne, *The United States and East Asia*, 73–74; Young, *Rhetoric of Empire*.

62. For accounts that belittle Foster's role at Shimonoseki see Young, *Rhetoric of Empire*, 32–33; McCormick, *China Market*, 58, 67–68. Young views Foster's presence at the negotiations as insignificant and credits Li Hung-chang's clever phrases and pathetic begging with softening the Japanese position. McCormick argues that Foster's only mission in China was to act as a front man for American bankers.

63. Foster's *American Diplomacy in the Orient* remained the standard treatment of the subject until the publication twenty years later of Tyler Dennett's classic *Americans in Eastern Asia*. Foster's views on Asian affairs are also forcefully presented in "China," *National Geographic*, 15 (Dec. 1904), 463–478; "The Chinese Boycott," *Atlantic Monthly*, 97 (Jan. 1906), 118–127; "Questions of the Far East," *Atlantic Monthly*, 97 (April 1906), 542–546; "Present Conditions in China," *National Geographic*, 17 (Dec. 1906), 651–672, 709–711.

64. Foster to Wilson, April 11, 1904, Wilson Papers. Also see Foster to Wilson, April 8 and June 25, 1904.

65. See chapter 8.

66. Foster to Wilson, Jan. 10, 1916, Wilson Papers. The similarities in views held by Foster and Lansing are analyzed in Daniel Smith, *Robert Lansing and American Neutrality, 1914–1917*, 179, and Burton F. Beers, *Vain Endeavor: Robert Lansing's Attempts to End the American-Japanese Rivalry*, 28.

67. John F. Fairbank, *The United States and China*, 401–403.

CHAPTER VIII

1. This remark is attributed to Chauncey Depew by Foster's biographer, William R. Castle, in "John W. Foster," *American Secretaries of State and Their Diplomacy*, vol. 8, 223.

2. Events surrounding Foster's appointment to act as the agent for the United States government are discussed in chapter 4. While serving as Secretary of State, Foster worked with the staff preparing the fur seal case. Castle, "John W. Foster," 193–202.

3. William Williams, "Reminiscences of the Bering Sea Arbitration," *American Journal of International Law*, 37 (Oct. 1943), 562–584.

4. Foster, *Memoirs*, vol. 2, 40–41. Callahan, *Policy in Canadian Relations*, 477. The Petroff affair, while detected in time to avoid the appearance of fraud on the part of the United States, did weaken Foster's confidence regarding the chances for success. Foster to Henry White (personal), Nov. 10, 1892, White Papers.

5. Gresham to Foster, July 14, 1893, Foster Papers; Foster to Gresham, July 27, 1893, National Archives, USDS, Bering Sea Despatches.

6. Malloy, ed., *Treaties*, vol. 1, 753. Callahan, *Policy in Canadian Relations*, 488–489. Foster's critics claimed that his concern for the welfare of the fur seal herds was a result of his association with the North American Commercial Company, which was engaged in the seal industry and resented Canadian competition. There is no evidence, however, that Foster was in the company's pay at the time the tribunal was hearing the case. For harsh criticism of Foster's management of the ful seal case, see Matilda Gresham, *Walter Q. Gresham*, vol. 2, 728–730. For a more judicious evalutaion, see Charles S. Campbell, *Anglo-American Understanding, 1898–1903*, 83–84.

7. Lansing to E. J. Phelps, Oct. 12, 1893, Gresham Papers. Foster left Paris for a world tour upon the completion of the negotiations in Paris. Before departing he wrote to Henry White at the legation in London, stating, "[my journey will be] purely of a personal character and devoid of all political significance; but I want to keep my eyes and ears open. . . . And I have thought that if I was in an informal manner put in contact with the British officials, for instance at Cairo, Bombay, Calcutta, Ceylon and Hong Kong, it would be profitable for me." White Papers.

8. Gresham to Foster, Oct. 9, 1893, Foster Papers.

9. For an analysis of United States–Canadian relations during the Cleveland administration, see Callahan, *Policy in Canadian Relations*, 449–451, 455–457. Tansill, *United States and Canada*, 341–352.

10. John A. S. Grenville, *Lord Salisbury and Foreign Policy: The Close of the Nineteenth Century*, 370–371.

11. Cridler (3rd Assistant Secretary of State) to C. S. Hamlin, June 28, 1897, National Archives, USDS Special Missions, vol. 4.

12. "Handed to Mr. Sherman by General Foster and by the Secretary of State shown to the President", April 20, 1897, USDS Special Agents, vol. 48.

13. Sherman to Foster, July 30, 1897, USDS Special Agents, vol. 48: Sherman to Hay, May 10, 1897, USDS, *Foreign Relations, 1897*, 280–290.

14. Foster to Sherman, June 16, 1897, USDS Special Agents, vol. 48. The social details of Foster's trip to St. Petersburg and London are recorded in Foster, *Memoirs*, vol. 1, 216–238.

15. "England and the Fur Seals," New York *Tribune* (July 14, 1897); John Hay felt Foster was undiplomatically blunt in his dealings with the British and in the note of May 10. Hay to Sherman, July 16, 1897, USDS Despatches, Great Britain; Hay to McKinley, July 16, 1879, McKinley Papers. Kelton Klymer, *John Hay: The Gentleman as Diplomat* 108–112.

16. Protocols of the conference, USDS Special Agents, vol. 48; Hay to Foster, Oct. 18, (confidential) Nov. 20, 1897, Foster Papers; Sherman to Hay, Nov. 28, 1897, USDS Instructions, Great Britain, vol. 32.

17. Sherman to Laurier, Nov. 12, 1897, Great Britain, Notes to, vol. 24; protocol of

the conference at Washington, May, 1898, in Malloy, ed., *Treaties*, vol. 1, 770–783. Also see Callahan, *Policy in Canadian Relations*, 457–458. Working with Foster at these sessions was John A. Kasson, a former minister to Germany and an expert on reciprocity. For a discussion of Kasson's role, see Edward Younger, *John A. Kasson: Politics from Lincoln to McKinley*, 371 ff.

18. Foster was extremely upset about the delays in the proceedings, realizing the importance of putting a treaty before the senate well in advance of March 4, 1899, when the composition of that body would change. Foster to Charles Fairbanks, Oct. 21, 1898, Fairbanks Papers. The best account of these lengthy proceedings is C. S. Campbell, *Anglo-American Understanding*, 88–137. Also see Grenville, *Lord Salisbury*, 272–273; Bradford Perkins, *The Great Rapprochement: England and the United States, 1895–1914*, 163–164.

19. Hay to Choate, April 19, 1899, USDS Instructions, Great Britain, vol. 33. For a detailed study of the long history of the border problem, see Tansill, *American-Canadian Relations*, 121–165. Also of interest on this matter is Foster's analysis of the border situation, presented in "The Alaskan Boundary," *National Geographic*, 10 (Nov. 1899), 425–456.

20. USDS *Foreign Relations, 1899*, 328–331, Malloy, ed., *Treaties*, vol. 1 787–792. Foster gave both Hay and Roosevelt great credit for submitting the Alaskan boundary question to international arbitration. Foster, *Memoirs*, vol. 2, 192.

21. W. R. Thayer, *The Life and Letters of John Hay*, vol. 2, 212. Foster expressed optimism about the chances for arbitration in "The Prospects for Arbitration with England," *Independent* (Dec. 24, 1903), 3025. He also expressed optimism about the chances for arbitration and praised the efforts of Hay and Roosevelt in a letter to the editors of the Washington *Post*. Hay was so delighted with Foster's letter that the secretary of state had it printed as a government document and distributed to each member of Congress. Foster, *Memoirs*, vol. 2, 194–195; Washington *Post* (Feb. 24, 1903); Senate Document No. 136, 57th Cong., 2nd Sess.

22. Foster to Choate, April 3, 1903, Choate Papers; Hay to Foster, July 2, August 5, 1903, Foster Papers, Foster to Wilson, August 21, 1903, Wilson Papers. Foster, *The Alaskan Boundary Tribunal*, 10–11.

23. The best analysis of the terms of the award is Foster's *Alaskan Boundary Tribunal*, 8–9; for the political side, Charles S. Campbell, *Anglo-American Understanding*, 311–318, 319–345; Thomas A. Bailey, "Theodore Roosevelt and the Alaskan Boundary Settlement", *Canadian Historical Review*, 18 (June 1937), 123–130.

24. Foster never intended his tough style to be taken personally by his diplomatic counterparts, and he was hurt when it was reported that he refused to visit British and Canadian diplomats to say goodbye at the conclusion of negotiations in 1899. Actually, Foster was ill and had asked his friend and colleague, Charles Fairbanks of Indiana, to extend his apologies. Foster to Fairbanks, Feb. 28, 1899, Fairbanks Papers. Foster was aware that his style of argumentation upset the British and Canadian commissioners, but he did not feel compelled to change his ways. Apparently, he believed the other side should accommodate themselves to the American approach. Foster, *Alaskan Boundary Tribunal*, 12; Foster, *Memoirs*, vol. 2, 201. Also see Campbell, *Anglo-American Understanding*, 83.

25. Hay to Roosevelt, July 2, 1903, quoted in Tyler Dennett, *John Hay: From Poetry to Politics*, 359.
26. Henry Cabot Lodge to Henry White, Nov. 19, 1897, in Allen Nevins, *Henry White: Thirty Years of American Diplomacy*, 187: Henry Adams to Elizabeth Cameron, Jan. 29, 1899, *Letters of Henry Adams*, vol. 2, 209; Hay to Foster (personal), Aug. 5, 1903, Foster Papers.
27. See chapters 4 and 5. Also see Foster's views expressed in *Memoirs*, vol. 2, 176-177.
28. C. S. Campbell, *Anglo-American Understanding*, 347.
29. *Alaskan Boundary Tribunal*, 14; Foster, *Memoirs*, vol. 2, 209.
30. Foster to Wilson, Jan. 3, 1898, Wilson Papers; Foster, *Memoirs*, vol. 2, 255-256.
31. Foster's candid views on John Sherman and William R. Day are present in Foster's, *Memoirs*, vol. 2, 275-276.
32. Louis M. Sears, "John Sherman," in *American Secretaries of State and Their Diplomacy*, vol. 9, 13, 19; in the same volume, see Lester B. Shippee and Royal B. Way, "William R. Day", 33-34.
33. See chapter VI.
34. Foster wrote that his association with Hay was "more intimate and prolonged than with any other of the secretaries of state." Foster, *Memoirs*, vol. 2, 279.
35. Hay to Foster, Oct. 3, 1898, Foster Papers.
36. Most important, see Hay to Foster, July 7, Sept. 26, 1899, April 17, Dec. 18, 1902, Foster Papers.
37. Foster confided to a personal friend that he had been advising Hay on Far Eastern affairs for a considerable period of time. Foster to Wilson, May 16, 1903, Wilson Papers. Regarding the U.S. involvement in the expeditionary force that put down the Boxer Rebellion, Foster wrote: "nothing should be done to cripple or impede the ability of China in the maintenance of a stable government and its territorial integrity. Hence it was necessary to continue in the concert of the powers and as far as possible control their action to that end." *American Diplomacy in the Orient*, 432.
38. Hay to Foster, June 23, 1900, Foster Papers; Dennett, *John Hay*, 233-234.
39. Hay to Foster (private), Oct. 30, 1900, Foster Papers.
40. Delber McKee, *Chinese Exclusion Versus the Open Door Policy, 1900-1906*, 59-61. Foster's work for the Chinese legation in the exclusion struggle is described in Wu T'ing-fang, *America Through the Spectacles of a Chinese Diplomat*, 48-50.
41. Quoted in McKee, *Chinese Exclusion*, 61.
42. *Chinese Exclusion: Testimony Taken Before the Committee on Immigration*, U.S. Senate, 57th Con., 1st Sess, Report No. 776 (1902), 33. Foster expanded his views on exclusion in later testimony by stating; "I recognize the wisdom of a limited exclusion of Chinese laborers to the United States. I accent the word 'laborers' because all the negotiations—the efforts—were devoted to the exclusion of laborers, and other Chinese were guaranteed free admission. My criticism of the law is that it does not have that effect. It excludes the laborers, and it practically excludes all others—students and merchants." (p. 67.)
43. *Chinese Exclusion*, Senate Report No. 776, p. 36.
44. Wu to Hay, April 29, 1902, USDS, *Foreign Relations, 1902*, 213-214; Hay to

Wu, April 30, 1902, USDS Notes to the Chinese Legation.
45. Quoted in McKee, *Chinese Exclusion*, 61.
46. Beal, *John Foster Dulles*, 200–201.
47. Foster, *Memoirs*, vol. 2, 299–301; Ingraham to Foster, May 27, 1905. T. Roosevelt Papers, "The China Development Company and the Open Door," *Journal of the American Asiatic Association* 5 (Aug. 1905), 198. W. K. Braisted, "The United States and the American China Development Company", *Far Eastern Quarterly* 11 (Feb. 1952), 159.
48. Beal, *John Foster Dulles*, 208–211. Foster observed that in working as legal counsel for foreign legations, he always advised against confrontations with the Department of State. *Memoirs*, vol. 2, 300.
49. Eleanor Lansing Dulles, *John Foster Dulles: The Last Year*, 61–62. Eleanor Lansing Dulles, a granddaughter of John Foster, described the Foster residence on Eighteenth Street in Washington as very grand, with reception rooms the size of ballrooms and filled with artifacts collected from around the world. Life in Washington was eventful, and on numerous special occasions Mrs. Mary Parke Foster would "preside like a duchess over the tea-table at five o'clock, as Senators, Justices, ambassadors and State Department officials came in early, with plenty of time for a relaxed hour of conversation before dinner." (p. 62.)
50. At the tender age of eight, Allen Dulles wrote a brief history of the Boer war that so impressed his grandfather that the old man had it published for private circulation. The former secretary of state also wrote a foreword in which he expressed his pleasure with young Allen's independence of thought, calling him "an ardent admirer of the Boers, and this in spite of the fact that all his immediate family favor the British cause." *The Boer War: A History* (copy in the Library of Congress). Also see Louis L. Gerson, "John Foster Dulles," in *American Secretaries of State and Their Diplomacy*, vol. 17, 334; R. D. Challener and John Fenton, "Which Way America? Dulles Always Knew," *American Heritage* 22 (June 1971), 84–85; John R. Beal, *John Foster Dulles*, 28.
51. Foster, *Memoirs*, vol. 2, 212. Eleanor Lansing Dulles, *John Foster Dulles*, 128.
52. Eleanor Lansing Dulles, *John Foster Dulles*, 128.
53. Quoted in Gerson, "John Foster Dulles," in *American Secretaries of State*, vol. 18, 10; Beal, *John Foster Dulles*, 55. In his letter Foster referred to Algernon Sullivan of Cincinnati, Ohio. Foster was associated briefly with Sullivan after the Civil War. Young Dulles began working with Sullivan and Cromwell for fifty dollars per month in 1911 and worked his way up to become head of the firm in 1927. Challener and Fenton, "Dulles Always Knew," 85–86.
54. Foster to John Foster Dulles, Aug. 22, 1913 and (personal) April 2, 1915. John Foster Dulles Papers.
55. Foster to John Foster Dulles, Aug. 20, 1911, John Foster Dulles Papers.
56. Foster to John Foster Dulles, Aug. 9, 1914, John Foster Dulles Papers.
57. Daniel Smith, *Robert Lansing and American Neutrality, 1914–1917*, 179; Julius Pratt, "Robert Lansing," in *American Secretaries of State and Their Diplomacy*, vol. 10, 47–48. "The Appointment of Mr. Robert Lansing of New York as Counselor in the Department of State," *American Journal of International Law*, 8 (April 1914), 336–337.

58. Phillip Jessup, *Elihu Root*, vol. 2, 320. Junior staff people in the State Department were impressed with Lansing's schooling and hoped that his appointment would mean that the president would give greater attention to foreign policy. Joseph Grew to T. Sergent Perry, April 6, 1914, in Grew, *Turbulent Era: A Diplomatic Record of Forty Years, 1904–1945*, 120–212. Also see Josephus Daniels, *The Wilson Era: Years of Peace, 1910–1917* (Chapel Hill; University of North Carolina Press, 1946), 437–439.

59. Upon Lansing's appointment Edith Bolling Wilson recorded the president as saying: "He is a counselor in the State Department and has had good schooling under old Mr. John W. Foster, his father-in-law, for whom I have great respect. I think he would steer Lansing, and the combination would be of great help to me," Wilson, *My Memoir* (Indianapolis; Bobbs-Merrill, 1939), 64. Also see Stuart, *The Department of State*, 238. There was also public speculation that Foster would play an important behind-the-scenes role, once Lansing became secretary of state. Vieillard, "Custos Custodis," *Nation* 100 (June 17, 1915), 680.

60. Foster to Bert (Robert Lansing), Sept. 4, 1914, Lansing Papers.

61. Foster to Lansing, Sept. 3 and Sept. 16, 1916, Lansing Papers. Also see Burton F. Beers, *Vain Endeavor: Robert Lansing's Attempts to End the American-Japanese Rivalry*, 28.

62. Foster to John Foster Dulles (personal), Feb. 16, 1917, Lansing Papers.

63. Lansing to Dulles, Jan. 29, 1913, Dulles to Lansing, Jan. 3 and Lansing to Dulles, Feb. 1, 1913, J. F. Dulles Papers.

64. For an entertaining account of the fledgling careers of the young Dulleses, see Leonard Mosley, *Dulles: A Biography of Eleanor, Allen, and John Foster Dulles and Their Family Network*, 44–62.

65. In his final letter to James Harrison Wilson, Foster stated; "I am not well enough to write you my views on the war situation. Though a Pacifist after a fashion, I am so bitter with Germany I rather hope we will get into the scrimmage." Foster to Wilson, Feb. 9, 1917, Wilson Papers. Foster to Iglehart, April 9, 1917, Willard Library, Evansville, Indiana. Foster to John Foster Dulles, Feb. 7, 1917, John Foster Dulles Papers.

66. Robert Lansing to United States Embassy in Paris (telegram to be forwarded to Allen Dulles at legation in Bern, Eleanor Lansing Dulles and Emma Dulles in Paris), Nov. 15, 1917, Lansing Papers. Evansville *Journal–News*, Nov. 15, 1917; Evansville *Press*, Nov. 15, 1917; Evansville *Courier*, Nov. 17, 1917; *New York Times*, Nov. 16 and 28, 1917. Rev. Charles Wood, D. D., *Gen. John W. Foster: A Memorial Sermon Delivered in the Church of the Covenant, Sunday Morning, December 2, 1917* (copy in the Library of Congress).

67. Evansville *Courier*, Nov. 17, 1917.

CHAPTER IX

1. "The Dedication Oration," in *Official Souvenir, Indiana Soldiers and Sailors Monument*.

2. *A Century of American Diplomacy: Being a Brief Review of the Foreign*

Relations of the United States, 1776–1876, iii.

3. *The Practice of Diplomacy as Illustrated in the Foreign Relations of the United States*, 1. This book was written as a companion to *A Century of American Diplomacy*.

4. "Review of *A Century of American Diplomacy*," *Independent*, 52 (Dec. 20, 1900), 3048; S. M. MacVane, "Review," *Atlantic Monthly*, 87 (Feb. 1901), 271; John Holloday Latane, "Review," *American Historical Review*, 6 (April 1901), 588; Richard Olney to Foster (personal), Nov. 16, 1900, Foster Papers; John Hay to Foster, Oct. 11, 1900, Foster Papers. Regarding Foster's close personal relationship with John Hay, see Foster, *Diplomatic Memoirs*, vol. 2, 276–280.

5. Foster, *American Diplomacy in the Orient*, 399, 436, 438.

6. Foster, *American Diplomacy in the Orient*, 399.

7. Walter LaFeber, *New American Empire*, 100–101.

8. Foster, *American Diplomacy in the Orient*, 434–437.

9. Foster, *American Diplomacy in the Orient*, 305. Foster records an unpleasant incident that occurred on his visit to China in 1895 when he was informed that he could not bring Chinese guests, including high ranking officials, into the foreigners' dining area of a restaurant in Shanghai. Foster was upset but solved the problem by having the Chinese served in his private quarters. Foster, *Memoirs*, vol. 2, 121–122. Foster was also an outspoken and often unpopular critic of American discrimination against Orientals, see for example, *The China Indemnity: Was It a Punitive Measure*; "The Chinese Boycott," *Atlantic Monthly*, 97 (Jan. 1906), 118–127; "Decision of the Most Profound Importance," *Independent*, 58 (June 8, 1905), 1292–1293.

10. Foster, *American Diplomacy in the Orient*, 412–414.

11. *Ibid.*, 435. Foster expressed similar views in an article entitled "Present Conditions in China," in which he stated that it seemed "perfectly natural that a feeling of resentment against foreigners should pervade the Empire . . . [and] in view of the spoliation of their territory, the enormous indemnities extracted, and the disposition to establish a foreign monopoly for the exploitation of their industries and mines, it must be admitted that this feeling is not without some justification." *National Geographic*, 17 (Dec. 1906), 671.

12. In reviewing *American Diplomacy in the Orient*, historian Theodore S. Woosley wrote that Foster's work was fair and "balanced," although he criticized the superficial treatment of American involvement in the opium trade and complete neglect of the Hawaiian annexation affair. *American Historical Review*, 60 (Oct. 1903), 180–182. The reviewer in the *Independent* found Foster's book "well written" and suggested that Foster's "diplomatic career has given him the power of stating unpleasant truths in courteous language." *Independent*, 50 (March 1903), 623.

13. F. Harvey Harrington, "The Anti-Imperialist Movement in the United States, 1898–1900," *Mississippi Valley Historical Review*, 22 (1935), 211–213; Robert E. Osgood, *Ideals and Self-Interest in America's Foreign Relations*, 50. LeFeber, *New American Empire*, 68.

14. "Annexation of Cuba," *Independent*, 61 (Oct. 25, 1906) 967. In 1899 Foster wrote to General James H. Wilson, a long-time friend, who was with the United States

Army in Cuba, expressing a pessimism about the ability of the United States to provide democratic institutions for the Cubans: "We have become responsible for good government there, and cannot allow its people to get into chaos. I do not have as high an opinion of the capacity of the Cuban for independent self-government as you seem to entertain; however, we must let him try to experiment. I fear if left alone he will tread the same road as San Domingo and the Spanish American republics generally." Foster believed that rather than attempt to govern Cuba, the United States should establish commercial reciprocity with Cuba to insure close economic ties. Foster to Wilson, Dec. 23, 1809; Dec. 19, 1902, Wilson Papers.

15. Foster viewed the Hawaiian situation as unique, since an Anglo-Saxon population had in large measure replaced the native peoples. *War Not Inevitable*, World Peace Foundation Pamphlet Series No. 3, part 2 (Oct. 1900), 8–9.

16. For a comprehensive analysis of this school of conservative amateur historians, see John Higham with Lenard Krieger and Felix Gilbert, *History: The Development of Historical Studies in the United States*, 147–158, 187–188. Also see Ralph Henry Gabriel, *The Course of American Democratic Thought* (New York, 1910), 372–380, 383–386. For an interpretation of Mahan suggesting that his work was intended to be neither a call for American expansion nor moral leadership abroad, see Peter Karsten, *The Naval Aristocracy* (New York, The Free Press, 1972), 326–347.

17. Foster, *The Practice of Diplomacy*, 9–10, 104–105. Also see Foster's "Letter Regarding Training in Universities for Diplomatic and Consular Service," *American Journal of International Law* 9 (Jan. 1950), 162–163.

18. *A Century of American Diplomacy*, 3–4.

19. Calvin D. Davis, *The United States and the First Hague Conference*, 16–17.

20. *Arbitration and the Hague Court*, 13. *The Independent*, 48 (May 7, 1896). For examples of Foster's early interest in the use of international law as a means of settling disputes between nations, see "Results of the Bering Sea Arbitration," *North American Review*, 161 (Dec. 1895), 693–702; "Permanent Method of Arbitration with Great Britain," *Independent*, 52 (June 4, 1900), 1420–1422; "Prospects of Arbitration with England," *Independent*, 55 (Dec. 24, 1903), 3025–3026. Also see Merle Curti, *Peace or War*, 141, 153.

21. Davis, *U.S. and the First Hague Conference*, 200–201, 202–203, 212–213.

22. *Arbitration and the Hague Court*, 68–69. Foster proudly pointed out that the United States and Mexico were the first nations to submit a case before the international tribunal at the Hague. This was the Pius Fund claim (see pp. 69–71). Also see Foster's pamphlet entitled *What Has the United States Done for International Arbitration?* address delivered before the New York State Bar Association, Jan. 9, 1904 (*Twenty-Seventh Annual Report of the Proceedings of the New York State Bar Association*, 1904), 3–25; "America's Contribution to the Literature of International Law and Diplomacy," *Yale Law Journal*, 13 (June 1904), 409–420; "Pan American Diplomacy," *Atlantic Monthly*, 89 (April 1902), 485–486.

23. *Arbitration and the Hague Court*, 97.

24. *Arbitration and the Hague Court*, 97–104.

25. *Arbitration and the Hague Court*, 79–86.

26. By 1904 Foster was recognized as a leading spokesman of the peace movement and the prestige of his presence was considered necessary for the success of national meetings. John Bassett Moore to Foster, Jan. 5, 1904 and enclosures, Moore Papers.

27. "Editorial Comment," *American Journal of International Law*, 1 (Jan. 1907), 130–133; George A. Finch, "The American Society for International Law, 1906–1956," *American Journal of International Law*, 2 (April 1956), 296–297. Sondra Herman, *Eleven Against War*, 22–23. For a history of the formative years of the Mohonk Conference, see Davis, *The United States and the First Hague Conference*, 25 ff.

28. "Editorial Comment," *American Journal of International Law*, 1, 134; Finch, "American Society for International Law," 297; Curti, *War or Peace*, 201–202.

29. Finch, "American Society for International Law"; Oscar Straus, *Under Four Administrations*, 333–336; Daniel Smith, *Lansing and Neutrality, 1914–1917*, 2.

30. Straus, *Under Four Administrations*. Also of interest is Foster's brief article "Objections Urged to Arbitration Treaties," *Independent*, 58 (Jan. 5, 1905), 9–11.

31. Roosevelt's views on the arbitration treaties are stated in a letter to Senator Shelby Cullom dated Feb. 10, 1905 and printed in *The Letters of Theodore Roosevelt*, ed. by E. E. Morison vol. 4, 1119. Also, see Shelby Cullom, *Fifty Years of Public Service*, 396–401.

32. Roosevelt to Hay, Feb. 6, 1905, *Letters of Theodore Roosevelt*, vol. 4, 1114.

33. Roosevelt to Silas McBee, Feb. 10, 1905, *Ibid.*, 1121. Foster knew that the president was angered, but he persisted in his belief that the administration was in error: "I am henceforth *persona non grata* with the Executive department of the Government, and I am sorry for it, but not sorry that I spoke my mind. Secretary Hay has no use for the Senate and would abolish it tomorrow if he could have his way. But the country never had more use for the Senate than now." Foster to Wilson, Feb. 20, 1905, Wilson Papers.

34. *Report of the Twelfth Annual Meeting of the Late Mohonk Conference, 1906*, 12–16, 139. *Resolutions of the Mohonk Conference on International Arbitration*, 1907, 141. Also see Merze Tate, *The Disarmament Illusion*, 313–314.

35. Theodore Roosevelt to George Otto Trevelyan (personal), Aug. 18, 1906, *Letters of Theodore Roosevelt*, vol. 5, 366. Roosevelt promoted the Second Hague Conference and favored arms limitations on terms agreeable to the United States. However, he rejected any notion of arms reduction or disarmament. For an insightful discussion of Roosevelt's views on the Hague Conference, see Howard K. Beale, *Theodore Roosevelt and the Rise of America to World Power*, 336–354.

36. Foster attended the conference as an advisor to the Chinese delegation. *Memoirs*, vol. 2, 211–212; James Brown Scott, *The Hague Peace Conference of 1899 and 1907*, vol. 1, 158; Eleanor Lansing Dulles, *John Foster Dulles*, 61–62. John Foster Dulles, because he spoke French, was made secretary of the delegation.

37. *Memoirs*, vol. 2, 212.

38. James Brown Scott, ed., *Proceedings of the Hague Peace Conferences*, vol. 3, 795.

39. William I. Hull, *The Two Hague Conferences and Their Contributions to International Law*, 134–137; Tate, *Disarmament Illusion*, 342–343.
40. *Memoirs*, vol. 2, 239. Scott, *The Hague Peace Conferences*, vol. 1, 178–179. As positive accomplishments of the Second Hague Conference, Foster listed the following: (1) creation of a prize court; (2) procedural improvements for commissions of inquiry and arbitration; (3) prohibition of the use of force in the collection of debts; (4) adoption of new regulations for the amelioration of land and naval warfare; (5) greater protection of neutral commerce during war; (6) some advancement towards a goal of obligatory arbitration and establishment of a permanent arbitral court; (7) provision for the periodic meeting of other world peace conferences. *Memoirs*, vol. 2, 240.
41. Foster accepted a position on the board of the Carnegie Endowment for International Peace. Foster to Andrew Carnegie, Nov. 15, 1910, Carnegie Papers. For some reason Foster became disenchanted with the organization but was encouraged to remain on the board by Elihu Root, who wrote in part: "[James Brown] Scott tells me you are thinking of withdrawing. . . . I shall really feel like chucking the whole business overboard if you back out now just when the real work is to begin. You have the knowledge of international affairs and experience which would be of immense service in a great experiment like this, and you have the position of authority to make your knowledge and experience effective, and you have time and strength and ability." Root to Foster, Jan. 31, 1911, Foster Papers. Also see David Patterson, *Toward a Warless World: The Travail of the Peace Movement 1887–1914*, 148.
42. For example, see *International Arbitration: An Address Delivered in Richmond, Indiana by Request of the Commercial Club, December 1, 1909*, 5–7, 11–12, 14, 28–32; *War Not Inevitable*, World Peace Foundation Pamphlet Series No. 3, part 2 (Oct. 1911); "Misconceptions and Limitations of the Monroe Doctrine."
43. *Proceedings*, American Society for Judicial Settlement of International Disputes (Dec. 15, 1910), 44.
44. In 1910 Foster saw no threat from Japan to the United States or to American interests in the Pacific and Far East; nor did he feel the Anglo-Japanese Alliance would be detrimental to U.S. policy. "The Japanese War Scare," *International Conciliation in the Far East*, 28–31.
45. Roosevelt to Philander C. Knox, February 9, 1909, *Letters of Theodore Roosevelt*, vol. 6, 1513. Roosevelt's views on Japan are described in Beale, *Theodore Roosevelt and America's Rise to World Power*, 324–334; Wallace Chessman, *Theodore Roosevelt and the Politics of Power* (Boston, Little, Brown and Co., 1969), 111–123.
46. Osgood, *Ideals and Self Interest*, 86–88. Herman, *Eleven Against War*, 24; Robert McCloskey, *American Conservatism in an Age of Enterprise, 1865–1910*, 22, 27–28; Lloyd C. Gardner, "American Foreign Policy, 1900–1921," 211.
47. Foster to Wilson, Nov. 21, 1903, and Wilson to Foster, Nov. 6, 1903, Wilson Papers.
48. Address delivered May 14, 1902, Indianapolis, Indiana, printed in Foster, *War Stories*, 181–190.
49. Foster to Wilson, Feb. 9, 1917, Wilson Papers.

50. LaFeber, *New American Empire*, 97–98. Foster's views on the need for an American christianizing mission in the world came at a time when this idea was widely accepted, see Julius Pratt, *The Expansionists of 1898: The Acquisition of Hawaii and the Spanish Islands*, 279–316.

51. Rev. Charles Wood, D. D., *General John Watson Foster*, 11, 14. Also see Foster's lecture on missionary efforts in China delivered at the First Presbyterian Church of Watertown, New York, and printed in the *New York Times*, September 9, 1895; *The Value of Investments in Foreign Christian Colleges: An Address Given on Behalf of American College for Girls at Constantinople, March 24, 1909*.

52. Rev. Wood placed Foster in the conservative school of Presbyterianism. In eulogizing his long-time parishioner, Rev. Wood remarked, "Inflexible, as some doubtless thought his Presbyterianism, it was not rigid or exclusive. He was tolerant even to an extraordinary degree to phases of Presbyterianism, with which, personally, he could not agree, . . . [but he looked] with some apprehension at even the suggestion of radicalism or liberalism." Wood, *General John Watson Foster*, 12; also see William Castle, "John W. Foster," in *American Secretaries of State and Their Diplomacy*, vol. 8, 208.

53. *The Civilization of Christ*, 14–15. Foster's views on the need to evangelize the world through the power of example and Christian missionary efforts were similar to those expressed by the popular preacher Josiah Strong. See Dorothea Muller, "Josiah Strong and American Nationalism: A Reevaluation," *Journal of American History* 3 (Dec. 1966), 487–503.

54. Foster, *The Civilization of Christ*, 7.

55. Foster, *The Civilization of Christ*, 6.

56. Foster, *The Civilization of Christ*, 6.

57. Warren Kuehl, *Seeking World Order: The United States and International Organization to 1920*, 38–39.

CHAPTER X

1. Andrew H. Berding, *Dulles on Diplomacy*, 13. Also see the remarks of John Foster Dulles in his address to State Department officials upon his inauguration as secretary of state. USDS press release 50 (Jan. 29, 1953).

Essay on Sources

Although Foster was a major figure in the formation and implementation of United States foreign policies for three decades, no complete biography of him has ever been written. The best account of Foster's diplomatic career is provided by William R. Castle, "John W. Foster," in *American Secretaries of State and Their Diplomacy*, ed. by Samuel F. Bemis and Robert Farrell (New York: Pageant Book Co., 1958), vol. 8, 185–223. Also of interest is a study of Daniel W. Snepp, "John Watson Foster, Soldier and Politician," *Indiana Magazine of History* 32 (Sept. 1936), which emphasizes Foster's military service in the Civil War. Foster has been the subject of two doctoral dissertations: Chester C. Kaiser, "John W. Foster: United States Minister to Mexico, 1873–1880 (American University, 1954) details Foster's role in Mexico during the first years of the Díaz regime, and a lengthy description of Foster's life in sympathetic and uncritical terms is presented in Francis M. Phillips, "John Watson Foster, 1836–1917," 2 vols. (University of New Mexico, 1956). Phillips' work is useful for genealogical details but provides no analysis of his diplomatic record.

Perhaps historians have neglected Foster because it is hazardous to attempt to make any assessment of his impact on the formation of foreign policy. Foster left very few personal papers; Foster's manuscript collection in the Library of Congress consists of two thin boxes containing only letters to him of a complimentary nature. Nevertheless, this small collection contains some valuable material, including several letters frequently cited by historians of late nineteenth-century American diplomacy. After completing his two-volume autobiography Foster apparently attempted to make certain that the recollections he published would not be challenged, and a year before his death he wrote: "I destroyed most of my voluminous papers and correspondence thinking them of no further use" (see Foster to Otto

159

Gresham, April 24, 1917, Otto Gresham Papers). One must assume that Foster had more sinister motives for destroying what must have been an exceptionally rich and insightful manuscript collection, possibly among the most comprehensive of any political figure of his era.

Fortunately, the scattered and diverse manuscript collections of Foster's contemporaries contain important letters from him that provide information on the political and diplomatic developments with which he was involved as well as insights into his social and family life. Of exceptional value are the papers of James Harrison Wilson, Walter Gresham, John Hay, Hamilton Fish, Robert Todd Lincoln, John Bassett Moore, and Robert Lansing; all are in the Library of Congress Manuscripts Division. The Rutherford B. Hayes Papers at the Presidential Library in Fremont include several letters from and about Foster dealing with political developments in Indiana during the campaigns of 1872 and 1876, and the Indiana Historical Society Library in Indianapolis maintains the papers of Conrad Baker, Oliver P. Morton, and other Indiana political leaders with whom Foster corresponded. Of value for material on Foster's years in Indiana is the Willard Library in Evansville, which holds an excellent collection of the city's newspapers and a small but useful manuscript file.

The John Foster Dulles Papers in the Princeton University library contain the largest single body of Foster's letters, and it is indeed fortunate for historians that Dulles did not share his grandfather's tendency towards pyromania. In addition to about a dozen letters to his grandson over a period of twenty formative years in the young diplomat's development, the Dulles Papers include a box of letters from Foster to his wife, written during his service with the Chinese government in Shimonoseki from December 1894 to June 1895 and a handwritten "Diary" covering the same period. This manuscript box also holds the handwritten memoranda and treaty drafts exchanged by the Chinese and Japanese plenipotentiaries. Further information about their grandfather is presented by the Dulleses, particularly Eleanor Lansing Dulles, in the oral history collection of the Butler Library of Columbia University, and I am grateful to Ms. Dulles for allowing me access to transcripts of her tapes.

In reconstructing and filling out Foster's diplomatic career, an invaluable source is the official record as it is presented in the general records of the Department of State in the National Archives, made available on microfilm. This material includes Despatches and Instructions as well as notes to and from foreign legations. Foster's voluminous thirty-year correspondence is detailed and erudite, and his views are always forcefully expressed. He did not hesitate to state his candid opinions on difficult issues. His characteristically blunt remarks often caused irritation in Washington, but his viewpoint was often the one adopted. The official correspondence presents a clear picture of Foster as a diplomat.

Various published reports of congressional investigations and hearings contain Foster's testimony. Of particular interest are *Mexican Border Troubles*, 45th Congress, 1st Session, House Executive Document No. 13, and *Report and Accompanying Documents of the Committee on Foreign Affairs on the Relations of the United States with Mexico*, 45th Congress, 2nd Session, House Report No. 701, both dealing with the problems along the United States border with Mexico and the recognition of Porfirio Díaz. Essential material relating to the attempted annexation of Hawaii in 1893 is printed in U.S. House of Representatives, House Executive Document No. 1, 53rd Congress, 2nd Session, and Senate Report No. 227, 53rd Congress, 2nd Session (known as the "Morgan Report"). Foster's testimony pertaining to Chinese exclusion is contained in Senate Report No. 776, 57th Congress, 1st Session. An overwhelming amount of detailed material relating to the fur seal controversy is presented in the sixteen-volume *Fur Seal Arbitration: Proceedings of the Tribunal, etc.* (Washington, D.C., 1895) and the record of the Alaskan boundary question is contained in the seven-volume *Proceedings of the Alaskan Boundary Tribunal* (Washington, D. C., 1903–1904).

A final source of primary material for the study of Foster's life and times consists of his voluminous published works, for in these he clearly put forth his personal views on contemporary diplomacy and the men who made it. Of particular importance is his classic *American Diplomacy in the Orient*, which for twenty years, until the publication of Tyler Dennett's *Americans in Eastern Asia*, remained the standard text on American foreign policy in the Far East. His books, articles, and printed speeches are full of subjective views on a wide range of topics. Of particular significance are those works dealing with United States diplomacy with Mexico and China, which offer Foster's evaluations of the personalities of Li Hung-chang, Porfirio Díaz, and Yuan Shi-kai. Foster's essays on Civil Service reform, international law, and the peace movement are also important.

In addition to his two-volume *Diplomatic Memoirs* published in 1909, Foster authored two other autobiographical books dealing with his early years in Evansville and his Civil War experiences. His biography of his father, *Biographical Sketch of Matthew W. Foster, 1800–1863*, provides glimpses of life in rural southern Indiana and in the rapidly growing river town of Evansville, while his *War Stories*, printed by his grandchildren a year after his death, offers a personal narrative of service in the Union army. All of Foster's autobiographical volumes contain excerpts from letters and fascimiles of documents that were apparently burned or otherwise destroyed. A brief autobiographical account of pre–Civil War life in Evansville is contained in volume 3 of Iglehart's edited work, *An Account of Vandenburg County from Its Organization*. "From the Reminiscences of John W. Foster" was written in the final year of the author's life.

Bibliography

ABBREVIATIONS: USGPO—U. S. Government Printing Office
USDS—U. S. Department of State

I. PUBLISHED WRITINGS OF JOHN W. FOSTER

A. Books:

American Diplomacy in the Orient. Boston: Houghton Mifflin, 1904.

Arbitration and the Hague Court. Boston: Houghton Mifflin, 1904.

Biographical Sketch of Matthew W. Foster, 1800–1863. Washington, D. C.: John W. Foster, 1896.

A Century of American Diplomacy: Being a Brief Review of the Foreign Relations of the United States, 1776–1876. Boston: Houghton Mifflin, 1900.

Diplomatic Memoirs. 2 vols. Boston: Houghton Mifflin, 1909.

The Practice of Diplomacy as Illustrated in the Foreign Relations of the United States. Boston: Houghton Mifflin, 1901.

War Stories for My Grandchildren. Cambridge, Mass.: Riverside Press, 1918.

B. Pamphlets and Printed Speeches:

Address by Hon. John W. Foster Delivered at the Indiana University Commencement, June 21, 1905. Bloomington: Indiana University, 1905.

The Alaskan Boundary Tribunal. Washington, D. C.: Judd & Detweiler, 1903.

The Annexation of Hawaii: An Address Delivered Before the National Geographic Society, at Washington, D. C. March 26, 1897. Washington, D. C.: Gibson, 1897.

Are or Is? Washington, D. C., 1901. (Copy in Library of Congress).

Armaments and the "Next War." The Opening Address at the Twelfth Annual Conference on International Arbitration, Mohonk Lake, N.Y., May 30, 1906. Washington, D. C.: Beresford, 1906.

Before the Congress of the United States: The Mexican Fraudulent Claims Argument of John W. Foster Before the Committee of Foreign Affairs of the House of Representatives, In Support of Senate Bills No. 539 and 606. Washington, D. C., 1892.

162

The China Indemnity: Was It a Punitive Measure? Washington, D. C.: Beresford, 1908.

The Civilization of Christ. Address delivered before Presbyterian Ministerial Association, Philadelphia, Oct. 16, 1899.

In re "La Candelaria": Supplemental Brief for the Government of Mexico. Washington, D.C.: Beresford, 1905.

International Arbitration: An Address Delivered in Richmond, Indiana by Request of the Commercial Club, Dec. 1, 1909. Richmond, 1909.

International Awards and National Honor. Washington, D. C.: John W. Foster, 1886.

Introduction to *The Boer War* (for Allen W. Dulles). Washington, D. C.: John W. Foster, 1902.

Limitation of Armament on the Great Lakes. Pamphlet no. 2. Washington, D.C.: Carnegie Endowment for International Peace, 1914.

Maximilian and His Mexican Empire. Washington, D.C.: George Washington University, 1906.

"Misconceptions and Limitations of the Monroe Doctrine." An Address by John W. Foster, April 23, 1914. *Proceedings of the American Society of International Law,* Washington, D. C., April 22–25, 1914. Washington, D.C.: Byron S. Adams, 1914.

The Proper Grade of Diplomatic Representatives. Washington, D.C.: Judd & Detweiler, 1904.

The Relation of Diplomacy to Foreign Missions: An Address at the 5th International Convention of the Student Volunteer Movement. Nashville: University Press of Sewanee, 1906.

The Value of Investments in the Foreign Christian Colleges: An Address Given on Behalf of American College for Girls at Constantinople, March 24, 1909. Nashville, Tenn.: University Press of Sewanee, 1909.

Venezuelan Claims: Appendix to the Letter of Mr. John W. Foster to Hon. S. M. Cullom, Chairman of the Committee on Foreign Relations of the Senate of the United States. Washington, D.C.: Beresford, 1908.

War Not Inevitable. Pamphlet series no. 3, part 2. n.p.: World Peace Foundation, Oct. 1911.

What the United States Has Done for International Arbitration. Address delivered before The New York State Bar Association, Jan. 19, 1904. *The Twenty-Seventh Annual Report of the Proceedings of the New York State Bar Association,* 1904.

C.   Articles:

"The Alaskan Boundary." *National Geographic,* 10 (Nov. 1899), 425–456.

"The Alaskan Boundary Tribunal." *National Geographic,* 15 (Jan. 1904), 1–12.

"America's Contribution to the Literature of International Law and Diplomacy." *Yale Law Journal* 13 (June 1904), 409–420.

"The Annexation of Cuba." *Independent,* 61 (Oct. 25, 1906), 965–968.

"Another Step towards International Peace." *Independent,* 68 (June 9, 1910), 1288–1290.

"Canada and the Monroe Doctrine." *Independent* 54 (March 27, 1902), 721–723.

"The Candidate of Indiana for the President." *Independent,* 64 (March 12, 1908), 558 562.

"The Case Against Intervention." *Independent,* 77 (March 30, 1914), 440.

"China." *National Geographic* 15 (Dec. 1904), 463–478.

"The Chinese Boycott." *Atlantic Monthly*, 97 (Jan. 1906), 118–127.

"Classics as a Training for Men of Affairs." *School Review*, 17 (June 1909), 375–380.

"Clayton-Bulwer Treaty." *Independent* 53 (May 23, 1901), 1167–1171.

"Commercial Reciprocity with Canada." *Independent* 53 (Dec. 5, 1901), 2874–2877.

"The Contest for the Laws of Reform in Mexico." *American Historical Review*, 15 (April 1910), 526–546.

"Cultivation of Coffee in Mexico." *Monthly Report of Department of Agriculture*, 14 (July 1876).

"Decision of the Most Profound Importance." *Independent*, 58 (June 8, 1905). 1292–1293.

"The Dedication Oration." *Official Souvenir, Indiana Soldiers and Sailors Monument*. Indianapolis: Indianapolis *Journal* Co., 1902.

"The Development of International Law." *University of Chicago Magazine*, 1 (Feb. 1909), 136–148.

"A Foreign Service in an American Court." *Yale Law Journal*, 60 (May 1900), 283–286.

"Franklin as a Diplomat." *Independent* 60 (Jan. 11, 1906), 84–89.

"The Great Chinese Viceroy and Diplomat." *International Quarterly*, 2 (Nov. 1900). 584–596.

"International Responsibility to Corporate Bodies for Lives Lost by Outlawry." *American Journal of International Law*, 1 (Jan. 1907), 4–10.

Introduction to *Memoirs of Li Hung-chang*, trans. and ed. by William F. Mannix. Boston: Houghton Mifflin, 1913.

"Is the Forcible Collection of Contract Debt in the Interest of International Justice and Peace?" *Proceedings of the American Society of International Law*, 1907.

"The Japanese War Scare." *International Conciliation in the Far East*. Pamphlet no. 35. New York: American Association for International Conciliation, Oct. 1910, 28–31.

"The Latin-American Constitutions and Revolutions." *National Geographic*, 12 (May 1901), 169–175.

"Letter Regarding Training in Universities for Diplomatic and Consular Service." *American Journal of International Law* 9 (Jan. 1915), 162–163.

"Marquis Ito: The Japanese Statesman." *International Quarterly*, 9 (June 1904), 261–273.

"Maximilian and His Mexican Empire." *Records of the Columbia Historical Society*, 14 (Washington, D.C.: 1914), 184–204.

"The New Mexico." *National Geographic* 13 (Jan. 1902), 1–24.

"Objections Urged to the Arbitration Treaties." *Independent*, 58 (Jan. 5, 1905), 9–11.

"Pan-American Diplomacy." *Atlantic Monthly* 89 (April 1902), 482–491.

"Permanent Method of Arbitration with Great Britain." *Independent*, 52 (June 14, 1900), 1420–1422.

"Porfirio Díaz: Soldier and Statesman." *International Quarterly*, 8 (Dec. 1903), 342–353.

"Present Conditions in China." *National Geographic*, 17 (Dec. 1906), 651–672, 709–711.

"President Roosevelt and the Hague." *Independent*, 61 (Dec. 20, 1906), 1471–1472.

"Prospects of Arbitration with England." *Independent*, 55 (Dec. 24, 1903), 3025–3026.

"Questions of the Far East." *Atlantic Monthly* 97 (April 1906), 542–546.
"The Reciprocity Treaties and the Senate." *Independent*, 52 (June 14, 1900), 2897–2899.
"Results of the Bering Sea Arbitration." *North American Review* 161 (Dec. 1895), 693–702.
"Review of *The British Empire and the United States* by W. A. Dunning." *American Journal of International Law*, 9 (Jan. 1915), 269–272.
"Review of *Diplomacy of the War of 1812* by F. A. Updyke." *American Journal of International Law* 9 (July 1915), 762–765.
"Review of *Notes of a Busy Life* by Joseph Benson Faraker." *American Journal of International Law*, 10 (April 1916), 451–457.
"Second Hague Conference and the Development of International Law as a Science." *Proceedings of the American Society of International Law*, 1907.
"Status at Washington of International Arbitration." *Independent*, 56 (May 26, 1904), 1186–1188.
"The Treaty-Making Power under the Constitution." *Yale Law Journal* 11 (Dec. 1901), 69–79.
"Unlimited Arbitration between Great Britain and the United States." *Report of the Lake Mohonk Conference*, 1911, pp. 118–125.
"The Viceroy Li Hung-chang," *Century*, 52 (Aug. 1896), 560–571.
"Were the Questions Involved in the Foreign Wars of the United States of Such a Nature That They Could Have Been Submitted to Arbitration or Settled without Recourse to War?" *Proceedings of International Conference, American Society for Judicial Settlement of International Disputes*, 1 (Dec. 15, 17, 1910), 44–68.
"The Year's Progress in Peace." *Independent* 55 (July 2, 1903), 1551–1553.

II. MANUSCRIPT COLLECTIONS

A. Library of Congress, Manuscripts Division

James G. Blaine Papers
Joseph H. Choate Papers
Hamilton Fish Papers
John W. Foster Papers
Walter Q. Gresham Papers
Benjamin Harrison Papers (Microfilm)
Robert R. Hitt Papers
Robert Lansing Papers
Robert Todd Lincoln Papers
John Bassett Moore Papers
John Tyler Morgan Papers
Richard Olney Papers
Elihu Root Papers
Carl Schurz Papers
Benjamin F. Tracy Papers
Henry White Papers
James Harrison Wilson Papers

B.   National Archives, General Records of the Department of State, Record Group
     59 (1873–1903)

C.   Princeton University Library
     John Foster Dulles Papers

D.   Dwight D. Eisenhower Presidential Library, Abilene, Kansas
     Eleanor Lansing Dulles Papers

E.   Rutherford B. Hayes Presidential Library, Fremont, Ohio
     Rutherford B. Hayes Papers

F.   Indiana Historical Society Library, Indianapolis
     Conrad Baker Papers
     Noble C. Butler Papers
     William Halloway Papers (Oliver P. Morton Material)

G.   Butler Library of Columbia University
     Eleanor Lansing Dulles Oral History Tapes

H.   Willard Library, Evansville, Indiana

                      III.   PRINTED MATERIALS

A.   Government Documents:
United States International Boundary Commission. *Joint Report upon the Survey
     and Demarcation of the Boundary between Canada and the United States from
     Tonglass Passage to Mount St. Elias in Accordance with the Convention of January
     24, 1903; the Award of the Tribunal, Appointed under the Convention, Signed at
     London, October 20, 1903; an Exchange of Notes between the Governments of
     Great Britain and the United States Relative to the Award, Signed at Washington,
     March 25, 1905; and the Treaty Signed at Washington, D.C., February 24, 1925.*
U.S. Congress. *Congressional Record.* Washington, D.C., 1873–1900.
     U.S. House of Representatives. *Affairs in Hawaii.* 53rd Congress, 3rd Session,
     House Executive Document No. 1. (*Foreign Relations of the United States, 1894,*
     Appendix II).
     ———. *Hawaiian Correspondence.* 53rd Congress, 2nd Session, House Executive
     Document No. 48.
     ———. *Mexican Border Troubles.* 45th Congress, 1st Session, House Executive
     Document No. 13.
     ———. *Mexican Claims.* 48th Congress, 1st Session, House Executive Document No.
     103.
     ———. *Providing Indemnity to Certain Chinese Subjects.* 49th Congress, 1st Session,
     House Report No. 2044, May 1, 1886.
     ———. "Reciprocity with Spain." *Reports from the Consuls of the United States.*
     52nd Congress, 1st Session, House Miscellaneous Document No. 18.

_____. *Relations with Chile.* 52nd Congress, 1st Session, House Executive Document No. 91.

_____. *Report and Accompanying Documents of the Committee on Foreign Affairs on the Relations of the United States with Mexico.* 45th Congress, 2nd Session, House Report No. 701.

_____. *Report of the Commissioner to the Hawaiian Islands* (known as the Blount Report). 53rd Congress, 2nd Session, House Executive Document No. 47.

_____. *Report upon the Present Condition of the Fur Seal Rookeries of the Pribilof Islands of Alaska* (sometimes referred to as the Elliot Report). 54th Congress, 1st Session, House Document No. 175.

U.S. Senate. *Clarification of John W. Foster's Status as Counsel for China, 1895.* 53rd Congress, 3rd Session, Senate Executive Document No. 25.

_____. *Commercial Agreements with Other Countries.* 52nd Congress, 1st Session, Senate Executive Document No. 119.

_____. *Chinese Exclusion.* 57th Congress, 1st Session, Senate Report No. 776.

_____. *Chinese Immigration.* 52nd Congress, 2nd Session, Senate Executive Document No. 54.

_____. *Hawaiian Islands.* 52nd Congress, 2nd Session, Senate Executive Documents Nos. 76 and 77.

_____. *Journal of the Executive Proceeding of the Senate of the United States,* 1789–1905. 90 vols. Washington, D. C.: USGPO, 1828–1948.

_____. *Morgan Report.* 53rd Congress, 2nd Session, Senate Report No. 227.

U.S. Department of State. *Appointment Papers,* 1861–1869.

_____. *Fur Seal Arbitration: Proceedings of the Tribunal of Arbitration Convened at Paris under the Treaty between the United States and Great Britain concluded at Washington, D.C., February 29, 1892, for the Determination of Questions between the Two Governments Concerning the Jurisdictional Rights of the United States in the Waters of the Bering Sea.* 16 vols. Washington, D.C.: USGPO, 1895.

_____. *Papers Relating to the Foreign Relations of the United States.* Washington, D.C.: USGPO, 1872–1903.

_____. *Proceedings of the Alaskan Boundary Tribunal.* 7 vols. in 6. Washington, D.C.: USGPO, 1903–1904.

_____. *Protocol First Conference between Hawaiian Commissioners and Secretary of State,* February 4, 1893.

_____. *Register of the Department of State Corrected to September 1, 1892.* Washington, D.C.: USGPO, 1892.

_____. *Register of the Department of State Corrected to February 17, 1893.* Washington, D.C.: USGPO, 1893.

U.S. Department of War. *The War of Rebellion: A Compilation of the Official Records of the Union and Confederate Armies.* Washington, D.C.: USGPO, 1880–1901.

U.S. National Archives. General Records of the Department of State. (Microfilm).

B. Contemporary Historical Narratives, Reminiscences, and Compilations:

Adams, Henry, *Letters of Henry Adams, 1892*–1918, ed. by Worthington Chauncey Ford. Boston: Houghton Mifflin. 1938.

Alexander, W. D. *A History of the Later Years of the Hawaiian Monarchy and the*

Revolution of 1893. Honolulu, 1896.

Basler, Roy P., ed. *The Collected Works of Abraham Lincoln*. 9 vols. New Brunswick, N.J.: Rutgers University Press, 1953-54.

Carnegie Endowment for International Peace. *Yearbooks*. Nos. 1-7, 1911-1918. Washington, D.C.: Carnegie Endowment, 1911-1918.

Castle, William R. *Hawaii, Past and Present*. New York: Dodd, Mead, 1917.

Cleveland, Grover. *Letters of Grover Cleveland*, ed. by Allen Nevins. Boston: Houghton Mifflin, 1933.

Cullom, Shelby M. *Fifty Years of Public Service*. Chicago: A.C. McClurg, 1911.

Denby, Charles. *China and Her People: Being the Observations, Reminiscences, and Conclusions of an American Diplomat*. 2 vols. Boston: L. C. Page, 1906.

Depew, Chauncey. *My Memories of Eighty Years*. New York: Charles Scribners Sons, 1924.

Díaz, Porfirio. *Archivo de General Porfirio Díaz:* Memoirs Documentos. (Prologo y Notas de Alberto Maria.) 30 vols. Carreno: Universidad Nacional Autonoma de Mexico, 1951.

Elliot, Joseph Peter. *A History of Evansville and Vandenburg County, Indiana: A Complete and Concise Account from the Earliest Times to the Present, Embracing Reminiscences of the Pioneers and Biographical Sketches*. Evansville: Keller Printing, 1897.

Foulke, Dudley W. *Life of Oliver P. Morton*. 2 vols. Indianapolis, Ind.: Bowen-Merrill, 1899.

Grant, Ulysses S. *The Papers of Ulysses S. Grant*, ed. by John Y. Simon. 6 vols. Carbondale and Edwardsville: Southern Illinois University Press, 1977.

Gresham, Matilda. *Life of Walter Quintin Gresham, 1832-1895*. 2 vols. Chicago: Rand McNally, 1919.

Hamilton, Gail (Mary Abigail Dodge). *Biography of James G. Blaine*. Norwich, Conn., 1895.

Harrison, Benjamin, and Blaine, James G. *The Correspondence between Benjamin Harrison and James G. Blaine, 1882-1893*, collected and edited by Albert T. Volwiler. Philadelphia: The American Philosophical Society, 1940.

Harrison and Reid, *Their Lives and Record: The Republican Campaign Book for 1892*, compiled and edited by Thomas Campbell-Copeland. New York: Charles L. Webster and Co., 1892.

Hart, Robert. *The I. G. in Peking: Letters of Robert Hart, Chinese Maritime Customs, 1868-1907*, ed. by John K. Fairbank et al. 2 vols. Cambridge, Mass.: The Belknap Press of Harvard University Press, 1975.

Hawaiian Historical Society. *51st Annual Report*, 1942. Honolulu, September, 1943.

Hay, John. *Letters of John Hay and Extracts from His Diary,* ed. by Clara S. Hay. 3 vols. Washington, D.C.: Clara S. Hay, 1908.

Hayes, Rutherford B. *Diary and Letters of Rutherford B. Hayes, Nineteenth President of the United States*, ed. by Charles R. Williams. 5 vols. Columbus: Ohio State Archaeological and Historical Society, 1922-1926.

Hayes: The Diary of a President, 1875-1881, ed. by T. Harry Williams. New York: David McKay, 1964.

History of the Peace Negotiations, Documentary and Verbal, between China and Japan, March-April, 1895. Tientsin, China: *Tientsin Times*, 1895.

History of Vandenburg County, Indiana, From the Earliest Times to the Present, with Biographical Sketches, Reminiscences, etc. Madison, Wisc.: Brant & Fuller, 1889.

Iglehart, John E., ed., *An Account of Vandenberg County from Its Organization.* 3 vols. Dayton, Ohio: Dayton Historical Publishing, 1923.

Indiana in the War of the Rebellion: Report of the Adjutant General. (A reprint of volume 1 of the eight-volume report prepared by W. H. H. Terrell and published in 1869.) Indianapolis: Indiana Historical Bureau, 1960.

Kuykendall, Ralph S., ed. *Hawaiian Diplomatic Correspondence.* Honolulu: Honolulu Star-Bulletin, 1926.

Lake Mohonk Conference on International Arbitration. Mohonk Lake, N.Y.: Lake Mohonk, Conference on International Arbitration, 1895-1916.

Liliuokalani. *Hawaii's Story by Hawaii's Queen.* Rutland, Vt.: C. E. Tuttle Co., 1964.

MacMurray, John V.A., ed. *Treaties and Agreements with and Concerning China, 1894-1914.* 2 vols. New York: Oxford University Press, 1921.

Malloy, William M., ed. *Treaties, Conventions, International Acts, Protocols and Agreements between the United States of America and Other Powers, 1776-1909.* 2 vols. Washington, D.C.: USGPO, 1910.

Moore, John B. *American Diplomacy: Its Spirit and Achievements.* New York: Harper & Bros., 1907.

———. *Collected Papers of John Bassett Moore.* 7 vols. New Haven, Conn.: Yale University Press, 1944.

———. *A Digest of International Law.* 8 vols. Washington, D.C.: USGPO, 1906.

———. *History and Digest of Arbitrations to Which the United States Has Been a Party, together with Appendices Containing the Treaties Relating to Such Arbitrations, and Historical and Legal Notes.* 6 vols. Washington, D.C.: USGPO, 1898.

National Party Platforms, 1840-1960, compiled by Kirk H. Porter and Donald B. Johnson. Urbana: University of Illinois Press, 1961.

Proceedings of the Banquet of the Spanish-American Commercial Union, New York, May 1, 1889. New York: Hispana-American Publishing, 1889.

Report of the Secretary of Finance of the United States of Mexico on the 15th of January, 1879, on the Actual Condition of Mexico, and the Increase of Commerce with the United States Rectifying the Report of the Hon. John W. Foster Envoy Extraordinary and Minister Plenipotentiary of the United States in Mexico. New York: N. Ponce de Léon, 1880.

Roosevelt, Theodore. *The Letters of Theodore Roosevelt,* ed. by Elting E. Morison, 8 vols. Cambridge, Mass.: Harvard University Press, 1951-1954.

Schurz, Carl. *Speeches, Correspondence and Public Papers of Carl Schurz,* ed. by Fredrick Bancroft, 6 vols. New York: The Knickerbocker Press, 1913.

Scott, James Brown. *The Hague Peace Conference of 1899 and 1907.* 2 vols. Baltimore, Md.: Johns Hopkins University Press, 1909.

———., ed. *The Proceedings of the Hague Peace Conferences: Translation of the Original Text.* 4 vols. New York: Oxford University Press, 1907.

Seward, Fredrick William. *Reminiscences of a War-Time Statesman and Diplomat, 1830-1915,* New York: Putnam's, 1916.

Sherman, John. *Recollections of Forty Years in the House, Senate, and Cabinet: An Autobiography.* 2 vols. Chicago: Werner, 1895.

Spring-Rice, Sir Cecil. *The Letters and Friendships of Sir Cecil Spring Rice: A Record*, ed. by Stephen Gwyn. 2 vols. London: Constable, 1929.

Straus, Oscar. *Under Four Administrations: From Cleveland to Taft.* Boston: Houghton Mifflin, 1922.

Thayer, William R. *The Life and Letters of John Hay.* 2 vols. Boston: Houghton Mifflin, 1915.

Thurston, Lorrin A. *Memoirs of the Hawaiian Revolution*, ed. by Andrew Farrell. Honolulu: Advertise Publishing, 1936.

Vallarta, Ignacio Luis. *La Labor Diplomatica de Don Ignacio Luis Vallarta como Secretario de Relaciones Exteriores.* con un Estudio Preliminar de Jorge Flores. Mexico: Publicaciones de la Secretaria de Relaciones Exteriores, 1961.

Vladimir (Zerone Volpicelli). *The China-Japan War.* London: Sampson Low, Marston, 1896.

White, Andrew D. *Autobiography of Andrew D. White.* 2 vols. New York: Century, 1906.

White, Edward, ed. *Evansville and Its Men of Mark.*Evansville, Ind.: Historical Publishing, 1873.

Witte, Count. *The Memoirs of Count Witte*, ed. by Abraham Yarmolinsky. London: William Heinemann, 1921.

Wu, T'ing-fang. *America Through the Spectacles of An Oriental Diplomat.* New York: Fredrick A. Stokes, 1914.

C. Contemporary Articles and Reviews:

"Editorial," *Nation* 55 (July 7, 1892), 1.

"Editorial Comment," *American Journal of International Law* 1 (Jan. 1907), 129-134.

Johnson, W. H. "Review of *Diplomatic Memoirs* by John W. Foster," *Dial* 48 (May 16, 1910), 353-355.

Knobe, Bertha Damaris. "The Daughters of the American Revolution." *Woman's Home Companion* 31 (May 1904), 15.

Latane, John Holladay. "Review of *A Century of American Diplomacy* by John W. Foster," *American Historical Review* 6 (April 1901), 587-589.

MacVane, S. M. "Review of *A Century of American Diplomacy*," *Atlantic Monthly* 87 (Feb. 1901), 269-271.

Moore, John Bassett. "The Chilean Controversy," *Political Science Quarterly* 8 (1893), 467-494.

———. "Review of *A Century of American Diplomacy* by John W. Foster," *Political Science Quarterly* 16 (1901), 655.

"The New Secretary of State," *Harper's Weekly* 37 (July 9, 1892), 655.

"Our First Professional Diplomat," *Outlook* 117 (Nov. 28, 1917), 488

"Personal." *Harper's Weekly* 36 (July 23, 1892), 703.

Phelps, Edward J. "The Bering Sea Controversy," *Harper's Magazine* (April 1891), 766-774.

"Portrait of John W. Foster," *Review of Reviews* 27 (April 1903), 501.

"Portrait of Mrs. John W. Foster," *Woman's Home Companion* 31 (May 1904), 15.

"Prominent Men in Pan-American Affairs," *Bulletin of Pan American Union* 45 (July-Dec. 1917), 646-648.

"Review of *American Diplomacy in the Orient* by John W. Foster," *Independent* 55 (March 12, 1903), 623-624.

"Review of *Arbitration and the Hague Court* by John W. Foster," *National Geographic* 16 (March 1905), 133.

"Review of *A Century of American Diplomacy* by John W. Foster," *Independent* 52 (Dec. 20, 1900), 3048–3050.

Schurz, Carl. "The Hawaiian Business," *Harper's Weekly* 37 (Feb. 25, 1893), 170.

Scott, James Brown. "John Watson Foster: An Appreciation," *American Journal of International Law* 12 (Jan. 1918), 127–134.

_____. "Review of *The Practice of Diplomacy as Illustrated in the Foreign Relations of the United States* by John W. Foster," *American Journal of International Law 1* (Jan. 1907), 257–260.

Tracy, Benjamin F. "The Bering Sea Question," *North American Review* 156 (May 1893), 438, 513–542.

Vieillard, "Custos Custodia," *Nation* 100 (June 17, 1915), 1 680.

Williams, William. "Reminiscences of the Bering Sea Arbitration," *American Journal of International Law* 37 (Oct. 1943), 562–584.

Wood, Rev. Charles, D. D. *General John Watson Foster: A Memorial Sermon Delivered in the Church of the Covenant, Sunday Morning, December 2, 1917.* Washington, D. C. Printed by the Family, 1917.

Woosley, Theodore S. "Review of *American Diplomacy in the Orient* by John W. Foster," *American Historical Review* 9 (Oct. 1903), 180–182.

IV.   SELECTED SECONDARY SOURCES

A.   Books

Bailey, Thomas A. *America Faces Russia.* Ithaca, N.Y. Cornell University Press, 1950.

Barnard, Harry, *Rutherford B. Hayes and His America.* Indianapolis, Ind.: Bobbs-Merrill, 1954.

Barrows, Chester L. *William M. Evarts: Lawyer, Diplomat, Statesman.* Chapel Hill: University of North Carolina Press, 1941.

Beal, John Robinson, *John Foster Dulles: A Biography.* New York: Harper & Bros., 1957.

Beale, Howard K. *Theodore Roosevelt and the Rise of America to World Power.* Baltimore, Md.: Johns Hopkins University Press, 1956.

Beers, Burton F. *Vain Endeavour: Robert Lansing's Attempts to End the American-Japanese Rivalry.* Durham, N.C.: Duke University Press, 1962.

Beisner, Robert L. *Twelve Against Empire: The Anti-Imperialists, 1898–1900.* New York: McGraw-Hill, 1968.

Bemis, Samuel F., and Ferrell, Robert, eds. *The American Secretaries of State and Their Diplomacy.* 15 vols. New York: Pageant Book, 1958.

Berding, Andrew H. *Dulles on Diplomacy.* Princeton, N.J.: Van Nostrand, 1965.

Brown, Robert Craig. *Canada's National Policy, 1883–1900: A Study in Canadian-American Relations.* Princeton, N.J.: Princeton University Press, 1964.

Callahan, James Morton, *American Foreign Policy in Canadian Relations.* New York: Macmillan, 1937.

_____. *American Foreign Policy in Mexican Relations.* New York: Macmillan, 1932.

_____. *American Relations in the Pacific and the Far East.* Johns Hopkins Studies in Historical and Political Science 19 (January-March 1901), Baltimore, Md.: Johns

Hopkins University Press, 1901.

Callcott, Wilfred Hardy, *The Caribbean Policy of the United States, 1890–1920.* Baltimore, Md.: Johns Hopkins University Press, 1942.

Campbell, Charles S. *Anglo-American Understanding, 1898–1903.* Baltimore, Md.: Johns Hopkins University Press, 1957.

———. *Special Business Interests and the Open Door Policy.* New Haven, Conn.: Yale University Press, 1951.

———. *The Transformation of American Foreign Relations, 1865–1900.* New York: Harper and Row, 1976.

Casío Villegas, Daniel. *The United States versus Porfirio Díaz,* trans. by Nettie Lee Benson. Lincoln: University of Nebraska Press, 1963.

Clymer, Kenton. *John Hay: The Gentleman as Diplomat.* Ann Arbor: University of Michigan Press, 1975.

Commager, Henry Steele. *The American Mind.* New Haven, Conn.: Yale University Press, 1950.

Coolidge, Mary Roberts. *Chinese Immigration.* Reprint of 1909 ed. New York: Arno Press and the New York Times, 1969.

Cooling, Benjamin Franklin. *Benjamin F. Tracy: Father of the Modern American Fighting Navy.* Hamden, Conn.: Anchon Books, 1973.

Cumberland, Charles C. *Mexican Revolution: Genesis under Madero.* Austin: University of Texas Press, 1952.

Curti, Merle. *Peace or War: The American Struggle, 1636–1936.* New York: Norton, 1936. Bancroft, Herbert Howe, *History of Mexico,* 6 vols. San Francisco: History, 1888.

Davis, Calvin D. *The United States and the First Hague Conference.* Ithaca, N.Y.: American Historical Association/Cornell University Press, 1962.

———. *The United States and the Second Hague Peace Conference: American Diplomacy and International Organization.* Durham, N.C.: Duke University Press, 1975.

Dennett, Tyler. *Americans in Eastern Asia: A Critical Study of the Policy of the United States with Reference to China, Japan and Korea in the Nineteenth Century.* New York: Macmillan, 1922.

———. *John Hay: From Poetry to Politics.* New York: Dodd, Mead, 1933.

Dorwart, Jeffrey, *The Pigtail War: American Involvement in the Sino-Japanese War, 1894–95.* Amherst: University of Massachusetts, 1975.

Dulebohn, George R. *Principles of Foreign Policy under the Cleveland Administration.* Philadelphia: University of Pennsylvania, 1941.

Dulles, Eleanor Lansing. *John Foster Dulles: The Last Year.* New York: Harcourt, Brace & World, 1963.

Dulles, Foster Rhea. *America in the Pacific.* Boston: Houghton Mifflin, 1937.

———. *The American Red Cross: A History.* New York: Harper & Bros., 1950.

———. *China and America: The Story of Their Relations Since 1784.* Princeton, N.J.: Princeton University Press, 1944.

———. *The Imperial Years.* New York: Thomas Y. Crowell, 1956.

———. *Prelude to World Power: American Diplomatic History, 1860–1900.* New York: Macmillan, 1965.

Duncan, Bingham. *Whitelaw Reid: Journalist, Politician, Diplomat.* Athens: University of Georgia Press, 1975.

Dyer, Brainero. *The Public Career of William M. Evarts*. Berkeley: University of California Press, 1933.

Evans, Henry C. *Chile and Its Relations with the United States*. Durham, N.C.: Duke University Press, 1927.

Fairbank, John K. *The United States and China*. 3rd ed. Cambridge, Mass.: Harvard University Press, 1971.

Fleming, Denna Frank. *The Treaty Veto of the American Senate*. New York: Garland, 1971.

Foner, Philip S. *A History of Cuba and Its Relations with the United States*. 2 vols. New York: International Publishers, 1963.

Garraty, John A. *Henry Cabot Lodge*. New York: Alfred Knopf, 1953.

_____. *The New Commonwealth, 1877–1890*. New York: Harper & Row, 1968.

Gerson, Louis L. *John Foster Dulles*. American Secretaries of State and Their Diplomacy, ed. by Robert H. Ferrell and Samuel Flagg Bemis. New York: Cooper Square Publishers, 1967.

Gilbert, Frank M. *History of the City of Evansville and Vandenberg County, Indiana*. 2 vols. Chicago: Pioneer Publishing, 1910.

Grabner, Norman, ed. *An Uncertain Tradition: American Secretaries of State in the Twentieth Century*. New York: McGraw-Hill, 1961.

_____. *Ideas and Diplomacy: Readings in the Intellectual Tradition of American Foreign Policy*. New York: Oxford University Press, 1964.

Gregg, Robert D. *The Influence of Border Troubles on Relations between the United States and Mexico, 1876–1910*. Baltimore, Md. : Johns Hopkins University Press, 1937.

Grenville, John A. S. *Lord Salisbury and Foreign Policy: The Close of the Nineteenth Century*. London: Athlone Press, 1964.

_____, and Young, George B. *Politics, Strategy and American Diplomacy: Studies in Foreign Policy, 1873–1917*. New Haven, Conn.: Yale University Press, 1966.

Grew, Joseph. *Turbulent Era: A Diplomatic Record of Forty Years, 1904–1945*, ed. by Walter Johnson. 2 vols. Boston: Houghton Mifflin, 1952.

Guhin, Michael A. *John Foster Dulles, A Statesman and His Times*. New York: Columbia University Press, 1972.

Healy, David. *U.S. Expansionism: The Imperial Urge in the 1890s*. Madison: University of Wisconsin Press, 1970.

Herman, Sondra R. *Eleven Against War: Studies in American Internationalist Thought, 1898–1921*. Stanford, Cal.: Hoover Institution Press, 1969.

Herrick, Walter R., Jr. *The American Naval Revolution*. Baton Rouge: Louisiana State University Press, 1966.

Hidemichi, Roy Akagi. *Japan's Foreign Relations, 1542–1936*. Tokyo: Hokuseido Press, 1937.

Higham, John, with Krieger, Lenard, and Gilbert, Felix. *History: The Development of Historical Studies in the United States*. Englewood Cliffs, N.J.: Prentice-Hall, 1965.

Hill, Lawrence F. *Diplomatic Relations Between the United States and Brazil*. Durham, N.C.: Duke University Press, 1932.

Holt, William Stull. *Treaties Defeated by the Senate*. Gloucester, Mass.: Peter Smith, 1964.

Hsü, Immanuel C. Y. *The Rise of Modern China*. London: Oxford University Press, 1970.

Hull, William I. *The Two Hague Conferences and Their Contributions to International Law*. Introduction by Warren F. Kuehl. New York: Garland, 1972.

Hummel, A. W., ed. *Eminent Chinese of the Ching Period, 1644-1912*. 2 vols. Washington, D.C.: USGPO, 1943, 1945.

Ilchman, Warren F. *Professional Diplomacy in the United States, 1799-1939: A Study in Administrative History*. Chicago: University of Chicago Press, 1961.

Iriye, Akira. *Pacific Estrangement: Japanese and American Expansion, 1897-1911*. Cambridge, Mass.: Harvard University Press, 1972.

James, Henry. *Richard Olney and His Public Service*. Boston: Houghton Mifflin, 1923.

Jessup, Phillip C. *Elihu Root*. 2 vols. New York: Dodd, Mead, 1938.

Josephson, Matthew. *The Politicos, 1865-1896*. New York: Harcourt, Brace & World, 1938.

Kajima, Morinosuke. *The Diplomacy of Japan, 1894-1922:* Volume 1. *Sino-Japanese War and Triple Intervention*. Tokyo, Japan: Kajima Institute of International Peace, 1976.

Keim, Jeannette, *Forty Years of German-American Political Relations*. Philadelphia: William J. Dornan, 1919.

Klymer, Kelton, *John Hay: The Gentleman as Diplomat*, Ann Arbor: University of Michigan Press, 1975.

Kuehl, Warren F. *Seeking World Order: The United States and International Organization to 1920*. Nashville, Tenn.: Vanderbilt University Press, 1969.

Kung, S. W. *The Chinese in American Life: Some Aspects of Their History, Status, Problems, and Contributions*. Seattle: University of Washington Press, 1962.

LaFeber, Walter. *The New Empire: An Interpretation of American Expansion, 1860-1989*. Ithaca, N.Y.: American Historical Association / Cornell University Press, 1963.

Langer, William. *The Diplomacy of Imperialism, 1890-1902*. 2nd ed. New York: Alfred Knopf, 1965.

Laughlin, James L. and Willis, H. Parker. *Reciprocity*. New York: Baker & Taylor, 1903.

Leopold, Richard. *Elihu Root and the Conservative Tradition*. Boston: Little, Brown, 1954.

————. *The Growth of American Foreign Policy*. New York: Alfred Knopf, 1962.

Logan, Rayford. *Diplomatic Relations of the United States with Haiti, 1776-1891*. Chapel Hill: University of North Carolina Press, 1941.

McCloskey, Robert G. *American Conservatism in the Age of Enterprise, 1865-1910*. New York: Harper Torchbooks, 1951.

MacCorkle, Stuart A. *American Policy of Recognition towards Mexico*. Baltimore, Md.: Johns Hopkins University Press, 1933.

MacCormick, Thomas J. *China Market: America's Quest for Informal Empire, 1893-1901*. Chicago: Quadrangle Books, 1967.

McKee, Delber. *Chinese Exclusion Versus the Open Door Policy, 1900-1906: Clashes over China Policy in Roosevelt Era*. Detroit, Mich.: Wayne State University Press, 1977.

McKenzie, R. D. *Oriental Exclusion*. Chicago: University of Chicago Press, 1928.

Malozemoff, Andrew. *Russian Far Eastern Policy, 1881-1907*. Berkeley: University of California Press, 1958.

May, Ernest R. *Imperial Democracy: The Emergence of America as a Great Power.* New York: Harcourt, Brace and World, 1961.

May, Ernest R, and Thomson, James C. Jr., eds. *American East Asian Relations: A Survey.* Cambridge, Mass.: Harvard University Press, 1972.

Merk, Fredrick. *Manifest Destiny and Mission in American History.* New York: Vintage Books, 1963.

Montague, Ludwell Lee. *Haiti and the United States, 1714–1938.* Durham, N.C.: Duke University Press, 1940.

Morgan, H. Wayne. *From Hayes to McKinley: National Party Politics, 1877–1896.* Syracuse, N.Y.: Syracuse University Press, 1969.

———. *William McKinley and His America.* Syracuse, N.Y.: Syracuse University Press, 1963.

Mosley, Leonard. *Dulles. A Biography of Eleanor, Allen and John Foster Dulles and Their Family Network.* New York: The Dial Press, 1978.

Muzzey, David S. *James G. Blaine: A Political Idol of Other Days.* Reprint of 1934 ed. Port Washington, N.Y.: Kennikat Press, 1963.

Nevins, Allen. *Henry White: Thirty Years of American Diplomacy.* New York: Harper & Bros., 1930.

Osgood, Robert E. *Ideals and Self-Interest in America's Foreign Relations.* Chicago: University of Chicago Press, 1953.

Parkes, Henry Bamford, *A History of Mexico*, 3rd. ed. Boston: Houghton Mifflin, 1966.

Patterson, David S. *Toward a Warless World: The Travail of the American Peace Movement, 1887–1914.* Bloomington: Indiana University Press, 1976.

Perkins, Bradford. *The Great Rapprochement: England and the United States, 1895–1914.* New York: Atheneum, 1968.

Pike, Fredrick B. *Chile and the United States, 1808–1962.* South Bend, Ind.: Notre Dame University Press, 1963.

Plesur, Milton. *America's Outward Thrust: Approaches to Foreign Affairs, 1865–1890.* Dekalb: Northern Illinois University Press, 1971.

Pletcher, David M. *The Awkward Years: American Foreign Relations under Garfield and Arthur.* Columbia: University of Missouri Press, 1962.

———. *Rails, Mines and Progress: Seven American Promoters in Mexico, 1867–1911.* Ithaca, N.Y.: American Historical Association / Cornell University Press, 1958.

Portell Vilá, Herminio. *Historia de Cuba en sus Relaciones con los Estados Unidos y España.* 4 vols. Miami, Fla.: Mnemosyne Publishing, 1969 (1941).

Pratt, Julius W. *Expansionists of 1898: The Acquisition of Hawaii and the Spanish Islands.* Baltimore, Md.: Johns Hopkins University Press, 1936.

Relyea, Pauline S. *Diplomatic Relations between the United States and Mexico under Porfirio Díaz, 1876–1910.* Smith College Studies in History 10:1. Northampton, Mass.: Smith College, 1924.

Russ, William A. *The Hawaiian Republic (1894–1898) and Its Struggle to Win Annexation.* Selinsgrove, Pa.: Susquehanna University Press, 1961.

———. *The Hawaiian Revolution, 1893–1894.* Selinsgrove, Pa.: Susquehanna University Press, 1959.

Russell, Henry B. *International Monetary Conferences: Their Purposes, Characters and Results.* New York: Harper & Bros., 1898.

Ryden, George H. *The Foreign Policy of the United States in Relation to Samoa.* New Haven, Conn.: Yale University Press, 1933.

Schlesinger, Arthur M., Jr. *History of American Presidential Elections, 1789–1968.* New York: Chelsea House, 1971.

Schmidt, Karl M. *Mexico and the United States, 1821–1973: Conflict and Coexistence.* New York: Wiley, 1974.

Schonberger, Howard B. *Transportation to the Seaboard: The "Communication Revolution" and American Foreign Policy, 1860–1900.* Westport, Conn.: Greenwood Publishing, 1971.

Seeds, Russell M., ed. *A History of the Republican Party of Indiana,* vol. 1. Indianapolis: Indiana History, 1899.

Sherman, William R. *The Diplomatic and Commercial Relations of the United States and Chile, 1820–1914.* Boston: Gorham Press, 1926.

Sievers, Harry J. *Benjamin Harrison.* 3 vols. New York: University Publisher, 1959.

Smith, Daniel M. *Robert Lansing and American Neutrality, 1914–1917.* Berkeley: University of California Press, 1958.

Sprout, Harold, and Sprout, Margaret. *The Rise of American Naval Power, 1776–1918.* Princeton, N.J.: Princeton University Press, 1939.

Stampp, Kenneth. *Indiana Politics During the Civil War.* Indianapolis: Indiana Historical Bureau, 1949.

Stevens, Sylvester K. *American Expansion in Hawaii, 1842–1889.* Harrisburg: Archives Publishing of Pennsylvania, 1945.

Stuart, Graham H. *The Department of State: A History of Its Organization, Procedure, and Personnel.* New York: Macmillan, 1949.

Suarez, José León. *Mr. John W. Foster.* Con una introducción del Dr. Luis M. Drago. Buenos Aires, Argentina: Imp. "Suiza," 1918.

Tansill, Charles C. *Canadian-American Relations, 1875–1911.* New Haven, Conn.: Yale University Press, 1943.

———. *The Foreign Policies of Thomas F. Bayard, 1885–1897.* New York: Fordham University Press, 1940.

Tate, Merze. *The Disarmament Illusion: The Movement for a Limitation of Armaments to 1907.* New York: Macmillan, 1942.

———. *Hawaii: Reciprocity of Annexation.* East Lansing: Michigan State University Press, 1968.

———. *The United States and Armaments.* Cambridge, Mass.: Harvard University Press, 1948.

———. *The United States and the Hawaiian Kingdom: A Political History.* New Haven, Conn.: Yale University Press, 1965.

Taussing, Frank W. *The Tariff History of the United States.* 8th ed. New York: Putnam's, 1931.

Terrill, Tom E. *The Tariff, Politics and American Foreign Policy, 1874–1901.* Westport, Conn.: Greenwood Press, 1973.

Thomas, Hugh. *Cuba: The Pursuit of Freedom.* New York: Harper and Row, 1971.

Tompkins, Pauline. *American-Russian Relations in the Far East.* New York: Macmillan, 1949.

Treat, Payson. *Japan and the United States, 1853–1921.* Boston: Houghton Mifflin, 1921.

Tyler, Alice Felt. *The Foreign Policies of James G. Blaine*. Minneapolis: University of Minnesota Press, 1927.

Van Alstyne, Richard W. *The United States and East Asia*. New York: Norton, 1973.

Van Dusen, Henry P., ed. *The Spiritual Legacy of John Foster Dulles: Selections from His Articles and Addresses*. Philadelphia: Westminster Press, 1960.

Varg, Paul A. *The Making of a Myth: The United States and China, 1897–1912*. East Lansing: Michigan State Univeristy Press, 1968.

Vinacke, Harold M. *A History of the Far East in Modern Times*. 6th ed. New York: Appleton-Century-Crofts, 1959.

White, Andrew D. *Autobiography of Andrew D. White*. 2 vols. New York: Century, 1906.

Williams, Charles Richard. *The Life of Rutherford B. Hayes, Nineteenth President of the United States*. 2 vols. Columbus: Ohio State Archaeological and Historical Society, 1928.

Williams, William A. *The Roots of the Modern American Empire*. New York; Vintage Books, 1969.

Woodburn, James Albert. *A History of Indiana University, 1820–1902*. Bloomington: Indiana University Press, 1940.

Young, Marilyn Blatt. *The Rhetoric of Empire: American China Policy, 1895–1901*. Cambridge, Mass.: Harvard University Press, 1968.

Younger, Edward. *John A. Kasson: Politics and Diplomacy from Lincoln to McKinley*. Iowa City: State Historical Society of Iowa, 1955.

Zabriskie, Edward. *American-Russian Rivalry in the Far East, 1895–1914*. Philadelphia: University of Pennsylvania Prss, 1946.

B. Articles

Bailey, Thomas A. "Japan's Protest Against the Annexation of Hawaii." *Journal of Modern History* 3 (March 1931), 46–61.

———. "The North Pacific Sealing Convention of 1911." *Pacific Historical Review* 4 (March 1935), 1–14.

———. "Theodore Roosevelt and the Alaskan Boundary Settlement," *Canadian Historical Reivew* 18 (June 1937), 123–130.

———. "The United States and Hawaii During the Spanish-American War." *American Historical Review* 36 (April 1931).

Campbell, Charles S. "The Bering Sea Settlement of 1892." *Pacific Historical Review* 32 (Nov. 1963), 347–367.

———. "The Anglo-American Crisis in the Bering Sea, 1890–1891," *Mississippi Valley Historical Review* 48 (Dec. 1961), 393–414.

Campbell, John P. "Taft, Roosevelt and the Arbitration Treaties of 1911." *Journal of American History* 53 (Sept. 1966), 279–298.

Casío Villegas, Daniel. "El porfiriato, era de consolidación." *Historia Mexicana* 13 (1963), 76–87.

Challener, R. D. and Fenton, John. "Which Way America? Dulles Always Knew." *American Heritage* 22 (June 1971), 12–13, 84–93.

Dozer, Donald M. "Benjamin Harrison and the Presidential Campaign of 1892." *American Historical Review* 54 (Oct. 1948), 49–77.

———. "The Opposition to Hawaiian Reciprocity, 1876–1888," *Pacific Historical Review* 14 (June 1945), 157–183.

Duniway, C. A. "Training in Universities for Consular and Diplomatic Service." *American Journal of International Law* 9 (Jan. 1915), 153–156.

Field, James A. "American Imperialism: The Worst Chapter in Almost Any Book." *American Historical Review* 83 (June 1978), 644–668.

Finch, George A. "The American Society for International Law, 1906–1956." *American Journal of International Law* 50 (April 1956), 293–312.

Gardner, Lloyd C. "American Foreign Policy 1900–1921: A Second Look at the Realist Critique of American Diplomacy." In *Towards a New Past: Dissenting Essays in American History*, ed. by Barton J. Bernstein. New York: Vintage Books, 1969.

Garraty, John A. "Henry Cabot Lodge and the Alaskan Boundary Tribunal." *New England Quarterly* 24 (1951), 469–494.

Gignillat, John L. "Pigs, Politics and Protection: The European Boycott of American Pork, 1879–1891." *Agricultural History* 35 (Jan. 1961), 3–12.

Hackett, Charles W. "The Recognition of the Díaz Government by the United States." *Southwestern Historical Quarterly* 28 (July 1924), 34–55.

Hardy, Osgood. "The Itata Incident." *Hispanic American Historical Review* 5 (May 1922), 195–226.

———. "Was Patrick Egan a Blundering Minister?" *Hispanic American Historical Review* 8 (Feb. 1928), 65–81.

Harrington, Fred Harvey. "The Anti-Imperialist Movement in the United States, 1898–1900." *Mississippi Valley Historical Review* 22 (1935), 211–213.

Hunter, Charles H. "Statehood and the Hawaiian Annexation Treaty of 1893." *Hawaiian Historical Society, 59th Annual Report*, 1950. Honolulu: Hawaiian Historical Society, 1951.

Lewis, W. R. "The Hayes Administration and Mexico." *Southwestern Historical Quarterly* 24 (Oct. 1920), 140–153.

Livermore, Seward. "American Strategy and Diplomacy in the South Pacific, 1890–1914." *Pacific Historical Review* 12 (March 1943), 33–51.

McClendon, R. Earl. "The Weil and La Abra Claims Against Mexico." *Hispanic American Historical Review* 19 (Feb. 1939), 31–54.

MacCormick, Thomas J. "American Expansion in China." *American Historical Review* 75 (June 1970), 1393–1396.

Mahon, John K. "Benjamin F. Tracy: Secretary of the Navy, 1889–1893." *New York Historical Society Quarterly* 46 (April 1960), 179–201.

Plesur, Milton. "American Looking Outward: The Years from Hayes to Harrison." *The Historian* 22 (May 1960), 280–295.

Pletcher, David M. "Mexico Opens the Door to American Capital, 1877–1880." *The Americas* 16 (July 1959).

———. "Reciprocity and Latin America in the Early 1890s: A Foretaste of Dollar Diplomacy." *Pacific Historical Review* 47 (Feb. 1978), 53–89.

Pratt, Julius. "The Hawaiian Revolution: A Reinterpretation." *Pacific Historical Review* 1 (Sept. 1932), 285–292.

———. "The 'Large Policy' of 1898." *Mississippi Valley Historical Review* 9 (1932), 219–242.

Rowland, Donald. "The Establishment of the Republic of Hawaii, 1893-1894." *Pacific Historical Review* 4 (March 1935), 201-220.

Russ, William A. "The Role of Sugar in Hawaiian Annexation." *Pacific Historical Review* 12 (Dec. 1943), 339-350.

Snepp, Daniel W. "John Watson Foster, Soldier and Politician." *Indiana Magazine of History* 32 (Sept. 1936), 207-225.

Snyder, L. L. "The American-German Pork Dispute, 1879-1891." *Journal of Modern History* 17 (March 1945), 16-28.

Spetter, Allan. "Harrison and Blaine: Foreign Policy, 1889-1893." *Indiana Magazine of History* 65 (Sept. 1969), 214-227.

Swisher, Earl. "Chinese Representation in the United States." University of Colorado Studies Series in History 5 (Jan. 1967).

Tate, Merze. "Great Britain and the Sovereignty of Hawaii." *Pacific Historical Review* 31 (1961), 337-344.

Volwiler, Albert T. "Harrison, Blaine, and American Foreign Policy, 1889-1893." *Proceedings of the American Philosophical Society* 79 (1938), 637-648.

Weigle, Richard D. "Sugar and the Hawaiian Revolution." *Pacific Historical Review* 16 (Feb. 1947), 41-58.

Wilgus, A. Curtis. "James G. Blaine and the Pan American Movement." *Hispanic American Historical Review* 5 (Nov. 1922), 662-708.

Williams, F. W. "Review of the Memoirs of Li Hung-chang." *American Historical Review* 19 (April 1914), 633-635.

Williams, John A. "Stephen B. Elkins and the Benjamin Harrison Campaign and Cabinet, 1887-1891." *Indiana Magazine of History* 68 (March 1972), 1-23.

Young, Marilyn Blatt. "American Expansion, 1870-1900: The Far East." In *Towards a New Past*, ed. by Barton J. Bernstein. New York: Vintage Books, 1969.

Index